1984

Michael A. Faletti‚
117 Seeser Street
Joliet, Illinois 60436‚

BOOKS BY

MAX WILK

THE WIT AND WISDOM OF HOLLYWOOD

THE WIT
AND WISDOM
OF HOLLYWOOD

From the Squaw Man to the Hatchet Man

Assembled, recorded, footnoted & edited by

MAX WILK

New York 1971 ATHENEUM

Excerpts have been taken from the following: *Total Recoil*, by Kyle Crichton, copyright © 1960 by Kyle Crichton, reprinted by permission of Doubleday & Company, Inc.; *This Was Hollywood*, by Beth Day, copyright © 1960 by Beth Day, reprinted by permission of Doubleday & Company, Inc.; *Confessions of a Hollywood Columnist*, by Sheilah Graham, copyright © 1968, 1969 by Sheilah Graham, reprinted by permission of William Morrow & Company, Inc., and Bantam Books; *Charlie*, by Ben Hecht, copyright © 1957 by Ben Hecht, reprinted by permission of Mrs. Ben Hecht and Harper & Row, Publishers, Inc.; *A Child of the Century*, by Ben Hecht, copyright © 1954 by Ben Hecht, reprinted by permission of Simon & Schuster, Inc.; *Hollywood Without Makeup*, by Pete Martin, with introduction by Nunnally Johnson, copyright © 1948 by Pete Martin; *Merely Colossal*, by Arthur L. Mayer, copyright © 1953 by Arthur L. Mayer, reprinted by permission of Simon & Schuster, Inc.; and *King Cohn: The Life and Times of Harry Cohn*, by Bob Thomas, copyright © 1967 by Robert Joseph Thomas, reprinted by permission of G. P. Putnam's Sons.

Library of Congress catalog card number 73-124983
Published simultaneously in Canada by McClelland and Stewart Ltd.
Manufactured in the United States of America by
Kingsport Press, Inc., Kingsport, Tennessee
Designed by Harry Ford
First printing May 1971
Second printing May 1971
Third printing August 1971

FOREWORD
BY JUDITH CRIST

THE decline and fall really got going, I suppose, when some academic began calling the movies an "art form" and was completed when, as Bill Ludwig suggested, M-G-M made the mistake of auctioning off its props instead of its producers.

By no small coincidence, Max Wilk, purveyor of the Ludwig comment, has chosen the report of the auction as the fadeout for his anthology of the wisdom and the wit once rampant in our favorite factory town. That event certainly underlined the bitterest of ironies, that it is the artifacts (movie stars included) rather than the artists that a sentimental generation dotes on, that the materials rather than the minds of Hollywood are cherished. For just as there has been, since that damned cineastic "art form" label, decreasing evidence of art or form in film, so we have been getting little wit and less wisdom from the creators thereof. Who, after all, can be witty, let alone wise, when the sheriff is part of the front-door decor, the fifth mortgage is long overdue, the maintenance men have taken over from the lunatics who were once running the asylum, and Harry Kurnitz's apocalyptic vision of machine-written movies, "Untouched by Human Hands," has seemingly come upon us, at least in the "untouched by human minds" phase?

Well, the more it changes . . . The "monsters and pirates and bastards" of yore are still around, even though, as Richard Brooks suggests, they'd be better cast these days as gas jockeys; Nunnally Johnson testifies that the clichés of the early Hollywood satires, "the drunk writers, the stupid producers, the arrogant directors," are still on hand. Since the diaspora that followed the big-studio disintegration, of course, they're scattered the world over most of the time, returning, like homing pigeons, for the great art-form tasks of money raising, cost accounting and budget brawling, or to pick up a fast bundle via the television quickie, today's B movie. The sense of community in moviemaking is gone—for good or ill and to enable the born-yesterday young to harbor notions that one man can ever make a movie.

No such delusion afflicted the wise and witty men and women whom Max Wilk recalls in these pages. Trapped in the fortune-cookie-factory world of moviemaking, but fully aware of why and how and to what purpose they were caught therein, they were articulate about themselves and others. Their distinction, and their anthologizer's, is that they were and are products of the pre-audio-visual era, when words were a human form of communication, when there was kinship among those who could read and write and talk and who reveled in the expertise of doing all three, on the job or off. These are verbalizers, perceptive and precise pros, whose touch of fine madness and sense of *le mot juste* take them beyond Hazlitt's concept of humor as "the growth of nature and accident" to fulfill his definition of wit as "the product of art and fancy." And the soul thereof is the one-liner, scores of which Wilk has memorialized herein, from Dorothy Parker's classic on the British "schedule" and the American "skit," to Arthur Caesar's "dace" versus Zoe Akins's "mace," with the lovely lingual mayhem of the Goldwyns or the Curtizes for underlining.

Beyond the one-liner, there's the anecdote to bring flesh and blood to the factory scene, to fill out a personality, vivify a phase of moviemaking and, time and again, put the lie to all the artsy-smartsy legendry and teary-eyed nostalgia that has befogged our memories of Hollywood's heyday. And beyond these there are the commentaries and critiques (who but Wilk would remind us that there were critics like Bob Benchley and Robert Sherwood, or critics of any kind, before James Agee?); the firsthand reactions ("I don't know which makes me vomit worse—the horned toads from the cloak-and-suit trade, the shanty Irish, or the gentlemen who talk of Screen Art," wrote Stephen Vincent Benét, starting on the fifth version of *Abraham Lincoln*); the recall of the great original wits and the witties they've lost claim to by now.

Admittedly, there's nothing funny about the movie business in the Seventies—unless you get your guffaws out of box-office grosses and international banking. And all the other decades may have seemed as grim in contemporary terms. But there were giants—and, fortunately, the right man is on hand to anthologize them. What qualifies Max Wilk for the job is not that he's one of the rare "word-men" in the medium today or that he has chosen dove-gray rather than black comedy as his métier (a pretty gutsy choice these dark days), or even that he's the author of the one funny Jerry Lewis movie I've seen. It's simply that he's a movie-lover—and nothing about movies is alien to him. And like the giants, he laughs best when it hurts a little.

ACKNOWLEDGMENTS

THE AUTHOR is grateful for permission to reprint substantial excerpts from the following books:

Laughter Is a Wonderful Thing, by Joe E. Brown. Quoted by permission of A. S. Barnes & Company, Inc.

Voices Offstage, by Marc Connelly. Quoted by permission of the author and Holt, Rinehart and Winston, Inc.

Total Recoil, by Kyle Crichton. Quoted by permission of Doubleday & Company, Inc.

This Was Hollywood, by Beth Day. Quoted by permission of Doubleday & Company, Inc.

Stephen Vincent Benét, by Charles A. Fenton, and *Selected Letters of Stephen Vincent Benét*, edited by Charles A. Fenton. Quoted by permission of the Yale University Press.

The One with the Mustache Is Costello, by George Frazier. Quoted by permission of the author.

The Fifty-Year Decline and Fall of Hollywood, by Ezra Goodman, quoted by permission of the author.

Confessions of a Hollywood Columnist, by Sheilah Graham. Quoted by permission of William Morrow & Company, Inc., and Bantam Books.

Charlie, by Ben Hecht. Quoted by permission of Mrs. Ben Hecht and Harper & Row, Publishers, Inc.

A Child of the Century, by Ben Hecht. Quoted by permission of Simon & Schuster, Inc.

"The Notebook of a Schnook," from *Pencil in the Air*, by Samuel Hoffenstein. Reprinted by permission of David Hoffenstein.

Introduction by Nunnally Johnson to *Hollywood Without Makeup*, by Pete Martin. Quoted by permission of the author.

Merely Colossal, by Arthur L. Mayer. Quoted by permission of Simon & Schuster, Inc.

The Bathtub Hoax, by H. L. Mencken. Quoted by permission of Alfred A. Knopf, Inc.

Silent Star, by Colleen Moore. Quoted by permission of Doubleday & Company, Inc.

Hello, Hollywood! by Allen Rivkin and Laura Kerr. Quoted by permission of the authors and Doubleday & Company, Inc.

King Cohn, by Bob Thomas. Quoted by permission of G. P. Putnam's Sons.

Writers on Writing, edited by Robert Van Gelder. Quoted by permission of Charles Scribner's Sons.

Grateful acknowledgment is also made for the use of the following:

"Let's Forget Pearl Harbor," by Art Buchwald, quoted by permission of the author.

"Roman Candle of MGM," by Ezra Goodman, first published in *Esquire,* quoted by permission of the author.

"Gene Fowler's Ten Commandments for the Motion Picture Industry," "Testament of a Dying Ham," and "Hollywood's 23rd Psalm," by Gene Fowler, reprinted by permission of Will Fowler.

Ben Hecht's newspaper columns, first published in *PM,* quoted by permission of Mrs. Ben Hecht.

Interviews with Mitchell Leisen and Ralph Bellamy from *Film Fan Monthly,* quoted by permission of Leonard Maltin.

Material first published in *The Hollywood Reporter* and quoted by permission of Tichi Wilkerson Miles.

"1938," by Harry Ruby, reprinted by permission of the author.

An interview with Hal Roach from *The Silent Picture,* quoted by permission of Anthony Slide.

Material first published in *The Screen Writer, Point of View* and *WGAw News,* quoted by permission of Writers Guild of America West, Inc., and the authors (or their executors).

INTRODUCTION

THIS giant assortment of Hollywood jokes, toasts, anecdotes, letters, footnotes and *feuilletons* which you hold in your hands, is the end result of a pleasant conversation which took place some time back between yours truly and that eminent wandering wit, Mr. S. J. Perelman.

It was on a dark and stormy London afternoon, in November. The year was 1969; the locale, an elegant town house in Mayfair. In that Green Street drawing room, where Restoration fops once practiced their intrigues, where Victorian heads of government plotted the course of empire, where Edwardian dandies gorged, Mr. Perelman and I sat and spoke. And what did we discuss? World events, the welfare state, pollution, ecology, or any such subject? No. We discussed the present state of the movie business.

We reviewed a few of the more massive bank-busting turkeys then being peddled to apathetic audiences by desperate film producers, we gossiped about our various unemployed writing pals, and then, after a decent interval of such masochistic chat, Mr. Perelman began to reminisce about his early days in Hollywood where he toiled as a gagman and writer. (Does anyone who is a true Perelman fan need to footnote the fact that Mr. P. was a major contributor to the early Marx Brothers' comedies? I have often encountered certain mnemonically gifted Perelman-Marx aficionados who can, without the slightest effort, recite entire sequences of certain Marx Brothers' lunacies.)

Unfortunately I did not have a tape recorder with me on that dark November afternoon, so I must reconstruct most of our conversation from memory. I remember Perelman discussing a story conference he'd once had with that great language-mauler, Mike Curtiz the director, which led me to remember an anecdote about a Darryl Zanuck story conference told to me by Leland Hayward, which is reprinted in this book. We talked of Thalberg and Jack Warner and other such legendary figures. We mused on certain foreign film stars imported during the thirties, whose careers usually consisted of one horrible film, after which they were returned to sender. Mr. Perelman's favorite failure was a long-lost Balkan temptress named Lil Dagover, while mine was a male Gallic Boyer-imitator named Fernand Gravet. How can one forget him, when the studio billing of his name always sternly cautioned: "Pronounced *Gravy*"?

In the ordinary course of events, when two writers have killed time so successfully, we might have proceeded to the corner local and had a few pints and let it go at that, but suddenly there flashed through my head what Mr. Sam Goldwyn is alleged to have referred to as "the mucus of an idea."

"Sid," I said, "all of this stuff about your early days in Hollywood would probably make a marvelous book."

"I've already written about it," he said. "I did a piece about Thalberg, and then another one about the Garden of Allah apartments for *The New Yorker,* just a couple of months ago."

"Of course," I said, "but there must be a mountain of other unpublished material about Hollywood—all those great stories about the people who suffered and bled at $1500 a week—for all those years—"

"Absolutely," nodded Perelman. "Why don't *you* do the book?"

"Oh no, it should be *you*," I said. "You remember a lot more than *I* do."

"Wilk," he snapped waspishly, "you are not *that* young."

We met again a few days later, and Perelman again regaled me with another set of anecdotes that dealt with his Hollywood years. When I once again brought up the subject of his working on a book, Perelman reiterated his claim that I should do it. As for himself, he was far too busy, being at the time involved in preparing a magazine article which was to be a profile of a baby albino gorilla. (I am certain, despite the lack of a tape recorder, that's what he said.)

I returned home on an antique Boeing 707. A few days later, while riding on an even more antique Penn Central commuter train, the one which leaves Grand Central every evening around 5 P.M. and on some random evenings arrives in Westport a few hours later—a trip which I refer to as Penn Central Roulette—I reported my Perelman conversations to the gentleman seated next to me, who is a book publisher. (I know he is definitely a publisher because he smokes a pipe and reads *The Wall Street Journal.*)

When I finished a few of the Hollywood stories that Perelman and I had swapped, the publisher's eyes lit up and he said, "How soon can you get started?" It was a few days before Christmas, and I had spent two hours that afternoon with my agent, who passed the time by filling me in with gloomy tales of his out-of-work clients, one of whom seemed to be me.

"Oh, I don't really know," I said coyly. "You see, I'm really much too busy to take on such a massive project—I have so many different irons in the fire—"

"Fine," said the publisher. "I'll call your agent and discuss the terms with him tomorrow. Perelman is absolutely right—you should do the book. Get to work."

I did as I was told. I got to work.

Why not? I have been a movie fan for some forty-three years, and my earliest memory is of cowering beneath a theatre seat in an infantile panic, while waiting for doom to strike lovely Renée Adorée, in a picture which was called *The Flaming Forest.*

I spent my formative years at Loew's State and RKO-Keith's, in White Plains, New York; was the movie critic of my prep school newspaper, and while attending Yale, found New Haven to be a moviegoer's paradise. There were six movie houses which changed their programs once each week. On the seventh day I rested.

Not only did I watch movies incessantly, but for years I have voraciously collected documenta dealing with films: magazines, books, autographed photos, *Film Daily* yearbooks, and other assorted material. During the summers of 1938 and 1939 I worked as office boy at the Warner Bros. studio in Burbank, later was assigned by the Air Force to serve as a G.I. writer at the First Motion Picture Unit at Culver City, and have at various times in the past two decades been in and out of studios as a scenarist.

I purchased one of the Radio Shack's best Japanese tape recorders, plus a stack of blank tapes, and started talking to a list of people whom I assumed would be knowledgeable about Hollywood and the film business. I went to Beverly Hills and tracked down a representative list of people who have to be called "survivors"—talented men like Harry Tugend, Nat Perrin, Harry Ruby, Richard Fleischer, Jackie Cooper, Ken Englund, Irving Brecher, Arthur

Sheekman, Hal Kanter, Earl Felton, George Burns—to mention a few—most of whom not only remember a good deal of Hollywood's wit, but also have been responsible for talking and writing a lot of it.

I scanned the files of *The Hollywood Reporter* with Mrs. Tishi Wilkerson Miles' kind permission, and *Daily Variety's* bound copies, courtesy of Tom Prior, and I dug out long-buried pieces by writers such as Benchley, Herman J. Mankiewicz, Harry Ruby and Frank Scully. I spent many pleasant hours with Ken Englund, who was delighted to allow me access to his two valuable reminiscences: one about working with Leo McCarey, and the other, the heretofore undocumented story of Sam Goldwyn's dealings with James Thurber during the production of *The Secret Life of Walter Mitty*. I prowled through the Academy of Motion Picture Arts and Sciences Library and turned up more buried treasure.

Back home I spent time with Connecticut neighbors John Cromwell, whose career as a director and actor started in 1915, and Joseph Mankiewicz, who is a gold mine of authentic movie history, having made a good deal of it himself.

In New York I was fortunate to get to talk with Goodman Ace, Jerry Chodorov, and Leland Hayward, whom I'd been nagging for years to write his memoirs. Arthur L. Mayer and Jules Levey gave me fascinating sidelights on the distribution and selling of movies over the years. Irving Caesar, the great songwriter, was delighted to talk about his brother Arthur, who was a legendary Hollywood wit.

The Library of the Lincoln Center of Performing Arts is a mother lode of clippings and source material. A low bow to its efficient staff, and another to the helpful people at the Museum of Modern Art Film Library.

My friend Spencer M. Berger, of New Haven, Connecticut, has one of the most complete libraries of books on the movies that I've ever been fortunate enough to browse through. His library has a unique feature. He shows marvelous old films on its wall.

For the past seven or eight years London has become a suburb of the old Hollywood, and so back I went, tape recorder in hand, tracking down and interviewing screenwriter Donald Ogden Stewart, who lives in Ramsay MacDonald's old house up in Hampstead. "I don't remember much any more," he apologized. "It all happened thirty or forty years ago." Mr. Stewart then proceeded to regale me with four hours of marvelous reminiscence.

I went to see Bob Parrish, Mel Frank, I. A. L. Diamond and

George Axelrod. Sam Jaffe had a lot to tell me about the days when he was studio manager at Paramount. Jack Benny was at the Dorchester and he sat and talked for almost two hours about his contemporaries in comedy. Dave Golding had stories about his years as a Goldwyn press agent, and Walter Shenson had tales about Harry Cohn. Larry Adler had stories about everybody. Ben Lyon and Bebe Daniels were a movie fan's treat. Miss Daniels, who suffered several strokes a few years back, was in great shape, I am delighted to report. And how that lady did remember! Sam Spiegel interrupted a busy production schedule on *Nicholas and Alexandra* to present me with an anecdote about John Huston.

I brought back twelve reels of tape on Pan Am's new 747. Norman Krasna came dashing through New York, and I pinned him against his hotel-room wall for three hours of reminiscence about his Hollywood days. Robert Emmett Dolan took time off from conducting *Coco* to provide me with endless stories about his thirty years in California. Pat Englund, who grew up in the movie business, gifted me with time and memories. At the Running Footman, Henry Ginsberg talked about running Paramount.

Everybody has been perfectly wonderful. I have to say that, even though it sounds like the traditional speech that's made by an Academy Award winner. In this case it's absolutely true.

Now let me toss a few special bouquets. The first goes to Mr. Allan Rivkin. Allan, who's been a top screenwriter for years, worked very hard with his wife, Laura Kerr, back in 1962, to produce a wonderful book about the movies called *Hello, Hollywood!* It's a massive assemblage of reminiscences and anthologized material by all sorts of authors.

When I went to Hollywood and first broached my project to Allan, who's in charge of public relations for the Writers Guild of America, West, Inc., our union, I did so with a certain amount of justifiable nervousness. After all, the Rivkins are old Hollywood hands, their book is pretty definitive, and they are certainly entitled to regard a Connecticut carpetbagger with a somewhat jaundiced eye.

When I finished telling Allan what I had in mind, over a luncheon which he insisted on paying for, his reaction was amazing. He grinned and said, "Okay, Max—I'll be glad to help you with whatever I can. Anything that's good for writers . . ."

And he was not as good as his word, he was better. With Allan's help, I was able to locate the various authors who had contributed pieces to the old *Screen Writer* back in the Forties—some of whose work is reprinted herein—and he also assisted me in securing the proper reprint permissions through the Guild. And finally, he lobbied with the Guild Council to allow me—for the very first time—to reprint copyrighted material from the fabled Writers Guild annual awards shows of the past few years.

I realize that Mr. Rivkin hails from Minnesota, which is also the birthplace of both my parents, but I think he rates an award of his own for services above and beyond the call of old Gophers.

I will toss another bouquet in the direction of Mr. Nunnally Johnson. When I called him up in February 1970, and told him I'd come out to California to talk to him for my forthcoming book, he was friendly but not too receptive. He told me he hadn't been feeling too well lately, and that he'd announced his retirement from the movie business. "After all," he said somewhat morbidly, "you've got to remember that I'm seventy-two years old."

"Nunnally," I said, "I really don't happen to think seventy-two is so damned old."

"Well, I'll tell you one thing," snapped Mr. Johnson. "I don't expect to hang around like Bertrand Russell!"

Having delivered himself of that ultimatum, he consented to have me come around. He then spent almost four hours talking into my tape recorder, piling one marvelous anecdote onto another. Under the circumstances, it was a large favor.

One further bouquet is in order. I cannot hand it to the gentleman in person since he is no longer with us. So, in absentia, let me mention Jacob Wilk, my father.

He started his career in show business at the age of fifteen, as an usher in the legitimate theatre in Minneapolis, so he could get to see the plays. He remained stage- and screen-struck for the rest of his life, which led him to serve as drama critic on the *Minneapolis Tribune,* and then to a job as an advance agent for the Frohman office in New York, and for William A. Brady.

He went to work for Brady's World Film Co. in the old Fort Lee, New Jersey studios. He distributed independent films, among which were John Barrymore in *Raffles,* and Mabel Normand in Mack Sennett's *Mickey,* then went on to be associated with the great director, Maurice Tourneur.

As an independent literary agent for ten years in New York, he sold film properties to every company, so successfully that in 1928

Jack and Harry Warner decided that it would make good sense for Warner Bros. to have *him* buying for *them*. They were absolutely right. Came January 1929 and he went to work for Warner Bros. as story editor. In the turbulent motion-picture pecking order my father's length of service with the Warners is remarkable; he stayed with the company twenty-three years.

In those years he built up an awesome record of successful deals. His keen sense of story values and his wide acquaintanceship among authors and publishers and Broadway people gave Warner Bros. a long edge over other studios when it came to snaring screen rights to first-rate books and plays. Space doesn't allow for a detailed listing of his "picks," but I can mention *I Am a Fugitive from a Chain Gang*, which he picked up from an unknown ex-convict, and *The Maltese Falcon*, which he snatched from a pulp magazine, *Black Mask*. He nagged at Jack Warner until he persuaded him to buy *Anthony Adverse*, at a hitherto unheard-of price. He funneled Warner money into play production of such hits as *Three Men on a Horse, Boy Meets Girl, Brother Rat,* and *White Horse Inn*. Add to the list *Life with Father*, which he got for the Warners, and *This Is the Army*, which he snatched from beneath L. B. Mayer's very nose, and the list can go on indefinitely. His last and probably most successful coup, after leaving Warner, was to put together a three-way package deal of *Giant*, forming a partnership of Henry Ginsberg, Edna Ferber and George Stevens.

My father had a reputation throughout show business, and even today, some fourteen years after his passing, all sorts of doors have been opened to me in the past six months—doors that might have remained shut to others—simply because my last name is Wilk and at fifty, to many people, I am still "Jake's son."

He keeps cropping up in so many of the interviews I have had with various people. John Cromwell took pleasure in recalling the days when he and Jake worked together for William A. Brady— that was in 1916. Sam Jaffe, who was the first Hollywood agent to set up the "package deal" concept, said to me, "Your father was the best negotiator I ever dealt with. He also had the best taste in the whole movie business. He was a pleasure to do business with, believe me . . ."

Arthur Mayer, who was Jake's luncheon companion at Sardi's for thirty years, cheerfully recalls how Jake handed him a two-page *Reader's Digest* article as the basis for a film, and how the story was later expanded by "Doc" Golden and Mayer into a blockbuster film success called *Hitler's Children*. Norman Krasna, who served his time at Warner Bros., said, "He was a quiet guy—none of that phony Hollywood front—but he knew just what he wanted, and he never quit until he got it." And my good friend Leland Hayward, who before becoming one of Broadway's most successful play producers was one of Hollywood's most inventive and shrewd agents, told me, "I never had fights with anybody the way I went to the mat with Jake—but he was the fairest man in the whole movie business."

Annie Laurie Williams, who has been a top literary agent for many years and is a legend in her own right, was a firm friend. "Jake helped me so much when I was just getting started," she once told me. "I was just a simple little Texas girl who didn't know my way around. Well, I had to repay the favor somehow, so I brought him Margaret Mitchell's *Gone with the Wind* in galley proofs and told him that I'd give Warner Bros. a forty-eight-hour exclusive on it for $50,000. He read it in a hurry and immediately got in touch with Jack Warner about grabbing it. Then he called me back and sadly reported that Warner turned it down. Warner had said, 'I wouldn't pay $50,000 for any damn book anytime.' Jake was so depressed about Warner's lack of foresight that I ended up cheering *him* up about it."

But possibly the highest tribute that was paid to Jake came in 1956, when Eliot Hyman and a Canadian syndicate bought from Warner Bros. the entire backlog of Warner films that had been made up to 1948. One day the phone rang in my father's apartment, and it was Eliot Hyman calling. He introduced himself and then explained that it was he who had just taken possession of the hundreds of Warner films that dated back to the early Twenties. "I was wondering if you'd be interested in a consultant's deal with us," said Hyman. "You see, we've got all this stuff now, but we desperately need somebody to go through it all with us—and tell us what we've bought!"

The movie business has been going for a long time. The saddest truth about it is that it never had much of a sense of history about itself.

True, today there are collectors and scholars and students who are hard at work, picking through the ruins and trying to assemble definitive histories of the studios and the stars and the men who ran the front offices and shipped out fifty-two pictures a year, but, unfortunately, most of the truth—not the press-agent handouts and the waves of phony verbiage on which the business thrived—remains only in the memories of the people who lived it. Too many of them are gone, and with them, the history.

I once mentioned to my father that I'd just finished reading Mack Sennett's autobiography, and how interesting it had seemed.

"Half a book," he said.

When I asked him what he meant, he shrugged and said, "The other half is more interesting. What Sennett left out."

"When are you going to sit down and write *your* reminiscences?" I demanded. "I'll even give you a title: *Tickets in the Name of Wilk.*"

Again Jake shrugged. "I'll get around to it someday," he told me, but then his business sense, so pragmatic after all those years, came to the fore. "First, of course, I'll want a publisher who'll give me a good advance," he said.

He died in 1956, and with him went half a century of personal reminiscences that future students of the motion picture will, alas, never have for reference. Which is probably my fault. I should have been sitting there with a tape recorder, getting him to tell about Darryl Zanuck and John Barrymore, Paul Muni and George Arliss, Bette Davis and Jolson, and all the rest of the people he knew.

His book never got written. But this one has been. So bouquets to you, Mr. Perelman, for insisting I do it, and to Messrs. Knopf and Bessie of Atheneum for underwriting. And to all the rest of my friends and to the people who have become friends—long may you stay survivors.

Thanks to Jessica Silvers, who taped some people as my proxy, to Jesse Kahn Culberg, who has always shared stories of her Hollywood years with me, to Diane Daniels, who was willing to undertake the hideous job of helping me to assemble some 575 loose pages of manuscript into some semblance of order, and, last but far from least, a large bouquet to my wife, Barbara, who miraculously enjoys listening to these stories before, during and after their transcription.

But I am sure that none of you will object if I dedicate the rest of this book to my father, the late Jacob Wilk.

MAX WILK

CONTENTS

SILENT DAYS, NOISY NIGHTS

"A rock is a rock, a tree is a tree—shoot it in Griffith Park!"

THE STERN BROTHERS,
UNCLES OF CARL LAEMMLE

"Our comedies are not meant to be laughed at." IBID.

*"My head is buried in the sands of tomorrow, while my tail
feathers are singed by the hot sun of today."*

JOHN BARRYMORE

MOVIE VAMP: *"Haven't you a tighter gown than this?"*
TIRED WARDROBE MANAGER: *"No, madam, I am a costumer, not
a taxidermist."*

LIFE, 1922

"**THERE** never was a *silent* film," said [Irving] Thalberg. "We'd finish a picture, show it in one of our projection rooms, and come out shattered. It would be awful. We'd have high hopes for the picture, work our heads off on it, and the result was always the same. Then we'd show it in a theatre, with a girl down in the pit pounding away at a piano, and there would be all the difference in the world. Without that music, there wouldn't have been a movie industry at all."

(*from* TOTAL RECOIL, *by Kyle Crichton, Doubleday, 1960*)

David Selznick's father, Lewis J. Selznick, was an enormously resourceful and somewhat flamboyant showman. When news came that the Czar of Russia had been overthrown by the Russian revolution, Selznick fired off the following cable: WHEN I WAS A BOY IN RUSSIA YOUR POLICE TREATED MY PEOPLE VERY BADLY. HOWEVER NO HARD FEELINGS. HEAR YOU ARE NOW OUT OF WORK. IF YOU WILL COME TO NEW YORK CAN GIVE YOU FINE POSITION ACTING IN PICTURES. SALARY NO OBJECT. REPLY MY EXPENSE. REGARDS YOU AND FAMILY, LEWIS J. SELZNICK. No reply was ever received.

Selznick's early empire eventually collapsed, but the family name persisted for the next four decades. Son Myron Selznick became Hollywood's first talent agent, and before his early death, was instrumental in prying huge prices for his clients' services from grudging studio heads. Son David O. Selznick created his own feudal empire, and persisted in producing *Gone with the Wind,* which will serve as his masterwork for as long as there are projection machines and screens on which to show it.

"I went out to Hollywood in the middle Twenties as a humorous lecturer," Donald Ogden Stewart recalls. "There I was, a Yale man, and what did they do first? They asked me to work on *Brown of Harvard*. And then, when sound came in and Thalberg sent for me, what did he ask me, a humorist, to write? *Smilin' Through,* a great tear-jerker."

3

* * *

Cecil [B. De Mille], never to be outdone by anyone else, began pouring money into his newest effort, *The Ten Commandments,* with boundless energy. . . . One evening at dinner I did let him know that the bosses felt we had already sunk in the picture more than we could ever recover, and wanted me to clamp down on his spending. Cecil's eyes blazed. "What do they want me to do?" he snapped. "Stop now and release it as *The Five Commandments?*"

(*from* I BLOW MY OWN HORN, *by Jesse Lasky, Doubleday, 1957*)

De Mille took his producer-director chores quite seriously, and when in conference was often sealed off from the mundane world outside. While *The Ten Commandments* was being made, Theodore Roberts and James Neil, two of his actors, were summoned to an audience with De Mille. In Biblical costume, they sat in his outer office for what seemed like an interminable time, and finally sent in word: "Moses and Aaron are still waiting to see God."

COLLEEN MOORE

Since 1917, when Charlie Chaplin had gone into independent production, writing and directing his films as well as acting in them, he had been releasing his films through First National and had been one of their most valuable properties.

This was no longer so. As a founding member, along with Mary Pickford, Douglas Fairbanks, and D. W. Griffith, of a new releasing organization, United Artists, Charlie had left First National when his contract with them expired in September of 1922.

Nevertheless, he invited Mr. Rowland and three of First National's owners to lunch at his studio while they were in Hollywood—I suppose they thought just for old times' sake—and since Charlie's former bosses were now my bosses—I had signed with First National in 1922—they invited me to go with them.

When we arrived, Charlie ushered us into his studio living room. On one wall was a large bay window, the bright California sunshine streaming through. It was a beautiful day.

We were all sitting there chatting, waiting for lunch to be served, when Charlie stood up and, turning to Robert Leiber, the president of First National, said, "I hear you've bought Papini's *Life of Christ.*"

Mr. Leiber nodded.

Charlie nodded, too. "I want to play the role of Jesus."

4

If Charlie had bopped Mr. Leiber over the head with a baseball bat, he couldn't have received a more stunned reaction. Not just from Mr. Leiber. From all four of them. They sat there like figures in a waxworks. Even their faces had turned sort of waxy yellow.

"I'm a logical choice," Charlie went on. "I look the part. I'm a Jew. And I'm a comedian."

The bosses looked more stunned, if possible, than before.

Charlie explained to them that good comedy was only a hairline away from good tragedy, which we all knew to be true. "And I'm an atheist," he added, "so I'd be able to look at the character objectively. Who else could do that?"

They had no answer for him.

He stretched his arms high over his head, his fists clenched, and in a blood-curdling tone of voice screamed. "There is no God! If there is one, I dare Him to strike me dead!"

The five of us sat there chilled and tense, holding our breath, but nothing happened, not even one small clap of thunder. The California sun shone outside, the chirp of birds came through the window, and I suppose God was in His Heaven, and all was right with the world—all but for five very shaken people in the Chaplin studio.

There was silence in the car going back until Richard Rowland said, "He's the greatest actor alive, and he'd give an historical performance, but who of you would have the nerve to put in lights on a theater marquee: Charlie Chaplin in *The Life of Christ?*"

Mr. Leiber said wistfully, "It would be the greatest religious picture ever made, but I'd be run out of Indianapolis."

(*from* SILENT STAR, *by Colleen Moore, Doubleday, 1968*)

At one point in his career, the great Florenz Ziegfeld was in California. Temporarily strapped for cash, he remembered a large collection of costumes he had stored in a warehouse, and discussed with Nat Goldstone, a good friend of the Laemmle family, the possibility of selling his surplus costumes to Universal.

Goldstone approached Carl Laemmle with the proposition, but Uncle Carl was uninterested. He did not need any costumes. Goldstone, who was later to become a successful agent and Broadway producer (*Bloomer Girl*), brought the news back to Ziegfeld.

"Find out what they want for the studio," countered Ziegfeld.

With sweet dreams of a multimillion-dollar deal, Goldstone brought the message to Laemmle. He told Uncle Carl that the great

5

Ziegfeld wanted a price for Universal—lock, stock and barrel. Laemmle was interested. He sent bookkeepers and accountants into conference with instructions to give him an assessment of Universal's property. Goldstone, who now envisioned a fat commission for his part in the affair, was instructed to arrange a meeting between Laemmle and Ziegfeld.

The day arrived, and Ziegfeld came into Laemmle's office, where the diminutive Laemmle brought in all his financial advisors for a full-dress meeting. The formalities dispensed with, Laemmle informed Ziegfeld that Universal could be bought, and he mentioned the price—a several-million-dollar sum. He waited expectantly for Ziegfeld's reply.

Ziegfeld nodded, unperturbed. "I'm going to think it over for a bit," he told Laemmle. Then he rose to leave the office. "Oh, by the way," he said, as an afterthought, "I have a batch of costumes in my warehouse that I thought might be of some use to your studio, Mr. Laemmle, and I could let you have them for a very reasonable price—say, fifty thousand."

"Sounds like a good deal," remarked Laemmle jovially. He turned to one of the bookkeepers. "Make Mr. Ziegfeld out a check," he instructed.

There was a bit more conversation, the bookkeeper appeared with the check, Ziegfeld pocketed it—and left Universal. Laemmle waited for Ziegfeld's reply to his offer. He got no further response. But the costumes were promptly delivered to Universal.

The late Josef Von Sternberg, best remembered for the remarkable series of films in which he starred Marlene Dietrich, recalled, "What influenced me most was an anecdote about D. W. Griffith. 'Move these ten thousand horses a trifle to the right,' he was quoted as saying in a grand manner to his assistant, who rushed to obey, while the master tried to breathe a little easier by relieving some obstruction from his large nostrils. 'And that mob out there three feet forward'—this to another of his eager assistants, while his thumb was still in his nose. While his orders were being carried out he looked down benevolently at a small boy who had ventured admiringly to his side. 'Young man,' he said, 'when you grow up, would you like to be a director?' 'Naw,' drawled the youngster, 'my father doesn't let me pick my nose.' "

(*from* FUN IN A CHINESE LAUNDRY, *by Josef Von Sternberg, Macmillan, 1965*)

* * *

"I've heard it quoted for years, usually attributed to John Barrymore," said George Axelrod, "but my mother, who was Betty Carpenter and worked in silent pictures in the early Twenties, has always sworn it was she who said it. She was working for Sam Goldwyn in one of his early films, and Sam got into an argument with her, waving his finger at her to make his point. 'Don't you point that finger at *me*,' she said. 'I knew it when there was a thimble on it!' "

Francis X. Bushman was one of the brightest of all the male silent-screen stars. He starred in 424 films and in his peak earning period piled up $6,000,000 in five years. He is probably remembered best for his performance in the silent MGM classic *Ben-Hur*.

"*Ben-Hur* was a great joke on Mussolini," recalled Bushman some years later. "When we went to Italy to shoot the picture, he was most hospitable. He thought we were about to recreate the grandeur that was Rome. He couldn't do too much for us. Then, when we were done and had gone home and he saw the film, he almost had a stroke. The hero was a young Jewish follower of Christ, and a Roman was the villain of the picture.

"In the old days," said Bushman, "there were as many as seven companies working on the same set. I might be having a death scene in which I knelt heartbroken beside my little daughter whose life was flickering out, while next to me they would be shooting a noisy comedy. Cameramen would be yelling—there was no sound track to pick it up—and directors barked through megaphones. I had come from the thitt-tuh, where all was silence and respect when an artist was engaged in his art, where even the stagehands wore sneakers and spoke in whispers, and I said I couldn't stand the racket of this new medium. Now there were chalked lines drawn, giving me a space of only four feet in which to act, and I was constantly wandering off the set and disappearing where the cameras couldn't pick me up. Almost everybody doubled or tripled in brass to help out. We didn't sit around between shots. We pulled this or moved that. I remember a stunt man who told me 'I get twenty-two dollars a week, and they've broken twenty-two of my bones. That's a dollar a bone.' "

(*from* PM)

* * *

How did one become a Hollywood star?

The most persistent American fantasy, the one which brought thousands of young hopefuls into Los Angeles for decades, was the discovery legend—i.e., lovely young thing serves producer lunch, producer looks up, his sharp eyes widen, he asks, "How would you like a screen test for my next picture?" etc., etc.

There was no such formula for becoming a director. Some, like George Stevens, began as cameramen. Others worked their way up from cutting. Some talked their way into the job by sheer bluff and maintained the bluff for the rest of their lives.

In that Cloud-Cuckoo Land of the Twenties, young William A. Wellman, who had been a World War I fighter pilot, drifted into Hollywood and got a job as a laborer at the Goldwyn Studios. Later Wellman was to become a top-rank director (Wings, Battleground, Public Enemy, *etc.*).

Wellman's first promotion followed General Pershing's grand visit to the Goldwyn studio. All ex-servicemen on the lot were ordered to appear in uniform as a reception committee "so that the General would have a safe journey from the entrance of the studio to where the stars and producers were assembled and waiting." Wellman headed the line of sixty-odd ex-soldiers because he had a resplendent blue French uniform (the studio thoughtfully repaired the badly torn seat of his pants).

In Wellman's words, "The general and entourage swept through the gates and he got out. He saw this sight that had greeted him and he wasn't interested in it. He was interested in what was down the line. So he quickly shook my hand and then the hand of the man next to him, whereupon he turned and he looked back at me and he said, 'Where have I seen you before?'

"I said, 'General, I'd better not tell you,' and he snapped his fingers and said, 'That's it. What can I do for you?' And I said, 'Take me over behind that fig tree and talk to me for a few minutes and make me important.' He said, 'That I will do,' and he did.

"Well, the next morning, I was called into the office of the vice-president of the company, Abraham Lehr, and I was introduced to Mr. Goldwyn, and I was told I was the kind of man they wanted on that lot, and they made me an assistant director. I didn't tell them Black Jack and I had got together when we were both on a toot in Paris."

(*from* ROMAN CANDLE OF MGM, *by Ezra Goodman, Esquire, March, 1956*)

Among the giants of early movie business was Carl Laemmle, who started with nickelodeons and carved out a feudal barony called Universal Pictures. Diminutive in stature, Uncle Carl could be a tiger when it came to survival in the New York-Hollywood jungle. Operating a company staffed largely with his relatives, the little old film-maker of Universal City combined shrewdness with a sharp sense of what the public would pay to see.

"I was a young kid, an assistant sales manager at Universal in the East," recalls Jules Levey. "In those days, Adolph Zukor with his Famous Players Co. was the king of the business. One day Uncle Carl called me into his office. He spoke with a thick German accent. 'Yulius,' he said, 'vat's de matter ve don't get Zukor's prices for our pictures?'

"I was a brash, outspoken kid and I wasn't worried about losing my job, so I told him the truth. 'If we had good pictures, we'd get good prices,' I told him, 'but the truth is, Mr. Laemmle, our pictures are lousy.'

"Laemmle nodded his head. 'Well, Yulius,' he said, 'if you can't get the prices, you get the wolume.'

"I remember another day, it was a Sunday, and Laemmle called a special meeting—everybody in the place came in. I had a date to go to the ball game, and I was impatient to get it over with—I had a guy in a car waiting downstairs. Laemmle called the meeting to order and he said, 'I vant to make a picture called *The Hunchback of Notre Dame* vit Lon Chaney. Now, I vant you boys to giff me your opinion.'

"He went all around the table," says Levey, "starting with the Eastern Sales Manager, who was a guy named Schmidt. Schmidt didn't like the idea at all—he said he thought it would be offensive to the Catholic Church. Laemmle turned to the next guy, and he said he didn't think Lon Chaney was a big enough star—he was strictly a B star, and this picture would cost too much to gamble on

9

with Chaney. One by one everybody had an objection to the idea. Finally, Laemmle turned to me. 'Vat do you think, Yulius?' he asked.

"I was in a hurry to get to the ball game, so I said, 'Listen, it sounds okay to me, why not go ahead with it?'

"Laemmle nodded, and then he said, 'All right, now I'll tell you—yesterday ve *started* the picture!'

"Why did he hold the meeting? I guess because he wanted to put everybody on the spot—and then prove who was boss."

One day a director came in to Laemmle and informed Uncle Carl that he absolutely had to have a quartet for the next day's shooting. Laemmle tried to dissuade his director from spending the money, but the director insisted—a quartet was vital to the action of the scene. "All right!" said Laemmle. "You can have a quartet—but don't get too many!"

WILL ROGERS

There is only one thing that can kill the movies, and that is education.

If the movies want to advance, all they have to do is not to get new stories but do the old ones over as they were written.

You can't spring a new plot on an audience the first time and expect it to go. It takes a movie audience years to get used to a new plot.

(*from* AUTOBIOGRAPHY OF WILL ROGERS, *Houghton Mifflin, 1949*)

One of the more thriving businesses today is motion-picture criticism. Toward the end of this past decade, alas, there were times when more people were writing about certain films than were actually paying to see them. Why not? Anyone with a heritage of Late Show viewing, a card to his local Film Society, and a typewriter could become, de facto, a film critic.

In France you could even do without the typewriter. All you needed for your credentials was to develop a critical monograph on the complete cinematic works of some obscure American B-picture director, circa 1936 to 1940—the more obscure, the better. Your monograph could refer to his "lean and taut cinematic thrust" (brought about by his seven-day shooting schedules at

Monogram), his "sensitive feeling for the problems of the confused contemporary young" (as evidenced by his direction of Bonita Granville in Nancy Drew and the Hidden Staircase), and his "empathetic probing of the forces of the supernatural" (viz., his work with Bela Lugosi, John Carradine and George Zucco in The Attack of the Devil Bat's Daughter), and voilà—you were now a full-fledged Cahiers du Cinéma man, available for lectures, round tables and demonstrations.

It wasn't always that simple.

To begin with, in the early days of the silent motion picture, nobody paid much attention to film criticism. To be an honest film critic was even more difficult. The film producers specialized in flamboyant publicity and hoopla, but they cared little for truth. The newspapers cheerfully accepted motion-picture advertising, but left out any serious criticism of this upstart medium. Creativity, it was felt, belonged to such respectable fields of the arts as the drama and the concert stage. If you wanted to find out whether a new film was good, bad or indifferent, you might read an honest review of it in Sime Silverman's Variety, but rarely in any other paper.

When Robert E. Sherwood began writing his film criticisms for the old Life magazine, in the early Twenties, he was indeed a rara avis. A man of talent, taste and wit, who wrote knowledgeably about the films of the day, both out of admiration for the screen's possibilities and despair for its creative waste, Sherwood was always honest, often hilarious. In a time when movies were being sneered at by the intellectuals, he dared to take them seriously. His critical remarks of that day remain pungent, pointed, and remarkably up to date.

In later years, Sherwood was to become one of our major playwrights (Idiot's Delight, There Shall Be No Night, Abe Lincoln in Illinois) and, during the war years, one of President Roosevelt's confidants and speechwriters. His two-volume history, Roosevelt and Hopkins, is a massive and lasting piece of work.

An amusing anecdote about Sherwood is recounted by Buster Keaton in his own book, My Wonderful World of Slapstick. According to Keaton, such was the mutual admiration between him and Sherwood that in 1924, *during Sherwood's summer vacation, he lured the six-foot-four critic out to Hollywood to work on a film idea for a comedy.*

Sherwood labored for several weeks and evolved a comedy idea that would trap Buster and a girl friend on the top of a half-finished skyscraper in midwinter and subject them to a series of misadventures high on the Manhattan skyline. Alas, Sherwood was never able to come up with the indispensable wind-up of the story—how to get Buster and his girl safely off the scaffolding in the midst of a nighttime blizzard.

Sixteen years later Sherwood ran into Keaton in the lobby of the Dorchester in London. He leaned down and patted the great comedian's shoulder. "Don't worry, Buster," he soothed, "I'll get you down off that building yet!"

Here are some of Sherwood's peerless film reports.

SCHOOL DAYS

The Famous Players–Lasky Corporation has started the Paramount Stock Company and School for the purpose of raising the intellectual tone of its employees. Regular courses are given in the various branches of Philmology, including "Photodramatic Theory," "Cinematography and Lighting," "Motion Picture History," etc.; and all members of the organization are required to take a certain number of these studies.

There are regular report cards, on which are recorded the student's rating in the various courses, together with remarks on his or her General Deportment, Health, Times Absent and Times Tardy at Classes.

It is a worthy idea and, if carried out, should do a vast amount of good. But one can be pardoned for sensations of skepticism concerning the spirit with which the film stars will accept this innovation. I cannot refrain from picturing the situation which would arise if Wallace Reid arrived late at the studio some morning with a note from his mother, informing teacher De Mille that he had been kept home on account of the measles epidemic scare.

However, I shall be the last one to ridicule any attempt to inject a little gray matter into the silent drama; and if hearty co-operation is what the Paramount School desires, here is a suggested examination paper which might well be administered to the students when Commencement rolls around:

What foreign authors suggested the stories of *Male and Female* and *The Affairs of Anatole* to Jeannie Macpherson? What did she do with these stories?

Define the following words: "Taste," "Repression," "Intelligence," "Simplicity."

Account for the financial failure of these pictures: *Sentimental Tommy. The Golem. Dr. Jekyll and Mr. Hyde. Broken Blossoms.*

Account for the success of these: *Fool's Paradise. Where Is My Wandering Boy Tonight? Dream Street. Over the Hill.*

What is a moron? Name eleven examples from your intimate acquaintance.

Who invented "hokum"? How much money would he have made from the film producers if he had sold his invention on a royalty basis?

KEATON'S COPS

In *Cops* Buster Keaton develops the old police-chase idea to the nth power by staging his antics in the midst of a police parade, and the resultant mob effect is as stupendous as anything in Mr. Fox's spectacles. What is more, it is actually funnier—and that is no faint praise.

There is a popular misconception to the effect that so-called highbrow critics are prejudiced against red-blooded Western pictures as a matter of principle. All critics are necessarily puny, shriveled, anemic old crabs who have never stepped outside the city limits, and therefore know nothing of the ways of clean, two-fisted he-men. As a matter of fact, some of my best friends are he-men, and moreover, I once rode in the stagecoach that used to whirl around the sawdust track in Buffalo Bill's show; so that I have at least as good a working knowledge of the Great West as most of the movie cowboys. I have no more prejudice against pictures of this type than I have against Cecil B. De Mille's dramas of life in Fifth Avenue mansions with the proverbial eucalyptus in the back yard. . . . But I am tired to death of Western melodramas with stories written on a mimeograph machine, and with stars whose sole claim to dramatic fame is their Swobodian muscular development. . . .

BLOOD AND SAND

There are a number of strikingly effective bullfight scenes . . . although it is quite evident that the expensive Signor Valentino is absent from the more strenuous episodes. He is shown making passes at a bull which is only half in the picture. As Will Rogers observes, we shall probably never learn the identity of the hero who held the bull's tail.

In a recent issue of *Screenland,* H. L. Mencken is quoted as follows: "The kind of jackass who likes the movies as they are is the man who keeps them as they are." That observation will serve from now on as the motto of this department.

Marion Davies! I have yet to encounter a single movie fan with the slightest respect for her ability—and yet the coal that has been used to keep her name flaming on the electric signs would probably run the city of Syracuse for a whole year.

Those incurable lowbrows who agree with me that Ben Turpin's eyes are infinitely more interesting than Rudolph Valentino's will derive a considerable amount of satisfaction from *Home Made Movies,* the latest Turpinian photo-drama.

Of course you can argue that it is crude, that it is slapstick, that it does not demonstrate the inevitable triumph of virtue over vice, that it possesses no heart interest: and if that's the way you feel about it, you can have *Rags to Riches* while I take *Home Made Movies.* And then we'll all be happy.

Buster Keaton's motto seems to be "Fall, and the world laughs at you." In his three latest comedies, he dives as he has never dived before, landing on everything but his feet.

Keaton . . . is a distinct asset to the movies. He can attract people who would never think of going to a picture palace to see anything else. Moreover, he can impress a weary world with the vitally important fact that life, after all, is a foolishly inconsequential affair.

ROBIN HOOD

Out of the muck of misunderstood heroines, Royal Northwest Mounted Policemen, property mothers, rising young district attorneys, wandering boys, amorous sheiks and strong silent men of the open has come a real motion picture.

Robin Hood . . . this year, when the general trend of the silent drama has been steadily downward . . . appears as an oasis in the desert . . . a radiator at the North Pole, a breeze in the doldrums, or four aces on an unlucky Saturday night.

14

EAST IS WEST

Constance Talmadge is one of the few film stars who can be cute without being revolting—fresh, but not offensive. She is the world's champion in the standing broad wink.

THE PRIDE OF PALOMAR

Get down your old musket, Uncle Ned, and keep your powder dry: Mr. Hearst says that the Japs are coming. If you don't find any Japs to shoot at, Mr. Hearst wouldn't be such a bad target himself.

OLIVER TWIST

Presenting the extraordinary spectacle of a great dramatic artist who has reached the apex of his career at the age of seven. Jackie Coogan could retire today, secure in the knowledge that he has touched the heights.

NANOOK OF THE NORTH

This remarkable picture was sponsored by a firm of fur dealers, Revillon Frères (if you must know), and directed by Robert J. Flaherty. Their success will doubtless inspire other merchants to enter the film business.

NERO

Rome is rebuilt in a day, under the personal supervision of Mr. William Fox.

THE STROKE OF MIDNIGHT

Splendid acting, but too much of it.

OVER THE BORDER

Endless views of Canadian Northwest Mounted Policemen trudging through blizzards, and then entering log cabins with flour sprinkled over their mackinaws.

YELLOW MEN AND GOLD

A rip-roaring melodrama, featuring Richard Dix, Helene Chadwick, a chest of buried treasure and a rejected manuscript.

SILVER WINGS

A mother-love story, featuring Mary Carr and several over-developed lachrymal glands.

WHILE SATAN SLEEPS

Jack Holt puts over a big moral lesson with both fists.

SOUTH OF SUVA

Little Miss Mary Miles Minter goes to an island in the Fijis and is subjected to some rough treatment by the natives and the scenario writer.

A FOOL THERE WAS

Revised edition of the famous vamp drama that made Theda Bara famous. Weakened by the absence of Miss Bara and the presence of censors.

(from issues of LIFE, *1922)*

SHERWOOD ON SHAW

It was more than thirty years ago that George Bernard Shaw started to convince the public that there is no Santa Claus. Now, through the medium of the Fox Movietone, he is attempting to establish the fact that there is no George Bernard Shaw. What a disillusioner the fellow is, to be sure.

His debut on the screen is cause for lamentation. He appears before an incredulous audience as a dealer in sunshine sayings, a peddler of whimsy; he speaks as though he had suddenly traded souls with J. M. Barrie. He even goes so far as to tell a pointless anecdote about a little girl in Wales who asked for his autograph.

I regret having seen this short film. It is disappointing to have to report that George Bernard Shaw, appearing as George Bernard Shaw, is sadly miscast in the part. Satirists should be heard and not seen.

(from LIFE, *July 12, 1928)*

John Barrymore made a film in which a monkey also appeared, and the great man took a definite shine to the monkey. He called in the animal's trainer and informed him that he would like to buy the monkey and keep her as a pet. "I like Clarabelle and I'd like to keep her," he said.

"How much do you make, Mr. Barrymore?" the trainer replied.

"I make $3,000 a week," answered Barrymore.

"Well, she likes *you* too," said the monkey's trainer, "and she makes $5,000 a week—she'd like to buy *you*."

Mary Pickford was such a shrewd businesswoman that she was known to some as "The Bank of America's Sweetheart."

* * *

"I first worked for Jack Warner back in the early Twenties," recalled Ben Lyon. "It was a picture called *Open Your Eyes,* which dealt with the problem of venereal disease and was made for the armed services. I played a good boy who was led astray by bad boys. One of the bad boys was played by our producer, Jack Warner.

"The picture was being made on the streets of New York, and we were all running from location to location. Jack had such a tight budget that he used 'short ends'—unexposed pieces of film left over from other companies' reels. He'd buy them from the lab for bargain prices. Sometimes the short ends were seventy-five feet, or maybe a hundred. Whatever they were, Jack's cameraman would put them into the camera, and then we'd have to time the action of each scene to fit the film we actually had. Sometimes, when we were really short, we'd have to rush through the scene like lightning. I suppose today you'd call that rapid-fire pacing.

"I think Jack gave up acting after he saw himself in that picture. We met a couple of years back, and I said, "Jack, I only wish I'd been as lousy an actor as you were—I could have ended up as head of a studio."

Back in the days when Gloria Swanson was a reigning star of the silents, she took as her husband a titled gentleman, the Marquis de la Falaise.

Legend has it that Miss Swanson's mother, upon hearing the news of her daughter's marriage, immediately phoned the family lawyer. "What" she demanded, "is a markee?"

"It's one of those things," said the lawyer, "that you hang in front of a theatre to keep the rain off the paying customers."

"My God!" cried the anguished lady. "Gloria married one of them this afternoon!"

Conrad Nagel was a superb example of the steely-eyed, wavy-haired, chiseled-profiled, elegantly turned-out leading man. He belonged to a lineal procession that included Francis X. Bushman, Creighton Hale, Neil Hamilton, and many other such Arrow-collar types of the early "heart-throb" school of the film academy. After the actor's death the following appeared as part of his obituary in The New York Times.

In a letter . . . [Nagel] denounced as a "hoary myth" a much-quoted story about a silent film in which he lifted a girl and carried her to a bed. According to the story, the girl looked at him tenderly but actually said, "If you drop me, you bastard, I'll kill you."

Mr. Nagel recounted that the silent pictures were a source of great joy to many thousands of deaf people and that, being expert lip readers, they would have deluged Hollywood with letters of protest. However, he conceded that there was a basis in fact for the story. He said that during rehearsal, another actor—who was suffering from a hangover—had to lift an actress from the floor. She told him, "Use your breath, that's strong enough to do the job."

Donald Ogden Stewart is fond of relating an incident that took place when he and actor John Gilbert took a weekend jaunt to Tijuana. It was at the time that Cecil B. De Mille was filming his version of the life of Christ, *The King of Kings,* in which H. B. Warner played the title role.

A great deal of publicity had been released by De Mille, underscoring the taste and dignity with which he was preparing his subject. One of the stories, which received great press acceptance, announced that Warner's contract stipulated he would take no strong drink while engaged in playing Christ before the cameras.

On this particular weekend Stewart and Gilbert spotted Warner drinking in a dark corner of a Tijuana café. Stewart crossed over to Warner's table and, with great dignity, placed a large glass of water before the actor. "Would you mind very much changing that into red wine?" he inquired.

Sam Jaffe (not to be confused with the actor) was studio manager at Paramount in the late Twenties—a very complex job for a young man, since the company was geared to ship a completed film to its exchanges at the end of each week.

One day he sought Jesse Lasky's advice on investing his money. Would Lasky advise buying California real estate or securities? Lasky's advice was simple and direct. "Sam," he said, "Paramount is a first-rate company. Who would know better how good it is than you and I, who work here every day? Invest your money in Paramount stock—it's the best buy I know. Every spare dollar I have goes right into Paramount."

Came the black days of October 1929, and Paramount stock

dropped in value to a dreadful point where it was selling for two dollars a share. Eventually the company was forced to go into bankruptcy.

"Everything Lasky had went down with Paramount stock," recalls Jaffe, "and there came a day when Lasky, one of the founders of the company, was pushed out. All that stock he was sitting with was just so much worthless paper."

One fine October day in 1929, Groucho Marx was playing golf with Max Gordon, the producer, at a Long Island country club. Gordon was suddenly overtaken by sensations of bliss.

"Marx," he said, strolling down the fairway and twirling his club, "this is the life! Why should we do any work at all? Here I am, a nobody, my real name is Salpeter, I am a kid from Rivington Street, but I can spend a fine day playing golf because I already made three thousand dollars this morning. Marx," Gordon demanded, hitting a ball and running happily after it, "how long has this been going on?"

A few days later, on the morning of the crash, Groucho's telephone rang. It was Max Gordon, and his voice was hollow. "Marx?" he said. "This is Salpeter. The jig is up."

(from THE VICIOUS CIRCLE, *by Margaret Case Harriman, Rinehart,*
1951)

In the late Twenties, exhibitors all over the country engaged in a fierce rivalry to see who could build the largest and most opulent movie theatre. Certain relics of this era—which spawned such monsters as the huge Fox Detroit, the New York Roxy, the Paramount, the Capitol, and the Metropolitan in Boston—still remain, although economically they no longer can exist as movie houses.

Possibly one of the greatest white elephants ever erected in this era was the Mastbaum (named after its founding father, Jules Mastbaum, a Philadelphia exhibitor). The Mastbaum was so huge that its physical dimensions elicited many derisive quips. It was Al Boasberg who said, "It's such a big theatre you need a license to shoot deer in the balcony." And he later added, "At the Mastbaum you don't hire a manager—you elect a governor." Unfortunately, the Mastbaum was built at the very end of this halcyon era of monster movie houses. Came the 1929 crash and the ensuing Depression, and the Mastbaum stood there mostly empty for many years.

Norman Krasna, the author-playwright, recalls a poker game with Jack Warner during the late Thirties. "I shouldn't have been in the game in the first place," says Krasna. "The stakes were huge, and I didn't know any better, but I was single and making good money, so there I was, locked in a hand with Jack Warner—and I thought I had him. So I thought I'd relieve the tension, and I said 'Listen, Jack—forget the table stakes, put in the Mastbaum!'

"Warner clapped his hand to his forehead. 'Oh *boy!*' he cried. "'If I could only put it in—it loses $11,000 a week when it's open and $6,000 a week when it's closed. That damn place has cost us a fortune. Believe me, I'd love to lose it to you—but damn it, the banks wouldn't accept you as the owner!' "

GARBO SPEAKS!

"Never buy anything you can't put on the Chief."
ACTORS' SAYING, CIRCA 1930

"Boy meets girl, boy loses girl, boy gets girl."
HOLLYWOOD PRODUCER'S FORMULA

*THE film revolution was headquartered in Brooklyn
at the Warner studio, where Sam Warner, along with a
dedicated crew of technicians and engineers from Western
Electric, developed a device called Vitaphone. Sam Warner
was to die of overwork, but Vitaphone made his three sur-
viving brothers rich and revolutionized the motion-picture
business. Ever since that night when Al Jolson sang and
talked in* The Jazz Singer, *film audiences have been inundated with a sea of sound effects, music and lyrics and
dialogue, good, bad and repetitive.*

*Dozens of books document the coming of sound to the
screen, but none of them contain the pithy comments of
Ernst Lubitsch, one of Hollywood's finest craftsmen
(*Trouble in Paradise, Desire, Angel, *etc.) who passed on
his wisdom to Joseph L. Mankiewicz, another top film
maker. The following was related by Mankiewicz.*

Lubitsch was a great man who was very kind to me. We met in
1929 when he was a big director at Paramount. I wasn't his protégé
—that's a self-serving thing to say—but we became very good
friends, and later, when I directed my first picture, he was the producer.

I used to have lunch with him almost every day, wangle invita-
tions to his house whenever I could—and I used to pester him, because I got out to Hollywood just *after* the change from silent films
to sound; in fact, my first job at Paramount was to write subtitles
for sound pictures that were being sent out to the thousands of
movie theatres that hadn't yet been equipped for sound films. And I
remember asking, "Ernst, what was it like when the actual decision
was taken by the producers to switch over from silent films to
sound?"

Lubitsch had a habit of crooking his forefinger over that enormous nose of his, and he said, "*Junge,* I want you never to forget
this. You must remember this as long as you work—what I am about
to tell you. When the decision was made to change from silent films
to talking films, the producers called together the greatest stars they

had—this was in each studio. And the producers said, 'You ladies and gentlemen who are the stars of the great silent screen, you must now learn to *talk*. You can no longer make faces and look camera left, camera right, up, down, what the director tells you to do, and then hope that he can put it together into a performance. You've got to learn to talk dialogue, to sustain scenes, to characterize, to remember dialogue and play it. Those of you who can—you'll be greater than ever. Those of you who can't—overnight, no matter how great you are, you'll be finished.'

"Then," said Lubitsch, "they called together all the great directors. And they said, 'All you directors of the silent screen, no more running out in the morning with that box, a camera and an assistant, you shoot something here and you shoot something there, and then bring it back . . . No, no. You gentlemen have got to learn to read scripts, to digest characterization, pace, and how to tell a story that is written—and those of you who do will be bigger than ever. Those of you who don't—overnight, you'll be forgotten.'

"And then," said Lubitsch, "they called together all the great title writers, those who'd been the biggest of the silent screen, and they said, 'You writers, no longer is it going to be something that you can bring in on the back of an envelope, it's no longer a question of waiting until the director gives you a film and has you write subtitles for it—you have to become *dramatists*—you have to learn how to write dialogue, conflict, and so forth. And again, those of you who learn will go on to fabulous wealth and fame. Those of you who can't —you're finished.'

"And," said Lubitsch, "that really happened, as you know. You could name the great stars of the silent screen who were finished— the great directors, gone—the great title writers who were washed up —but, boy, remember this as long as you live: The producers *didn't lose a man*. They *all* made the switch! *That's* where the great talent is. *Remember this*."

"We had great parties at our beach house," recalled Bebe Daniels, who made her first film, *The Common Enemy*, at the age of four. "It was during silent pictures, and we could play cards and dance or swim. Our nights were always free, you see. It wasn't until sound came in that our entire social pattern changed. With talkies, you couldn't play at night any more—you'd come home from the studio, have supper, and start studying your lines for tomorrow at eight A.M."

* * *

Al Lewis is in his mid-eighties. In his lifetime he has been a successful producer in every form of entertainment that show business has devised in America: as a vaudeville producer with Max Gordon, in the legitimate theatre (Cabin in the Sky, Banjo Eyes) *and as one of the pioneering producers of sound films, at Fox, Paramount and Metro.*

He is blessed with near-total recall, and has some sixty-odd years of experience from which to draw a remarkable series of incisive anecdotes like the following.

I was producing at Fox, and the studio signed Georgie Jessel to a three-picture contract at $50,000 a picture—a very big salary. I'd been friends with Jessel for many years in New York, so Winnie Sheehan put me in charge of finding a suitable property for Georgie.

I persuaded the front office to let me buy *Liliom* by Ferenc Molnár for Georgie, who would have been very good in it. Georgie came out from New York and established himself in Fannie Brice's house, which was an opulent layout—many bedrooms and an indoor swimming pool, huge landscaped grounds—the works. There he lived like some Eastern potentate, with his mother, his sisters, a couple of cousins, and all sorts of hangers-on. Why not? He was making big money and living it up—and he had all those women waiting on him hand and foot, cooking for him, treating him like a pasha.

Unfortunately, this was a period when the first talkies were being made, and there was a good deal of confusion about how to make them. Instead of letting Jessel make *Liliom,* the front office assigned him to another picture—a thing called *Live, Love and Laugh,* which was about an Italian organ grinder. I'd been working on something else, so I wasn't its producer, thank heaven, because it was really awful.

The picture was finished, and they took *Live, Love and Laugh* out and previewed it. Disaster. The next morning Georgie came in for a meeting with the bosses, and there ensued a discussion about his next two pictures. They never directly told Jessel they wanted out of the commitment, but they equivocated and told him they couldn't find proper material for him, and it would be quite a while until they did, and in the meantime, wouldn't it be a good idea if there was some sort of a re-negotiation about his services?

Georgie got the message. He told them he wouldn't discuss a settlement—they'd have to talk to his lawyer in New York. They agreed to do that right away.

25

Georgie left the studio and drove home to that huge house he'd rented. There everything was still going on—business as usual—his relatives lounging around the yard, kids jumping in and out of the pool, women in the kitchen cooking and bringing food into the dining room for other relatives, who were eating as if there was no tomorrow—and into this scene came Georgie, defeated and depressed.

He walked into this house and stood there, watching everybody enjoying his largesse, and then he yelled, "All right—*everybody out! The Egyptians are coming!*"

COLLEEN MOORE

I had just signed a contract to make four pictures for First National. In those days I got $12,500 a week—with very little taxes to pay on it, which made me one of the highest-paid stars in the business.

The sound thing had just begun, and everybody was really worried about the transition—everybody including my bosses, who ran twenty-six theatre chains all over the country. They all got on the train and came out to Hollywood, and the day arrived when I had to take a voice test.

We went over to Warner Brothers, and there was a stage on which was a kind of glass box. A young man had come out—he was from Western Electric—he couldn't have been more than twenty-seven or so—to be in charge of the test. My whole future depended on what that kid said about my voice.

There was a sort of balloon hanging above me, and I said, "What's *that?*" He said, "That's a microphone. You stand under it, and I'll go inside the booth, and then, when I give you the signal, you say something." "Say what?" I asked. "Oh, anything that comes into your head," he said. Then he went inside and put on some headphones, and I was all alone—standing under that thing.

He signaled me to talk, and I said the first thing that came into my head: "Little Bo Peep has lost her sheep, and doesn't know where to find them." He signaled me—*again*—and I said it again.

There was a long silence. All my bosses were standing on the other side of the stage. I looked at them. They weren't watching me, they were watching that young kid. Then he looked up, and he made a thumb and forefinger gesture with his hand, through the glass.

That's when one of the men said, "Thank God—*she can talk!*"

Poor John Gilbert—he was one of the real tragedies of the sound film era. And it wasn't because his voice didn't record well, although that's been the legend for years. I was talking to Ina Claire some years back, and she told me the actual story, which is actually much worse.

John's voice was fine—it was the same timbre as that of Ronald Colman or Doug Fairbanks, both of whom successfully made the transition from silents to sound. Metro put him into his first talking picture—it was called *One Glorious Night*—and when it was finished, they ran it in the projection room, and all the executives, Mayer and Thalberg and the others, were pleased as punch. They stood around congratulating John—and themselves—on the triumphant proof that he'd conquered the microphone.

Then they took his picture out and previewed it, and that's when the audience betrayed John. You see, for years and years movie audiences had been accustomed to *watching* romantic leading men as they made those ardent and passionate speeches to the heroines. But they'd never *heard the words.* Now on came John, and for the first time the audience heard him saying, "Darling, I love you—I love you," and when they heard that, they began to giggle nervously and to titter, and then they laughed at him. And the executives misunderstood it. They assumed the people were laughing at his voice.

That was it. The stories started going around about John's high-pitched voice, and they ruined him. But just you watch *Queen Christina,* that picture he finally got to make with Greta Garbo— she insisted they hire him—and you listen to John in the love scenes, and you'll realize that all that gossip about him is absolutely false.

In the midst of that transitional period, when several sound stages were being built especially to house talking-picture production, fate dealt Paramount a cruel blow. An accidental fire broke out at midnight and the highly incendiary rock-wool insulation used in the new sound stages went up in a disastrous blaze.

"We were out of business," recalls Sam Jaffe, then studio manager at Paramount. "Four sound stages gone, and no place to make talkies—we couldn't compete. We had stars, we had scripts, but we had no place to make film. Mr. Zukor came out and he asked me for a schedule on rebuilding the sound stages. I told him four to five months. He looked at me and said, 'We're through.'

"It was a terrible situation—remember, in those days we shipped a picture out to the exchange every week, and here we were, completely stymied.

"I took a walk around the wreckage one night about 11:00 P.M., and it was ghostly and quiet. Not a sound anywhere. I don't know where it came from, but suddenly I had a brainstorm. *Turn night into day*, make films at *night* when it was quiet, let the construction gangs work during the day!

"I ran to a telephone and called Jesse Lasky and I explained my notion. We could use the old silent stages, drape them with blankets, and shoot all night! Maybe the sound quality wouldn't be as perfect, but that didn't matter. What was important was that we could make sound film.

"It didn't take Lasky very long to realize that the idea was feasible, and he ordered me to get going. We got going. We kept the studio commissary open and served a meal at midnight. The actors reported for work at 7:00 P.M. when the streets around the studio were quiet, no traffic, and within a week we had three pictures in production on our all-night schedule. And they were good pictures, too —one was *The Wolf of Wall Street*, with George Bancroft, the next was *Interference*—and we kept in production on that crazy schedule for four months until the new sound stages, which were being built during the day, were completed.

"It was just one of those lucky ideas," says Jaffe with modesty, "but there's no doubt that it saved Paramount Pictures from folding up in 1928."

BEN LYON

When Howard Hughes hired me to play the lead in *Hell's Angels*, the original deal called for me to work for three months. The actual shooting took 104 weeks—because we had made an entire silent version of the picture when sound came in. Hughes insisted that we do the whole thing over again, so for two years I worked in one picture.

When I first went to work for Hughes, I was a pretty popular star at First National, and I was getting roughly 800 letters a day from fans. By the end of the two years in *Hell's Angels* I was getting about fifteen a day, most of which said "Dear Ben Lyon—where are you? What's happened?"

This was a time of great confusion. Sound films were the only thing that mattered, and established stars were being dumped right and left. Nobody had seen *Hell's Angels* and nobody wanted to hire me, so I went down to my friend Henry Duffy, the legitimate producer, and offered myself to him to play in a production at his theatre in Los Angeles.

Duffy said, "You've been getting $3,500 a week—I couldn't possibly afford you, Ben." I said, "Never mind the salary, I'll do it for nothing." We compromised—he ended up paying me $125 a week, and scheduled a revival of a play I'd done on Broadway ten years before, called *The Boomerang*. He hired Tom Moore to play the lead, and I played the juvenile. On opening night Bebe [Lyon's wife of forty years] and I bought out the house and invited all the people we could think of—producers, directors, Jack Warner, Louis Mayer—everybody.

I came out on the stage in my first entrance and you could hear the buzzing in the audience: "My God, he can *talk!*"

By the end of the first week with Duffy, I had three offers for pictures, and I was a movie star again.

After the success of Sam Warner's Vitaphone, the major film companies all began frantically tying up "technology" for talking pictures. Radio Pictures (later RKO) had RCA to assist it. Fox had Movietone. But the smaller companies were momentarily adrift.

Carl Laemmle, like so many of his contemporaries, had been dubious of the lasting quality of sound films. At first they seemed merely a fad. Eventually his son, Junior, and the studio executives convinced Laemmle that Universal must take the plunge and make a sound film.

Bryan Foy, then at Universal, had a film script called *Melody Lane* which could be adapted into a half-talking, half-silent film, but the big problem was to find sound equipment with which to shoot the talking sequences.

Nat Goldstone, who was then a "trouble-shooter" at Universal, was in on all the crisis conferences. Eventually he came up with an improvising solution. "Just don't ask me where the equipment's coming from," he advised Laemmle. "Give me three or four studio trucks, and have the cast and the director stand by to shoot at night. I'll be back later with the equipment."

That night, at 7:00, the Universal trucks rolled into the studio laden with the necessary equipment. Stagehands unloaded the hardware, it was rushed onto the sound stage, and the director began to film his "talking" sequences. The crew and cast worked all night. At 5:00 A.M., Goldstone ordered everything loaded back on the trucks, and out of the studio gates went the equipment. Every night, for the following two weeks, the Universal trucks rolled in at 7:00 with the equipment, and rolled out again at 5:00 A.M.

When *Melody Lane* was finished, Goldstone revealed his strategy. He had bribed several studio policemen at the Fox Studios, and every night, when the Fox crew had finished with the equipment and gone home, Goldstone would arrive at Fox, "borrow" the Fox equipment for Universal, and return it the following morning by 6:00 A.M.—in time for the Fox crew to use it! With the inadvertent assistance of Fox Movietone, Universal was able to turn out its first "talkie."

Many successful silent directors were unable to make the leap from silent technique to sound films. One of those who did was Lloyd Bacon. "But until the day he died," recalls Joe Mankiewicz, "Bacon would finish a scene, and call, 'Cut,' and then he'd turn to his script girl and say, 'Did you get the titles right?' With Bacon, dialogue would always be titles."

"I can remember vividly how tough it was on actors and actresses when the silent pictures gave way to talkies," adds Joe Mankiewicz. "That microphone was a nemesis—if you didn't record well, you were finished. There was a fire one day at Paramount, and Clara Bow ran out screaming, 'I hope to Christ it was the sound stages!' "

ABOVE THE
TITLE

"The only thing you owe the public is a good performance."
HUMPHREY BOGART

"Two of the cruelest, most primitive punishments our
town deals out to those who fall from favor are the
empty mailbox and the silent telephone."
HEDDA HOPPER

"What is success? It is a toy balloon among
children armed with pins."
GENE FOWLER

"Sex appeal is fifty percent what you've got and fifty
percent what people think you've got."
ATTRIBUTED TO SOPHIA LOREN

"They've great respect for the dead in Hollywood, but
none for the living."
ERROL FLYNN

GEORGE ROSENBERG was a Hollywood talent agent who possessed a Damon Runyonesque turn of phrase. For years he specialized in selling the talents of some of the brightest comedy writers in town, and his loyalty to his clients was legendary.

One evening, when one of his clients had stopped by the office on his way home, George solicitously inquired, "Hey, whatcha doing tonight, baby? If you're alone, come to the house for dinner."

"No thanks," said his friend, and with ill-disguised bravado, added, "It happens I have a date tonight. With a *star*."

George nodded soberly, as yet unimpressed. "Above or below the title?" he asked.

As a boy, the successful comedian Jackie Vernon was a passionate fan of the great Charlie Chaplin. He wrote fan letters to Chaplin week after week, all of which went unanswered. Time after time Vernon wrote, with no response from Hollywood.

Years later Vernon was in London for a professional engagement. Chaplin had emerged from retirement in Switzerland to direct *The Countess from Hong Kong,* with Sophia Loren and Marlon Brando. At a restaurant Vernon spotted the white-haired Charlie in person. Still a passionate fan, he walked across the restaurant and introduced himself. "Mr. Chaplin," he said, "please excuse me, but I had to come over and say hello. I'm one of your biggest fans—my name is Jackie Vernon."

Chaplin looked up at the rotund Vernon. "Vernon? . . . Vernon?" he mused. Then he nodded. "Tell me," he asked, "why did you stop writing?"

The relationship between the screen's great beauties and their cameramen has always been primary. Make-up, costuming and publicity were all basic ingredients of a female star's success, but the wizardy of the cameraman was indispensable.

Marlene Dietrich once did a portrait sitting for one of Hollywood's best photographers. She did not like the proofs. "I don't understand it," she said. "The last time I posed for you—six years ago—the photographs were superb! Now . . ." She shook her head.

"Ah yes, Miss Dietrich." The photographer smiled. "But you must remember that I was six years younger then."

Hedda Hopper, who spent many years reporting the Hollywood scene, was especially fond of recalling a day in which she watched Mae West and the late Alison Skipworth making a scene together. Miss Skipworth, no mean scene-stealer herself, was justifiably nervous of Miss West's abilities in that line, and the tension mounted during the rehearsal.

Finally, just before the cameras rolled, Miss Skipworth turned to Mae and said, with hauteur, "I'll have you know—I'm an actress!" Miss West smiled. "It's all right, dearie," she said. "I'll keep your secret."

Later Hedda interviewed Miss West and asked her how she knew so much about men. "Baby," said Mae, "I went to night school."

On the subject of Audrey Hepburn, Billy Wilder once said: "She's like a salmon swimming upstream. She can do it with very small bozooms. Titism has taken over this country. This girl single-handed may make bozooms a thing of the past. The director will not have to invent shots where the girl leans way forward for a glass of Scotch and soda."

(*from* THE FIFTY-YEAR DECLINE AND FALL OF HOLLYWOOD, *by Ezra Goodman, Simon and Schuster, 1961*)

RAYMOND CHANDLER

I remember Harry Tugend's wonderful crack about a certain film star, during World War II, when Tugend was trying to be a producer and hating it. He said, "You know, this is a lousy job. You got to sit and talk to that bird brain seriously about whether or not this part is going to be good for her career and at the same time you got to keep from being raped." Whereat a rather innocent young man piped up, "You mean to say she's a nymphomaniac?" Harry frowned off into distance and sighed and said slowly, "Well, I guess she would be, if they could get her quieted down a little."

(*from* CHANDLER SPEAKING, *by Raymond Chandler, Houghton Mifflin, 1962*)

34

* * *

The young Gary Cooper, a raw youth from Montana, became a popular leading man in the early Thirties. The Countess di Frasso became enamored of him, and in the course of their romance she took him to a good tailor for clothes, introduced him to the social high life and, in general, remade him into a more chic young fellow. When Cooper accompanied her to Europe, it was Bill Goetz who remarked, "The best way to go to Europe is on the Countess di Frasso."

After a run of successful films in which he had specialized in portraying the tight-lipped Westerner, Paramount assigned Gary Cooper to play in his first drawing-room comedy, Ernst Lubitsch's production of Noel Coward's *Design for Living.*

With Fredric March and Miriam Hopkins as his co-stars, the tall young Montanan found himself in rather elegant company. It was indeed a long way from straddling his trusty horse and riding across the prairie to romping in white-tie-and-tails with Hopkins and March, with dialogue by Coward. Cooper was justifiably nervous.

Under Lubitsch's understanding guidance, however, his first few days of shooting passed without any basic problem. During a break, Cooper strolled up to Lubitsch and asked, in customary Cooper monosyllabic style, "How'm I doin'?"

"I'm glad you asked me that," said Lubitsch, and beckoned his tall young star into a secluded corner. "You're fine, Coop, just fine —and you're getting better all the time. But if you don't mind my saying this, you're just a little bit uncertain of yourself."

"Yup," grinned Cooper.

"But you don't need to be!" urged Lubitsch. "I want you to remember that you are a *star*. Make me feel that you know this about yourself! Play your scenes with the authority of a star! You're just as big a star as Freddy March—and you make as much money as Miriam Hopkins—so be a star—act like one—and keep giving me more of that authority. All right?"

Cooper nodded slowly, as he thought over Lubitsch's advice. Finally he spoke. "But I *don't* make as much money as Miriam Hopkins," he said.

"I was preparing a picture for Gary Cooper," says Nunnally Johnson. "It was called *Along Came Jones,* and it was the first I'd done for a new company called International Pictures. It was also my first job as a producer-writer, and I'd gone to work on the screenplay before we were even certain that Coop would do it.

"Halfway through the script, I ran into Coop at lunch, and I figured it would be a good idea if he knew what the devil the thing was all about, so I asked him if he'd like to read the novel that my script was based on.

" 'Sure, why not?' said Coop. He was an uncomplicated fellow, one of the best guys I've ever worked with. He picked up the book and went away with it, and I went back to writing.

"I met him in the studio commissary a couple of weeks later. By that time I'd almost finished the first draft. 'How did you like the book, Coop?' I asked him.

" 'Oh, fine, I'm about halfway through,' he said. 'I'm reading it word by word.' "

Marlon Brando was sipping tea in the foyer of the fashionable Prince de Galles Hotel in Paris. A passing waiter inadvertently poured some boiling hot water onto Marlon's lap. He jumped up, yelping with pain. The waiter was all apologies. After Marlon sat down, shifting his pants from the injured area, he said reflectively, "I'd like to write the headline for this story—Brando Scalds Balls at Prince de Galles."
(*from* CONFESSIONS OF A HOLLYWOOD COLUMNIST, *by Sheilah Graham, Morrow, 1969*)

When Hal Wallis was interested in signing Charlton Heston from Broadway, the actor was described to him as "another Burt Lancaster." The producer paused and said, "Yes, but do we need another Burt Lancaster?"

It should also be remembered how, after he hired Heston, Wallis billed him in his first film. Not content with the usual "and introducing" on a separate title card, Wallis insisted on a card which said: "and *Mr. Excitement Himself*—Charlton Heston!"

One evening, director Bob Parrish and his wife were guests at Charlie Chaplin's home. After dinner Chaplin inquired whether they would like to hear some music he had composed for his forthcoming film, *Limelight*.

36

The Parrishes accompanied the Chaplins to his studio, where he led them into a projection room. Through the sound system came the music, not on a piano, but fully scored and played by a forty-piece orchestra.

"We sat through the entire score of the picture," recalls Parrish, "and Charlie told us the story as it was to happen, acting out each sequence. It was a remarkable performance—remarkable, hell, it was fantastic! When it was over, Chaplin asked what we thought of it. We said, quite honestly, that it was great, and then I asked him, 'Why do you do it in this order? Most music is written after the film is finished, and then the picture is scored.'

"Chaplin nodded. 'Of course,' he said. 'But I will do this film to the musical score, like a ballet. It is all choreographed in my mind —all that remains is to film it.' "

Marlon Brando was to have starred in *Lawrence of Arabia*, but Sam Spiegel wanted a new face for Lawrence and he created a new star, Peter O'Toole. Without naming names, Sam said, "You make a star, you make a monster."

The late glamorous sex-symbol Jayne Mansfield made her Broadway debut in George Axelrod's comedy *Will Success Spoil Rock Hunter?* The morning after the opening night, she dashed happily into the producer's office, exclaiming, "I'm a star! I feel marvelous!"

"Have you read the reviews?" asked the producer.

"What reviews?" she demanded.

The producer handed her the papers. She slowly read what the critics had to say. At last she looked up. "What does 'inept' mean?" she asked softly.

In a speech at the Masquers honoring Jimmy Stewart, Hal Kanter fondly remarked about the actor, "He has so many of his pictures being shown on the Late Show, he keeps more people up than Mexican food."

When asked if she would contemplate a fifth marriage, Bette Davis said, "If I found a man who had $15,000,000, would sign over half of it to me before the marriage, and guarantee he'd be dead within a year."

37

* * *

"Don't be hard on her," a friend cautioned William Wyler about the star of *Funny Girl*. "It's the first picture Miss Streisand's ever directed."

JOHN WAYNE

There's too much pretentious nonsense talked about the artistic problems of making pictures. I've never had a goddamn artistic problem in my life, never, and I've worked with the best of them. John Ford isn't exactly a bum, is he? Yet he never gave me any manure about art. He just made movies, and that's what I do. I go out there on the floor and make a picture. I don't sit around for days trying to Methodize my way into a part. I read what's in the script and then I go out there and deliver my lines. The director knows what he wants from me and he gets it. I don't have to have nine or ten takes before they get something they can print. It's rare for me to have more than three takes at the most, unless it's an elaborate set-up involving a number of actors. I don't go around shooting off my mouth about the problems of acting. In fact, I don't even call myself an actor. I'm a *re-actor*. I listen to what the other guy is saying, and I re-act to it. That's the John Wayne method. It's taken me through a whole lot of pictures. Don't ask me how many, I've lost count.

Ben Lyon tells of his trip to Paris in the early Fifties to hire Orson Welles for a Darryl Zanuck epic entitled *The Black Rose*.

"I went to the Lancaster Hotel, where Welles was staying, and I had an appointment with Welles, but he postponed it three times. Finally he deigned to see me, and I went up to the penthouse he was renting and sat down with him. I told him we wanted to make a deal for his services, and he said he wanted $150,000 for the picture. I suggested that he might take less—that most of it would go for taxes, and that the budget was stretched already. Orson became very angry at this, and ordered me out of his suite.

"He got on the phone and called Darryl in California and raised hell. What right did some minor functionary, some ex-actor like myself, have to come and try to bargain away his established price? I got an angry cable from the studio, directing me not to bargain with Welles, but to close the deal at $150,000, which I proceeded to do.

"Then I went back to London, where I was head of production for Fox. The *Black Rose* company was in Morocco, and we sent word to Welles that he was to proceed there to meet them. We got word back that he could not leave the Lancaster. The hotel would not release his baggage until he paid up his bill, which was $7,000—and which he didn't have! Welles, the $150,000 holdout, couldn't leave Paris until we cabled his hotel the money."

This recalls the show-business classic, involving Joe Frisco in his hotel, refusing to close a deal with a producer for less than $1,000 a week. When his agent called and said, "Okay, I got the $1,000 for you, come down to the office and sign the contract," Frisco said, "C-can't. If I leave my hotel, they'll l-l-lock me out of my room."

As repeatedly recorded, Tony Curtis began life in the Bronx and originally bore the name Bernard Schwartz.

An agent named Joyce Selznick brought him into the Universal offices in Manhattan and introduced him to Bob Goldstein, an executive. Goldstein was impressed by the young man's potential, and arranged for him to be tested.

Eventually, Schwartz was hired by Universal and sent out to California, where under the watchful eye of Bob Goldstein's brother Leonard, a fabulously successful producer of low-budget films, the young man's career as an actor was carefully nurtured. His name was changed to "Anthony Curtis," later shortened to the present "Tony," and he was cast in such staple fare as "desert adventures" where his leading lady was invariably Piper Laurie. (Miss Laurie was to prove her true talent later as the lead in *The Hustler*.)

It was in one of these epics that production executives were treated to the spectacle of Curtis and Laurie riding to the top of a desert dune, at which point Curtis waved his arm toward the horizon and informed his lady friend, in rich Bronxese, *"Yonda lies the castle from my fodda!"*

Some time later Curtis brought his family out to California, where they settled down. One day he was taking his father on a tour of the studio when they encountered Oscar Brodney, a Universal writer-producer. Curtis introduced his father to Brodney, who mischievously inquired, "Tell me, Mr. Schwartz, why didn't you like the name Curtis?"

One of the MGM musicals, *Music for Millions*, was filmed when Margaret O'Brien was the reigning child star on the lot. During a sequence in which Larry Adler was supposed to play "Clair de Lune"

39

on his mouth organ, the director, Henry Koster, set up various re-action shots, one of which was to show June Allyson. Since Koster planned to have Miss Allyson weep at the sound of Adler's music, it then was decided to have Miss O'Brien weep also.

Koster explained what he needed to little Miss O'Brien.

She nodded and asked, "When I cry, do you want the tears to run all the way, or should I stop them halfway down?"

"Put me in the last fifteen minutes of a picture," said Barbara Stanwyck, whose acting career has spanned four decades, "and I don't care what happened before. I don't even care if I was *in* the rest of the damn thing—I'll take it in those fifteen minutes."

MITCHELL LEISEN

Barrymore was wonderful [in *Midnight*]. He had his wife, Elaine Barrie, and she kept a tight rein on him. She was in the picture so she could keep an eye on him. One day, when we'd been shooting about three weeks, Elaine came to me and she said, "You know, John thinks this is a wonderful picture—he read the script last night."

This was my introduction to idiot cards, flying back and forth all over the place. And boy, he could start one and pick up the next like nothing. But we had this one scene where he had to walk down a narrow corridor, and with the cameras and lights and things, there was just no room for idiot cards. So I said, "John, I'm afraid you're going to have to learn this." He said, "Oh? Do you want me to recite the soliloquy from *Hamlet* for you?" And he did. So I said, "Then why the hell these idiot cards?" He said, "My dear fellow, why should I fill my mind with this shit just to forget it tomorrow morning?"

(*from an interview in* FILM FAN MONTHLY, *January 1970*)

Roland Young was a dapper little Englishman who suffered bores not at all. He might be jolly in his stage roles, but in real life he seemed to be protected by burrs and fishhooks. He spoke in a rasping, low voice of his own invention, and made no secret of the fact that he liked very few people.

Once, in the club car of a train going through Illinois, a young fellow tried to make conversation with him.

"Haven't I seen you somewhere before?" asked the eager young man.

Roland Young grunted and froze him with a look.

"Are you going to Chicago?" persisted the young fellow, a little desperately.

Young grunted again.

The poor fellow made one last attempt.

"I'm George P. Witherbee, of Grand Rapids, Michigan—" he began.

"So am I," said Roland Young.

(*from* TOTAL RECOIL, *by Kyle Crichton, Doubleday, 1960*)

At the time when Leland Hayward was one of the most successful talent agents in Hollywood, he married his beautiful and talented client Margaret Sullavan. One of his waggish friends sent him a telegram: CONGRATULATIONS ON GETTING THE OTHER 90 PERCENT.

Preston Sturges did one of his most successful comedies, *Sullivan's Travels,* with Joel McCrea. Together they did another, *The Great Moment,* and each man respected the other's ability.

At a cast party following the last scene of *The Great Moment,* Sturges took McCrea aside. "Joel," he said, "I want to tell you I loved working with you, and I want to do another picture with you as soon as possible, but, as one pro to another, can I tell you something?"

"Certainly, Preston," said McCrea.

"Well, what you do is very good," said Sturges, "but have you ever seen a man sit down at a piano and play one note over and over again?"

"Yes, Preston, I have," said McCrea.

"Well, have you ever seen a great concert pianist like, say, Rubinstein, play?" asked Sturges.

"Yes—at the Hollywood Bowl," said McCrea.

"Well, have you noticed that he uses all the notes—all the colors—all the gradations?" asked Sturges.

"Yes," said McCrea.

"Well, that's my story," said Sturges.

McCrea nodded.

"The way I figure it, Preston," he said slowly, "those other guys are looking for that one note . . . and I've already found it."

* * *

41

"When I first went to work at Warners," recalled Bebe Daniels, who appeared in *The Maltese Falcon* and *42nd Street*, among other hits, "Jack Warner and his insurance people changed the fire-insurance coverage, and we found big signs everywhere reading NO SMOKING ON THE SET.

"Well, instead of smoking out in the open, actors took to sneaking cigarettes behind the scenery. In the middle of their smoke, the director would send for them, and they'd leave the cigarette sitting on a table or another piece of furniture. Within one week there were four fires in the studio! When Warner figured out why, he immediately rescinded the order. For once the efficiency experts had to eat crow."

Alfred Lunt and Lynn Fontanne, the two reigning stars of the American theatre, were finally persuaded by MGM to lend their considerable talent to a motion-picture version of the famous Molnár comedy *The Guardsman.*

The Lunts had played it on the stage, but they approached the ordeal of facing the cameras with trepidation. They journeyed to Culver City, and finally there came the day when the MGM technicians made the first screen tests.

Alfred, it is said, refused to enter the projection room to witness the results on the following day, and so Miss Fontanne went alone.

When she emerged, he awaited her verdict.

"Alfred!" she exclaimed. "It was absolutely remarkable! The camera does such amazing things—you don't seem to have any lips —but the make-up and lighting were superb, and you looked absolutely marvelous! So handsome and striking, my darling, you have an entirely new career before you, I'm sure of it—if I were you, I'd be so delighted with what they've done! Whereas I—well, I'm absolutely *appalling!* Disaster! I looked like some dreadful old shrew— a hag—I simply couldn't bear to look at myself for another second!"

Lunt nodded thoughtfully. "No lips, eh?"

When Ben Lyon was hired by the neophyte producer Howard Hughes to play in *Hell's Angels*, his contract guaranteed first billing. "It was to be Ben Lyon, Greta Nissen and James Hall, in that order," Lyon recalls.

"Subsequently we remade the entire picture in sound—this time with an unknown girl named Jean Harlow, whom I brought to

Hughes. At first Howard was unimpressed by her, but after she tested, he hired her, and as we went along with the picture, he became more and more enthusiastic about her possibilities. Finally we finished the sound version, and then I got the message, through the grapevine, that Hughes was planning to change the billing. He was going to put the picture out as 'Jean Harlow in *Hell's Angels*, with Ben Lyon and James Hall.'

"I went up to see Howard. In those days he had a little office and he was easily reached, all you had to do was walk in. Nothing like the Howard Hughes of today. I told him I'd never agree to give up first billing, and we argued, and then he finally sent for his lawyer, and he came in—a man named Neal McCarthy—and pretty soon the discussion became heated, and we started yelling back and forth.

"Finally McCarthy lost his temper. 'All right, Lyon!' he yelled. 'You want first billing and, damn it, we'll give you first billing. We'll put your name in letters six feet high on twenty-four sheets from here to New York and back again—but we'll paint your name on in *watercolor*, and the first time it rains, your name *will wash off!*'

" 'Well, at least *I'll be safe in California!*' I yelled back.

"By the time we finished laughing, I said I'd abide by whatever Hughes decided. And Howard agreed—my name came first."

GEORGE BURNS

We were working in pictures at Paramount during the early Thirties, and there was a gentleman named Osterman who'd been sent West by the bankers to operate the studio. He was up in the office running the place when Claudette Colbert came in to see him.

She was a very big star, who got something like $125,000 for working eight weeks in a picture, and this day she was very upset because in some sort of an economy move they had just fired her stand-in, a girl who earned maybe $35 a week. She told Osterman that either the studio would rehire her stand-in or she wouldn't do the picture.

Osterman was amazed. He said, "Miss Colbert, do you really mean to tell me that you'd turn down $125,000 if that girl isn't working on the picture?" and she said that was exactly what she meant.

Osterman gave in. "Okay, I'll bring her back," he said. Claudette left, and I went into the office. I had a problem to discuss with him. Gracie and I were about to start a picture—we were doing very well then, getting $60,000 for ten weeks' work—but Gracie had trouble with migraine headaches. She couldn't stand certain colors, and our dressing room was painted blue, which gave her a headache.

I explained this problem to Osterman, and asked him if he could move us to another dressing room, or have the walls painted white or pale pink. He said he'd have to think about it, but they'd solve the problem later.

"It can't be later," I said. "Either you paint the walls or we quit."

He looked at me and said, "Mr. Burns, do you mean that if I don't paint the dressing room now, you'll give up $60,000 and quit?" and I said, "Absolutely."

Osterman shook his head, and then he asked me, "Mr. Burns, did you ever run a studio?"

I told him no, I hadn't, and he said, "Well, you're running one *now!*" and he put his hat on, walked out of the office and went back East."

An exchange of correspondence followed this story:

Letter from Max Wilk to George Burns: "Dear Mr. Burns: If I'm not mistaken, wasn't the name of the man who was running Paramount then *Otterson?*"

Letter from George Burns to Max Wilk: "Dear Mr. Wilk: About the New York banker, I knew that the name was Otterson, but the reason I made it Osterman, I didn't want you to get sued, because the story's not true. I forgot to tell you I'm also a liar."

IRVING CAESAR

I'd known Al Jolson a long time. He'd made a big hit out of *Swanee,* the song that George Gershwin and I did. Then, after he made *The Jazz Singer* and a few other pictures, he came back to do a Broadway show. It was called *Wonder Bar,* and I worked on the score. Later it became one of his movies.

Jolie was an electric personality on stage, and he took himself very seriously. We tried the show out in Baltimore, which was his home town, so one evening he insisted I go with him to visit his old father, the cantor.

Well, Al was really on with Cantor Yoelson. He talked and talked—mostly about himself—proudly telling his father what a hit he was in the show, how much money he was making, how the people loved him, and so on. Old Cantor Yoelson nodded and kept glancing at his watch, and all he said to any of this was "Almost seven. Almost seven o'clock."

On and on went Al, still bragging about himself. "Almost seven," repeated his father.

Finally Al stopped. He came over to the chair where Cantor Yoelson was sitting and he said, "Pop—what is this with the seven o'clock, seven o'clock?"

The old man looked up. "Time for Amos and Andy!" he said."

One evening Jimmy Durante was sitting between acts at a table with actor John Barrymore, artist John Decker, and other friends. Barrymore was a frequent visitor at Earl Carroll's [nightclub] for he liked to step out of his loneliness, as he put it, and see someone other than his creditors.

Barrymore said to the Schnozzola, "You should play Hamlet."

"To hell with them small towns," Durante replied. "I'll take New York."

After *Roadhouse Nights* [Durante's first picture] was released early in 1930, the old man [Durante's father, Bartolomeo] attended the picture show and sat through it three times. He did not understand the medium, but kept looking at Jimmy with great interest. When asked for his opinion of the picture, Bartolomeo uttered what might well have been the most profound criticism ever offered of the cinema—or of modern civilization, for that matter.

He said simply, "Talk! Talk! Talk!"

(*from* SCHNOZZOLA, *by Gene Fowler, Viking, 1951*)

Hollywood, which has demonstrated its willingness to accept [Errol] Flynn on his own terms, is sometimes brought up short by catching him in a truth. One afternoon shortly before he was to face trial for statutory rape, he was lying on the divan in a writer's office chatting dreamily about his life. "When I used to buy slaves in New Guinea . . ." he said.

"For *Christ's* sake, Errol!" the writer interrupted. "You're not talking to the publicity department, you know."

Flynn gazed at him with an expression of deep hurt. "But really, old boy," he said.

"Bull," said the writer, with such finality that Flynn dropped the subject.

A year or so later, the writer, having gone into the Army, found himself in New Guinea. One evening he fell into conversation with

45

an old half-breed sea captain who, upon discovering that the writer came from Hollywood, turned purple with rage. "Hollywood, huh?" he said. "You happen to know a fella named Errol Flynn?" The writer said that he did. "Well," said the captain, "I got a loaded rifle waiting for that dirty bastard Flynn."

Looking at him with surprise, the writer said, "Really? What did he do to you?"

The captain's eyes narrowed with hatred. "He bought some slaves from me," he said.

Astounded to hear Flynn's words confirmed, the writer said, "Oh, really? Well, what's so wrong about that? He paid you, didn't he?"

The captain nodded. "He paid me all right," he said, "but after he had sailed away I found the bastard had paid me with tokens from the St. Louis World's Fair."

When this was repeated to Flynn, he shook his head. "That isn't quite true," he said, very seriously. "They were tokens from the San Francisco Exposition."

(*from* THE ONE WITH THE MUSTACHE IS COSTELLO, *by George Frazier,*
Random House, 1957)

KYLE CRICHTON

About W. R. Hearst and Marion Davies' pictures, I got the lowdown from Dick Powell, who was her leading man in one of her small cinematic disasters. Hearst never allowed Marion to act unless he was on the set. With the great man were invariably three or four unknown gentlemen of bulky nature, who said nothing, but looked about with great intentness.

"The love scenes were sheer torture," said Powell. "If I didn't make them look real, the director would never use me again. If I made them too real, I was sure I was going to get a bullet in the back. Marion was doing her part in the long kissing close-ups, but I was damn near choking to death. That picture lasted ten weeks, and I thought I'd die before I got out. I was still shaking months afterward."

(*from* TOTAL RECOIL, *by Kyle Crichton, Doubleday,* 1960)

So huge was Miss Davies' Santa Monica beach house, and so lavish were her guest lists, that at one time a local joke was a headline, concocted by some Hollywood wag, which read: MARION DAVIES CLOSES BEACH HOUSE—THOUSANDS HOMELESS.

ROBERT EMMETT DOLAN

I guess one of the most typical actor stories I ever heard took place at Paramount when I was there. Alan Ladd, who was then a big star, was walking down the street and one of his friends stopped him and said, "Say, I read where your new picture starts Monday."

"Yeah," said Ladd, "and I haven't even read the script yet."

"That must be kind of disturbing," said his friend.

"Sure is," said Ladd. "I don't know what I'm going to wear."

As a guest on Rudy Vallee's radio program, John Barrymore was such a success that he was made a weekly "regular." For a while after that, the show's writers, who were Mel Frank and Norman Panama, Abe Burrows and Paul Henning, had a field day. All manner of subjects offered themselves for humor—Barrymore's fabled drinking, his divorce, his lady friend Elaine Barrie all made finding comedy premises relatively simple.

But as each week passed, there were complaints from offended ladies' clubs around the country, and the show's sponsor, Sealtest Dairies, were uniquely sensitive to public opinion. One by one, the controversial subjects were declared taboo.

Soon the writers found themselves running completely dry of ideas. On one particular week they left New York aboard a train headed for California, and closeted themselves in a compartment in order to prepare next week's script, but no inspiration was forthcoming.

In the middle of the night there was a knock on the compartment door. Mel Frank opened it, and there stood Barrymore. "Gentlemen," said their star, "I understand you are having trouble finding premises. If it will be of any help to you, I want you to know—I never take a bath."

A further anecdote about Barrymore's radio career. He was nowhere to be found prior to a 7:00 P.M. broadcast. As the clock ticked on, he was located, through the efforts of his good friend John Decker. Barrymore was monumentally drunk. He was brought to the studio, where doctors went to work on him. He was given cold showers, dosed with hot coffee, massaged, and given stimulants. Finally, as the hour for the show approached, Barrymore was sober enough to stand, and he walked out onto the stage.

When his first cue came, he opened his mouth and nothing

47

came out. There was a moment's hesitation, and then he tried again. This time the famous Barrymore voice echoed through the studio, the line got its laugh . . . and from that point on, Barrymore soared through the rest of the show. "It was something miraculous to see," says Frank. "He gave one hell of a performance."

When Will Rogers made *State Fair*, at Fox, during the Thirties, his co-star in the film was a mammoth championship hog from Iowa named Blue Boy. After the film was completed, the prop man came to Will and explained that Fox was anxious to sell Blue Boy. Since Will had a huge working ranch out in the Santa Monica canyons, would he consider purchasing Blue Boy and removing him to his home, for eventual transformation into ribs, chops, bacon and bristle? "Shucks," said Will, "I just wouldn't feel right, eating a fellow-actor."

The relationship between John Ford and Bob Parrish, who is also a successful director, goes back many years to the days in the early Thirties when Parrish worked as a child extra in Ford films. As a youth, he appeared in *The Informer*, and when he began to learn his trade as a cutter, he worked on several of Ford's films.

One day Parrish summoned up his courage to ask Ford a basic question. He mentioned having seen John Wayne in Ford's *Stagecoach*, and remarked on the fact that in his two following films Wayne had not given as good a performance. "Why is he better when he works for you than when he works for other directors?" he asked.

Ford glowered at young Parrish. "Why do you want to know?" he asked.

"Because someday I'd like to be a director," said Parrish.

"Then why the hell don't you get off this set and go back to your cutting room and find out how to cut first!" snapped Ford.

Several years later, when both Ford and Parrish were in the Navy during the war, they met again. Ford invited Parrish to see some of his films which he was screening that evening for Navy personnel.

Parrish joined Ford at the screening. Before the lights went down, Ford turned to Parrish and said, "Take a piece of paper and a pencil and count the number of times Duke Wayne talks in *Stagecoach* and in *The Long Voyage Home*."

Parrish sat in the darkened room and did as he was told.

When the lights came up, Ford turned to Parrish. "How many times?" he asked.

Parrish counted the check marks. They added up to fourteen speeches in both films.

"*That's* how you make 'em good actors," said Ford. *"Don't let any of 'em talk!"*

After a long and successful career in films, Norma Talmadge retired. One evening, she emerged from the Vendome Restaurant, a smart Hollywood spot, and was immediately surrounded by the customary crew of avaricious autograph hunters. "Go away, go away!" ordered Miss Talmadge. "I don't need you any more!"

FUNNY MEN

"I've been around so long, I knew Doris Day
before she was a virgin."

GROUCHO MARX

ONCE, in explaining his life of habit, and his basic parsimony (although he was open-handed to a fault with hordes of panhandlers), Fred Allen explained to Harry Tugend, "I never want to get used to anything I may someday have to do without."

BUSTER KEATON

. . . During the years we were trying to figure out what made movie fans laugh, and why, there was an extraordinary silent-pictures comic who made many successful one-reel and two-reel pictures. His name was Larry Semon, and he was so weird-looking that he could have posed either as a pinhead or a Man from Outer Space. His movies were combinations of cartoon gags, fantastic gags, and farcical plots.

Chaplin, Lloyd, and myself just couldn't make two-reelers as packed with laughs as Larry's. But when an audience got half a block from the theatre, after being convulsed by Semon's whammios, they couldn't have told you what they had laughed at. I would say this was because they were impossible gags. Only things that one could imagine happening to real people, I guess, remain in a person's memory.

(*from* MY WONDERFUL WORLD OF SLAPSTICK, *by Buster Keaton,*
Doubleday, 1960)

HAL ROACH

Laughter comes from children; it's an emotion. . . . The great comedians imitate children. That's their ability. . . . There is not a great visual comedian that I know of whose every movement is not that of a child. Nothing that Chaplin ever did! Nobody walked as he walked, no grown-up ever went around a corner on one foot. Hardy's action with the tie, Laurel scratching his head, these are the actions of a child. Laurel never cried when he was mad, he never cried when he was hurt, he never cried when he was scared. He only cried when he was confused—that's why it's so funny when he cries. . . .

Mack Sennett knew how to do slapstick, but he never knew why he did it. It was instinct with Mack. Mack had a great, great sense of humor. He had a writer, and this writer took a big salary—he was the dumbest guy you ever . . . They had writers in discussing a story, this guy would sit there and never open his mouth. Mack would make five or six suggestions, but they wouldn't seem to click. About an hour and a half later this guy would take the very thing that Sennett had said to start with, and say, "Supposing we did it this way." Sennett had forgot that he had already suggested it, and Sennett would say, "That's it! That's the idea we want." And he gave this guy the credit for the thing. He got big money out of Sennett for years."

(from an interview with Anthony Slide in THE SILENT PICTURE, *Spring 1970)*

In one of the Marx Brothers' comedies at Paramount, a scene was devised wherein an agreement was drafted. "This is no good without a seal," went the dialogue, at which point Harpo was to nod, disappear, and return with a live seal and dump it on Groucho's desk.

When the actual animal was brought in for the filming, he turned out to be far from docile. "He was one tough seal!" recalls Harry Ruby. "When they let him loose on the set and the director called for action, that seal chased me and Kalmar and all the Marxes all over the set!"

"What the hell kind of a seal is that?" complained Groucho, fleeing for his life. "That seal is a *lion!*"

"We finally had to tape the seal's mouth," says Ruby. "The trainer said the seal wouldn't mind a bit. But I'll never forget the sight of all of us running all over that sound stage, being chased by an angry seal . . . "

"The entire atmosphere at Paramount in the early Thirties was right for comedy," recalls Joe Mankiewicz. "We had expert prop men, technicians and directors who really knew their craft, and a whole group of comedians—Hank Mann, Andy Clyde, Edgar Kennedy, Hugh Herbert—all of whom had their characteristic 'bits' and gave us guaranteed laughs. There were writers like Grover Jones and William McNutt, who really knew their business. I was very lucky to break into picture-writing around all of those people.

54

"We'd get a memo from the front office saying that so-and-so had been signed up to perform, and did anyone on the writing staff have an idea for a picture. Once we got a memo saying Rin-Tin-Tin was set for a film, and did anyone have an idea?

"I sent in a plot outline I'd made up, in which Rin-Tin-Tin was psychotic and turned bad. He hated his master, Richard Arlen, and was crazy about Noah Beery, the villain. He'd go out and help Beery by tapping out the combination of a safe with his paw, and then Beery could rob it. The climax came when Rinty helped Beery take Mary Brian, Arlen's girl friend, to the hideout, and there was a big chase—with Rinty being pursued. That's how we used to kid around.

"Then one day Ben Schulberg, who ran production, sent a note around saying that the 1932 Olympic Games were to be held in Los Angeles, and how could we get a story out of that? Well, I went up and talked with him about it, and I said there were only certain set plots for athletic pictures—would Jack Oakie carry the ball over the goal line for a touchdown and win Mary Brian, and that sort of thing —and I suggested to Schulberg that he let me do a comedy about the Olympic Games, poke fun at the whole thing, and B. P. went along with it.

"That's how I got to write *Million Dollar Legs,* which had W. C. Fields and Ben Turpin and a whole batch of comics. Nowadays the art-film students say it was years ahead of its time—that's happened to me a lot since then—but when Paramount released *Million Dollar Legs,* nobody in the U.S. could figure out what the hell it was all about. It wasn't until the picture was sent over to Paris that it became a hit. It ran in one theatre in Paris for two years, and I got a letter from Man Ray, the photographer, telling me how marvelous and surrealistic he'd found the picture to be."

Harry Tugend once asked Harpo Marx, who had never gone very far in formal schooling, how he had managed to survive amid the wits and the intellectuals of the Thanatopsis poker club and the Algonquin Round Table. How did Harpo fit in? "Very simple," said Harpo. "They had to have someone to listen."

Tugend produced a TV show in which the two major parts were played silently by Harpo and in dialect by Chico. At the end Groucho made a cameo appearance.

The show's budget allowed $10,000 for stars. Tugend had the script in work and was preparing for a shooting date, when he got word from Zeppo Marx, their agent, that there was a hitch in the fee.

"What's the problem?" asked the perturbed Tugend.

"Well, it's pretty difficult," explained Zeppo. "It's a fight between Harpo and Chico. Harpo wants Chico to take $7,500 of the fee, and Chico says either it's a fifty-fifty split or he doesn't do the show."

Such was Harpo's loyalty to a brother who needed money more than he did, and such was Chico's loyalty to his brother.

Tugend also reports that Harpo would play golf in the hottest Palm Springs weather, wearing little if anything, and as they walked down the fairways adjoining homes with pools, Harpo would jump into them, one by one, and cool himself off.

In the years when Harpo was raising his four kids, he had a great rapport with them. His seven-year-old, Alec (named after Woollcott), appeared one morning in the kitchen, unannounced.

Harpo asked, "Hey, what are you doing home?"

"Well, I'll tell you, Harp," said the kid. "I'm playing hookey."

It was after the birth of Irving Thalberg's first son that Eddie Cantor sent him a congratulatory telegram, which read: CONGRATU-LATIONS ON YOUR LATEST PRODUCTION. AM SURE IT WILL LOOK BETTER AFTER IT'S BEEN CUT.

ROBERT EMMETT DOLAN

Charlie Butterworth was a very special sort of comedian. He was droll, the things he said were understated, and he had a wonderful way of making the ordinary hilarious.

We shared an apartment in New York, and one night we got a call from an actress. She was a self-proclaimed lesbian who was in a show, and she wanted to know what was happening at our place. "Well, we're going to have a party," Charlie told her.

"Wonderful, can I come?" she asked.

"Yes," said Charlie, "but you'll have to bring your own girl."

Charlie went to a cocktail party one night, and around six he excused himself—he had to go pick up a girl who lived a few blocks away. The hostess was insistent he return. "Do you promise to come back?" she asked. "Oh, sure, I just have to go pick up this girl," Charlie said. "You'll bring her back, then," said the hostess. "All right, then," said Charlie. "You *promise*?" persisted the hostess. "Well, if you like, I'll leave a little money on deposit," said Charlie.

When he got married, he drove his intended, Ethel, up to the Town Hall in Harrison, New York, to secure a marriage license. When the clerk turned to the future Mrs. Butterworth and asked, "Occupation?" Charlie quickly replied, "Adventuress."

Later we all gravitated to Hollywood. One afternoon Charlie and Harry Ruby were sitting in the back yard of Al Newman's house, watching the game on Newman's tennis court.

"If I put in a court," mused Ruby, "do you think I'd get the same crowd Newman gets?"

Charlie thought about that for a minute. "What size court were you thinking about?" he asked.

"Oh, regulation size," said Ruby.

"You'd get a better crowd," said Butterworth. "This isn't a very good court here."

Charlie had his own special solution for people he didn't like. He had developed an imaginary cruise ship, and it was ostensibly at sea—but, as he explained, it was perpetually sailing through the savage waters of the Tierra del Fuego, endlessly fighting waves and storms. And aboard that ship he relegated everyone he didn't like. I'd go up and say, "Listen, how about so-and-so?" and Charlie would say, "Corner suite on A Deck." Later on I'd say someone else's name he didn't fancy. "Oh, outside stateroom for *him!*"

Charlie was a big success in pictures, because his style was very well suited to the comedies of the Thirties. But producers would send him scripts in which the writers, who couldn't think of lines for him, would write in something such as "Butterworth gives the girl a look as only Butterworth can, and we fade out." This drove him crazy. "I need material just as much as anyone else!"

One day, at Metro, I was standing on a set when Bob Benchley came up to Charlie and drew him aside. In very low tones he said, "Well, Charlie, I had my opportunity, but I didn't have the courage."

"What happened?" asked Charlie, without cracking a smile.

"Well, I was in my car," sighed Benchley, "and there he was, between me and the sound stage. All I had to do was to put my foot on the gas pedal—and I had him."

"I can see that," said Charlie.

"Oh well, I just didn't have the guts," said Benchley.

"Well, don't feel too badly about it," said Butterworth. "Maybe next time you'll be able to go through with it."

Do you know who they were talking about? Freddie Bartholomew, the child star.

*　　*　　*

57

The Wit and Wisdom of Hollywood

1938
by Harry Ruby

From his snow-encrusted fastness
Santa starts upon his flight,
To traverse the star-lit vastness,
Under cover of the night.

Altho' he has everybody's
Address written on his slate,
Santa claus forgot where I lived,
Back in nineteen thirty-eight.

Sitting breathless by the chimney,
Drinking Ballantine and bimney,
Listening for his coming I
Heard a rustle in the sky,
It was Santa, going by.

Anxious to be doing chores for
Studios that dwell about me—
MGM whom Leo roars for
Found out they could do without me.

More than I once I told RKO
(Thinking they might need my stint)
That I lived on North Rodeo,
But they never took the hint.

Paramount, and others who
Turn out movies by the score-o!
Never found occasion to
Dial Oxford 3–8–4–o.

Once a phone call from my agent
From my fitful slumber freed me
Just to say—that distingué gent
Samuel Goldwyn didn't need me.

Granting that my pen will never
Rival Joyce or Ronald Firbank,
Not once, that year, was I ever
Summoned by the boss of Burbank.

Not one offer, bite or feeler
Came for me, I vow (L. Votum),
From that Twentieth Century-Fox's
Indefatigable factotum.

All the independent lots
Didn't care if I *farplatz.*

Altho' he has everybody's
Address written on his slate,
Santa Claus forgot where I lived,
Back in nineteen thirty-eight.

PRESENTING AL BOASBERG

Al Boasberg came from Buffalo, New York, where his father owned a jewelry store. Boasberg became stage-struck at an early age, and during the early Twenties he combined business with pleasure by selling jewelry to the vaudevillians who came through Buffalo each week. Early on, he began thinking up wisecracks, getting laughs—it was good for business—and eventually selling them.

A sample of an early Boasberg went thus:

"What do you think of a woman who sleeps with cats?"

"Who is she?"

"Mrs. Katz!"

From such humble beginnings are great comedy careers made. Boasberg came to New York in 1923 and went into the gag business. Vaudevillians thrived on his material, which included such classics as "I will now sing a new song, entitled "You Stole My Wife, You Horse Thief," and the dialogue between the comedian and the straight man (circa 1927):

"My brother slapped Al Capone."

"Gee, I'd like to meet him and shake his hand."

"No, we wouldn't want to dig him up just for that."

Such Boasberg lines as "There's no amusement tax on alimony" were quoted all over show business. He specialized in topical cracks: "The eclipse is just J. P. Morgan foreclosing on the sun."

Pilferage of material among comedians was rife. It was said that relatives of comedians playing in Denver or Seattle would attend each week's performance at the New York Palace, then step into a Western Union office and wire out the best gags. Boasberg once remarked, "Sometimes as many as two hundred night letters go out after a Palace opening—and most of what's in them is mine." He was capable of spontaneous ad-libs that were at once outrageous and hilarious.

A favorite Boasberg story, supplied by Goodman Ace, tells of the time he ran into an actor on a train trip. "The actor had just come from burying his wife, and was still weeping," says Ace. " 'You must have loved her very much,' said Boasberg. 'You were so overcome at the funeral.'

" 'You should have caught me at the grave,' said the actor.

"He always hung around with comics, wherever he went," says Ace. "If he went to a strange town, he'd head straight for the theatre and catch the show. Once in Chicago, he stopped in and caught a young comedian's act. The kid's chief claim to fame—and perhaps his only one at the time—was to appear onstage smoking two cigarettes in a special holder.

"Boasberg went backstage after the performance. 'Loved your act,' he told the kid, 'and I've got an idea for you that could really put you over big.' "

" 'Shoot,' said the comedian.

"Boasberg pointed at his twin-cigarette holder. 'Make that a candelabra,' he said."

He sold gags to so many comedians that it was said almost half the acts playing the Loew Circuit were using his material; for those acts using timely material, he developed a weekly service of new jokes that he would wire his clients as fast as he thought them up. He contributed material to legitimate shows produced by Ziegfeld, Earl Carroll, Sam Harris and the Shuberts. Top comics grabbed up his quips. Jack Benny and Burns & Allen were among his best customers.

Eventually Boasberg went West and became a prolific comedy title-writer for silent films. He went to work for Buster Keaton, producing not only titles but visual gags for the films Keaton was producing.

One evening Boasberg came down to visit Keaton, who was making scenes on a large outdoor set. There was no heat, and wind whistled through the scenery. "We could use a little heat around here, Buster," said Boasberg. Keaton agreed. Boasberg thereupon picked up a few pieces of scrap lumber and started a small fire.

The winds fanned his blaze, and before either of the two could control it, the fire proceeded to burn down Buster's entire set.

60

"What else could two funny men do?" asks George Burns. "They both stood there, watching the fire, and laughing."

Later, Boasberg moved to Metro and worked closely with another fertile comedy mind, Bob Hopkins.

One day Boasberg's producer called him in. He pointed at a page Boasberg had sent. "Listen," he said, "I know this takes place in a ritzy apartment house, but I'm a little worried about this line where you have the elevator boy say 'Ascending?' "

"What the hell, everybody knows what that word means," said Boasberg.

The producer refused to accept such a sweeping statement.

"All right, I'll prove it," said Boasberg, and threw open the office door. To the secretary outside he said, "Honey, do you know what the word 'ascending' means?"

"What word?" asked the secretary.

" 'Ascending—*ascending!*' " yelled Boasberg. "A-s-s-e-n-d-i-n-g!"

Boasberg developed certain eccentricities, one of which was building houses. After occupying them for a week or so, he would place them on the market. One of his houses went up in Beverly Hills, and he boasted to his friends that it had cost him $45,000. Since Boasberg was fond of bending truth slightly to make a better story, one of his friends questioned him about this. Boasberg's friend had seen the house and knew values; the house could not have cost that much. "The house cost $20,000," said Boasberg, "and I put a check for $25,000 in the cornerstone!"

Came sound, and Boasberg found a gold mine of employment at Metro. Irving Thalberg, a great admirer of his work, kept him busy on many comedies.

One evening, according to Ace, Boasberg got a call from Thalberg's secretary informing him that the head of the studio was leaving for New York on the Chief and that he expected Boasberg to come along. He should be at the station in time to leave that evening.

Boasberg hurried home, packed a bag and went down to the station. There were gathered a group of Metro functionaries, as well as other directors and writers from the studio. Each man was assigned a drawing room aboard the Chief. Boasberg got on the train, found his quarters, removed his shoes and relaxed. The Chief pulled out, bound for New York. A few minutes later a Thalberg minion summoned Boasberg to another Pullman car, where Thalberg was established with secretaries and a complete staff of assistants.

Thalberg waved Boasberg in. "It's about your new script," he said. "Here's how I want you to develop it, Al." Quickly, Thalberg outlined the basic situation. The heroine was extremely wealthy, an heiress, this must be established in the first three minutes of the film, after which the introduction of her boy friend took place, and then the complications.

"Have you got that all clear in your mind, Al?" asked Thalberg.

"Absolutely, Irving," said Boasberg.

"Fine, fine!" said Thalberg. "When the train stops at San Bernardino in about twenty minutes, you get off, and then tomorrow morning at the studio you can get started on the script." He ushered the bewildered Boasberg out of the compartment.

Boasberg got off the Chief at San Bernardino. It was pushing midnight. The only transportation back to Los Angeles consisted of a night bus that brought him home, disappointed and exhausted, at four in the morning.

Some years later Boasberg became a comedy contributor to the Marx Brothers, and it is said that the famous stateroom scene in *A Night at the Opera* was his idea. He never took screen credit, claiming "If it helps my pal Sam Wood [the director] get a great picture, forget me; they paid for it."

He continued to write jokes for comedians. One day the wife of one of his clients called up and asked Boasberg how much he charged per gag. "Honey, I don't do business that way," said Boasberg. "That's too bad," said the lady. "Tomorrow is my husband's birthday, and I was thinking of giving him three new gags."

In his last years Boasberg worked steadily as a trouble-shooter on Jack Benny's radio scripts. "Al was an amazing guy," says Benny. "I'd never ask him to do a whole script. But I could read a script and I'd feel that maybe on a certain page it was a little slow, and I'd give it to Al and ask him if he could fatten that section up a little—and he'd take the script away and come back in a couple of hours or so with two or three pages of solid laughs—he never failed me. It never mattered to me what I paid Al—he was always there when I needed him. I called him in one day and I told him I wanted to have him around for two years. I said, 'I'll give you $1,500 a week and you'll be free to do anything you want to do—movies, sketches, you can work for anybody else—just as long as you're there when I call you. How's that, Al?'

"He said, 'Jack, that's a marvelous deal.' No argument, no

nothing. We shook hands on it, and he went home. Next day I got word he'd died. Forty-five years old. What a helluva loss he was."

When Joe Frisco first arrived in Hollywood, a friend exclaimed about the place. "Look at that scenery, those beautiful hills—look at the Pacific Ocean!"

"Yeah," said Frisco, "b-but you can't put k-k-ketchup on it."

Frisco once remarked, "This is the only town where you can wake up in the morning and listen to the birds c-coughing in the trees."

At a Hollywood nightspot where he was dining, he glanced at a nearby table where a midget was standing, his head barely clearing the top of the tablecloth. "L-l-look at that," cracked Frisco. "He's doing the J-John the B-Baptist bit."

"I remember one day having a long and pleasant lunch at Lucey's, the restaurant down the street from Paramount," said Robert Emmett Dolan. "We were a convivial bunch—John O'Hara, Charlie Butterworth, Johnny Mercer, Bob Benchley and myself—and we enjoyed each other's company. I looked at my watch and it was four o'clock and we were still there. Benchley looked out Lucey's window. 'My God,' he said. 'We haven't even left the pier yet.'"

"Benchley was a very sound sleeper," said Mrs. Ethel Heyn, whose first husband was Charlie Butterworth. "I remember in the days when he lived at the Royalton, he had a male secretary who worked out a way of getting Bob up in the morning. Nothing else would do it. The secretary would lean over Benchley, who was dead to the world, and he'd whisper in his ear, 'Mr. Benchley, the men are here for the trunks.' And Bob would shake himself and sit up, bleary but awake."

Oscar Levant insists that it is he who was responsible for one of the great Hollywood put-downs, one which has been attributed to several other wits.

The scene was a Fox projection room, at which Darryl Zanuck was screening a film, with Levant as his guest. When the lights came up, Zanuck turned to Levant and asked, "Well, how do you like it?"

With his customary candor, Levant replied, "I think the picture stinks."

Zanuck began to burn. "Who the hell are you to think the picture stinks?" he demanded.

"Who the hell do you have to be to think the picture stinks?" Levant replied.

Levant once described the international jet-set agent Irving Lazar as the "Jewish Onassis of Beverly Hills—the only man to ride down Wilshire Boulevard in a yacht."

Oscar and Harpo Marx were driving in a car—it was Levant's first trip to California. Marx drove Levant out to the beach.

"In those days it was completely uncluttered by beach houses, boardwalks, hot dog stands, or human beings. It was just there, stark stretches of clean gray sand and blue water as far as you could see," Oscar recalled.

" 'There,' " said Harpo happily. " 'How do you like it?'

" 'Hey,' I said, 'a Gentile ocean!' "

Keenan Wynn, who was at MGM for many years, referred to a producer on the lot. "When he laughed, dust came out of his mouth," he said.

(*from* THE UNIMPORTANCE OF BEING OSCAR, *by Oscar Levant,*
Putnam, 1968)

Jimmy Durante had an argument with Sid Zelinka, a writer who brought in a joke for his radio show. He complained that the joke was far too raw. "It wouldn't go for my audience," he said. "Ya wanna know who my audience is? I'll tell ya. I was riding in a pullman and it was in a snowstorm. I opened the shade and looked out, and we was passing by a little house out there in Montana, and I could see in the window, there was a guy by a table with a light bulb hanging down, and plugged in there was a little radio, and he was listening. That's my audience—that guy in the shack in Montana—and I always gotta remember him!"

A week or so later, Durante himself came into a script conference and repeated to Zelinka a joke he wanted included in the script, but this joke was easily as raw as the one the writer had told the week before.

"Jimmy!" protested Zelinka. "What about that guy in the little shack out in Montana? Sure it's a funny joke, but what would *he* think?'"

"Ah—screw him!" said Durante.

JACK ROSE

Mel Shavelson and I had a script we'd done for Warner Brothers, and there was a good part in it for a comic like Jackie Gleason. Warner told me to go to New York and discuss it with Gleason, who was very big on television at the time.

I went to New York and they told me Gleason was up at Doctors' Hospital, where he'd go into a sort of retreat every few weeks, in a big suite, with everyone in attendance. He was supposed to get a few days of rest, and also to try to take off a little weight, but I gathered he had himself a pretty good time while he was there.

I went uptown to the hospital and got off on the floor where Jackie's suite was, and I started down the hall, and then a nurse stopped me and asked me where I was going.

I said, "I'm going to see Mr. Gleason—I believe he's a patient here."

And she said, "Oh, no, he's gone home. He wasn't feeling well."

In his early Hollywood days, Jerry Lewis was playing ball on the Paramount studio street when Adolph Zukor, then in his late eighties but still erect and brisk, strode by. "Hey, Adolph!" yelled the irrepressible Lewis, "run out for a long one!"

Hal Kanter reports another incident in the early history of the team of Martin & Lewis. The noisy Jerry was running down a hall at NBC studios in Burbank, calling out insults to all and sundry, when he rounded a corner and encountered a writer named Larry Markes, who is amiable, soft-spoken and possessed of ample bulk. Jerry stopped and stared at Markes and then yelled, "Hey—are you for *real*?"

"No," said Markes, "I'm a mural."

And when Jerry Lewis embarked on a solo career, one of the first ventures he attempted was the customary clown-plays-Hamlet job—this time, a TV version of the famous Al Jolson classic *The Jazz Singer*. The production ended with Lewis, in clown's make-up, singing at a purported Yom Kippur service.

At the dress rehearsal in the TV studios, Lewis reached his triumphant finale and then walked over to his writing staff, headed by Harry Crane. "How was I?" he demanded.

Without a moment's hesitation, Crane said, "Rudolph, the Red-Nosed Rabbi."

And, also without a moment's hesitation, Jerry said, "You're fired."

(Currently, Crane is happily and most gainfully employed as head writer for Dean Martin.)

HAL KANTER

Edward G. Robinson had stopped at the table to greet and chat with his old friend Ed Wynn. When he left to join the party with whom he was lunching that spring day in the Café de Paris at 20th Century-Fox, my companion turned to me.

"He looks wonderful," Ed whispered, "for a man his age."

I leaned closer to the new hearing device Ed had proudly shown me moments before he had replaced it in his ear. "You look wonderful, too," I said, "for a man your age."

Ed scowled that mock frown that only his face could make so outrageously funny.

"I look wonderful for a *woman* my age," he said, "but not for a man." Then he added, giggling, "I was downtown last week and saw a building as old as I am. It looked terrible!"

(*from* THE LAST TIME I SAW ED, *by Hal Kanter*, VARIETY)

One festive New Year's Eve, Wynn arrived at Hal Kanter's house. The Kanter living room was filled with guests, mostly writers, all of whom knew Wynn and were extremely fond of him.

Ed was accompanied by a lovely matron, whom he proceeded to introduce. "I'd like you to meet Mrs. Smith," he said. "I enjoy her company because she's very beautiful, and she's also very rich."

Leo Solomon, who had worked for Wynn on his television shows, nodded. "It's a cinch you wouldn't take her out if she got laughs," he said.

Woody Allen was also in *Casino Royale* [with Peter Sellers] and was also staying at the Dorchester. He had been in London three months waiting for his two weeks before the camera while Sellers rewrote the script, advised everyone on his role, and even sat in on the cutting, but Woody did not mind his wait. He loved London, he told me. "They have all the four seasons in one day." . . . One of the very top executives of the New York Columbia office was in London to see what in heaven's name was happening with the picture and the studio's money. He was also staying at the Dorchester. He saw Woody in the lobby and sat down with him, pouring out his problems with Peter.

"It's terrible," groaned the executive. "Look, Woody, I don't know how to tell you this, but Peter doesn't want you in the picture. But with all the trouble he's giving us, instead of getting rid of you, we really should get rid of him."

"Yes, you should," said Woody. "You can't put up with that sort of behavior. Get rid of him." And he walked away. The face was Woody's, and the voice was Woody's, but the taller body was unmistakably Peter Sellers'. This is the chief reason he did not return for the new ending.

(*from* CONFESSIONS OF A HOLLYWOOD COLUMNIST,
by Sheilah Graham, Morrow, 1969)

It was on a London visit that Jack Benny remarked, to a British audience, that he was well aware of his reputation for prudence. "It's absolutely true," he said. "I don't want to tell you how much insurance I carry with Prudential, but all I can say is—when I go, *they* go."

Benny freely admits that the best picture he ever appeared in was Lubitsch's savage satire *To Be or Not to Be,* in which Benny co-starred with the late Carole Lombard.

"No comic can be great in films without two things," says Benny, "a great story, which gives you a character to play—and a great director. I'm not knocking the people who directed me in other films in my early days, but truthfully, they couldn't come near a genius like Lubitsch. And no matter how big a star was, he didn't ask for Lubitsch—Lubitsch asked for *him.* So when I got word from my agent that Lubitsch wanted me to be in his next picture, I never even asked what it was—I just said of course I'd do it.

"His method of direction was perfect for me. He would act out the whole scene—and then he'd say, 'Now let's see how you'd do it.'

He'd give me the movements and then let me do them my own way. And he was great."

Benny points at the window. "If Lubitsch were to tell me to jump out that window, I'd jump."

As a child star of *Skippy*, etc., Jackie Cooper was booked by the Paramount executives to make personal appearances in New York at the flagship Paramount Theatre. Jackie, a youngster of about nine at the time, was possessed of a hard-driving stage mother. The show was to be emceed by Milton Berle.

As they arrived at the theatre, Jackie's mother took him aside for final instructions. All over the country, mothers were warning their kids to dress warmly, not to cross the street against the light, and to eat a hot lunch. Jackie's mother was saying to her nine-year-old son, "Remember, Jackie, when you get out there on the stage, *don't ad-lib with Berle!*"

When Jessel's marriage to Norma Talmadge broke up, Georgie was most upset. He loved the lady and wanted to patch things up. But it was no use; she ordered him out of their home.

A few days later, after brooding over the situation, Jessel decided to make *le beau geste*. He acquired a large diamond ring and drove to the home at midday. Securing entrance to the house through a back door, he made his way to the bedroom, surprised his estranged wife, and produced the diamond ring, hoping that the sight of it would bring her around.

It was no use. She told him to take his ring and leave the premises.

Jessel shrugged fatalistically. "Listen, Norma," he said, backing away, "as long as I'm here, could I use the pool?"

During this period Jessel was employed on a radio program, and Jerry Chodorov and Joe Fields were writing material for him.

Late one night they received a call from their employer. Distraught, he was contemplating suicide. "Come over here and help me with the suicide note," he pleaded.

Chodorov and Fields hurried to Jessel's home, where they found him deeply depressed. "I am absolutely serious about killing myself," he told them, "but I insist on a decent suicide note."

No amount of persuasion could change Jessel's mind. Finally, in desperation, Chodorov suggested a witty line for the note. Jessel approved of it. Fields came up with another. Jessel nodded and said, "Write those down."

The writers continued their therapeutic joking. Soon, carried away with the spirit of the comedy, Jessel contributed some lines of his own. Quip followed quip, jokes were concocted, Chodorov and Fields were busy making notes.

"Say, this is pretty good stuff," remarked Jessel. "Let's keep going with it!"

An hour or so later an entire routine had been blocked out and written. Jessel prepared to go to bed. Chodorov and Fields went home. And the suicide note?

"It ended up being Georgie's radio script for the following week," recalls Chodorov.

Groucho Marx is not often the receiver of wit, but one evening a few months back it finally happened. At a party in Beverly Hills he was approached by Mike Nichols, the director, whom he had never met before.

"Groucho," said Nichols, "I must tell you—I've seen *A Night at the Opera* seventeen times."

Very touched, all Groucho could manage was a "Really?"

"Yes," said Nichols. "I just couldn't get over that love story between Allan Jones and Kitty Carlisle!"

The movie community was rocked by the news that Elizabeth Taylor was to receive the unprecedented sum of one million dollars for *Cleopatra*.

Several executives at Columbia were lunching in the dining room and discussing this huge fee, pro and con. Comedian Buddy Hackett was also at the table.

"It's a helluva lot of money," said one producer. "Buddy, would you give Liz Taylor a million for a picture?"

"Nah," said Hackett. "I'd probably offer her $35,000."

"Only $35,000?" asked the surprised exec.

"Yeah," said Hackett, "and she'd say, 'Kiss my ass,' and that's all I want from her anyway!"

ROBERT BENCHLEY

If we were one, or all four, of the Marx Brothers, we would be a little confused by the judgments passed on us by the two visiting

British journalists now on the staff of the New York *World*. Mr. St. John Ervine, exercising his unquestioned prerogatives as the guest of a free country, was not pleased with the new Marx show, *Animal Crackers*. On the other hand, his countryman and colleague, Mr. William Bolitho, was so impressed by it that he wrote an appreciation in the same journal which must have thrown *Die Gebrüder* Marx into a panic of apprehension. We are afraid that from neither critic did they derive much practical help in their work.

Mr. Ervine had probably heard too much about how funny the Marx Brothers were, a fatal preparation for any critical viewing. Someone might have told him, however, that Zeppo Marx is not *supposed* to be funny and thus saved him from being so upset by the discovery when he made it. It must be difficult, in dealing with so strange a tongue as American, to tell whether an actor is supposed to be funny or not. We may also perhaps attribute a little of Mr. Ervine's coolness in the face of Groucho Marx's barrage of wise-cracks to a certain unfamiliarity with the words used. For, from Mr. Ervine's own genial attempts to be colloquial in the vulgate, we are quite sure that he couldn't have understood more than a third of Groucho's highly modern references. Chico Marx, in spite of having the answers in one of the most devastatingly made scenes in modern drama, left Mr. Ervine neither one way nor another, and it was only Harpo, who speaks the universal language of pantomime (and lechery), who registered with the visiting commentator. All in all, pretty nearly a wasted evening for Mr. Ervine.

But even Mr. Ervine's disapproval must have been more comprehensible to the Marx family than Mr. Bolitho's enthusiasm, for the latter understood them better than they probably understand themselves. As so often happens these days among earnest critics, deep and significant symbolisms were read into this harlequinade which, if generally accepted, would lower clowning to the level of a Channing Pollock morality drama. Harpo is, to Mr. Bolitho, "the simplest member to understand," and yet he is a "suppressed wish-complex." We wonder, or rather Mr. Bolitho wonders, "at the inviolable mutism he keeps proper to his extrahumanity, at his phantom tricks which belong to a largely incommunicable dream world." Harpo should know about this.

"Groucho," says Mr. Bolitho (and he may be right), "is at the same time less elemental and more complicated." We learn that he is the sublimation of the Jews' attitude toward life, "the exteriorization of this faithful power of laughing at themselves." The group, as a family, may possibly "immortalize themselves and become stock characters as enduring as the angel and the devil of the Talmudic legend." Of the two British opinions, we think we would rather have Mr. Ervine's condemnation. At least, he can plead ignorance of what it was all about.

The Marx Brothers ought to be very easy to enjoy. We find it absurdly simple. In the first place, we know the language, which is a great help, and, in the second place, we don't stop to think whether we are laughing at Harpo's inviolable mutism or because he is just comical. When Groucho says to Chico, "You look like Emanuel Ravelli," and Chico says, "I *am* Emanuel Ravelli," and Groucho retorts, "No wonder you look like him. But I still insist there is a resemblance," we detect no symbolism of an oppressed Jewry, but rather a magnificently disordered mind which has come into its own. And in Chico's suggestion that, in order to see if the stolen painting is perhaps hidden in the house next door they first *build* the house next door, we can find nothing which would qualify the brothers for participation in a Talmudic legend, but rather something that makes them a frantically transitory comet formation which we can proudly tell our grandchildren of having seen one night in 1928. For we doubt that the Marx Brothers have any successors.

(*from* HARPO, GROUCHO, CHICO, ZEPPO, AND KARL, *by Robert Benchley,* LIFE, *November 16, 1928*)

STARRING W. C. FIELDS

JOSEPH L. MANKIEWICZ

I wrote several episodes of *If I Had a Million.* I was a staff writer at Paramount, and that meant that everything I wrote belonged to the company. One of the sequences I wrote was for W. C. Fields and Alison Skipworth, and it was the one in which Fields bought a lot of old cars and went out to smash up roadhogs. When I wrote it, I invented a whole set of bird names for Fields to call Skipworth—"My little chickadee, my little tom-tit, and so forth."

After the picture was finished, Fields came into my office one day. He had under his arm a two-volume set of *Birds of America.* and he said "Kid, I'd like to buy that routine from you."

Fields was from the old vaudeville school, where you bought your material from a writer, and then it belonged to you, and nobody else could use it.

I told him he didn't have to buy it—it wasn't mine to sell. It belonged to the studio—just the same way *All About Eve,* which I

71

wrote and directed at Fox, belonged to Fox, and became *Applause,* a big hit on Broadway, without any of it coming to me.

"No," said Fields, "I'd feel better if I paid you, kid," and he made me take $50 cash. He may have been a difficult man, but he had a peculiar sense of what was right—and he stuck by it. Which also meant that later on, when he went to Universal, he could call his picture *My Little Chickadee* and feel he'd paid for the right."

A L   L E W I S

During the filming of the Paramount picture *International House,* starring W. C. Fields, Southern California was hit by a sudden series of violent earthquake tremors. Eddie Sutherland, the director, was putting his cast through a scene on a set which was a hotel lobby, replete with chandeliers and hangings, all of which began to sway ominously.

"Earthquake!" came the cry, and Sutherland ordered the sound stage evacuated, lest someone be hurt by falling objects. Actors and technicians stood fearfully in the studio street, waiting for the end of the tremors.

Several hours later, when it seemed safe, Sutherland decided to try and make the shot which had been interrupted. "Let's get Bill Fields back and start shooting," he ordered. A head count was taken; Fields was nowhere to be seen.

Assistant directors went in search of the missing comedian. One of them went into the deserted sound stage, calling "Mr. Fields? Mr. Fields?"

From Fields's dressing room came a muffled reply. Fields opened the dressing-room door and peered out. "Say," he asked, somewhat blearily, "where'd everybody go?"

With the assistance of certain pocket flasks and their contents, he had dozed peacefully in his dressing room throughout the entire earthquake and its attendant hysteria.

Letter from Max Wilk to George Burns: "Dear Mr. Burns: Al Lewis has given me a wonderful story about W. C. Fields sleeping through the earthquake while making *International House.* I recall that you and Gracie Allen were in that picture, and I wonder if you remember anything else that happened at that time."

Letter from George Burns to Max Wilk: "Dear Mr. Wilk: Yes, there was an earthquake during the making of *International House,* and if Al Lewis said that W. C. Fields slept through the quake, he must be right, because I think, I'm not sure, that Al Lewis was sleeping with him."

For a time the head of Paramount production was diminutive Manny Cohen, a bachelor who was fond of large cigars. He lived in an opulent house, and his cigars were shipped to him from the finest manufacturer in Havana.

Cohen wielded his power with customary firmness. When a film called *Lives of a Bengal Lancer* was completed, he threw a large party in honor of Gary Cooper. All of Paramount's stars were invited, and it was *de rigueur* at such bacchanales that studio performers should perform.

W. C. Fields was present. For years he had entertained his pals with stories of his old vaudeville juggling tricks. Cohen asked Fields if he'd do some of them. Fields demurred. Finally, Cohen persuaded Fields to perform.

"I'll do my old cigar-box tricks. Mind if I use some of your cigar boxes?" asked Fields.

He went over to a table which was piled with a dozen boxes of Cohen's finest, which had been set out for the guests. "Don't worry," soothed Fields. "I'll only use the sealed boxes."

He picked up a load of cigar boxes, retired to one end of the room, and then, with appropriate fanfare, he launched into a series of his famous cigar-box juggling tricks.

Manny Cohen watched, horrified, as his expensive Havanas began to flip out of the previously sealed boxes. The carpet, the furniture, the guests, all were sprayed with showers of cigars! Nothing could stop Fields—he continued flipping boxes this way and that, and Cohen watched his collection being systematically destroyed.

There had been no mistake on Fields's part. Before he began juggling, he had purposefully removed the tiny pins which securely fastened the lids of the expensive cigar boxes.

When Fields was working at Paramount, one of the few people he treated as a close friend was Paul Jones, a production manager who later became a very successful producer.

Fields trusted Jones to the extent of allowing him to go out at lunch hour and make deposits, sometimes amounting to as much as $3, in any of the local banks near the Paramount Studios. (It is well known that Fields had accounts in banks all over Los Angeles, as well as in every other place he'd ever passed through.)

In the mid-Thirties there arose in California a large controversy over the death penalty. Humanitarians were working to have hanging replaced by a more decent (?) method of execution—namely, the gas chamber.

The Hearst papers seized upon this issue, and as a referendum approached, the *Los Angeles Examiner* took it upon itself to headline the dilemma of a prisoner in the death house at San Quentin. The paper interviewed this hapless chap, and inquired as to whether he wanted death by hanging or by the gas chamber. When he opted for gas, the *Examiner* appeared with a front-page cartoon showing the prisoner in his cell cowering away from the shadow of a hangman's noose. Above the cartoon was a caption which read "GIVE ME GAS!"

On the set of the picture he was making. Fields perused the paper, and then, when Jones appeared, he beckoned him to his chair. "Do you think you could go out and get me one hundred copies of this newspaper?" he inquired.

Jones, who was by now completely accustomed to Fields's vagaries, nodded and went out to Marathon Street, where he picked up the specified number of *Examiners,* then brought them back to Fields.

Fields took a pair of scissors and laboriously cut out of each newspaper the front-page cartoon with its "GIVE ME GAS!" banner. Then, with a pen, he added, on each cartoon, "—AND CHECK MY OIL, TOO," and sent the cartoons out as his personal Christmas card.

Bob Hope was fond of relating this incident about W. C. Fields. He was in his dressing room at Paramount when he was visited by two ladies who were canvassing for donations to some worthy California charity.

"I am very sorry, mesdames," said Fields, "but I only give to one charity—F.E.B.F." And when pressed for the name of that cause, he elucidated: "Fuck Everyone But Fields."

Mark Hellinger had spent many years as a Broadway columnist before he came to work as a producer in Hollywood. He is probably best remembered for his first-rate production of Ernest Hemingway's *The Killers,* and for his large alcoholic capacity.

Even W. C. Fields was somewhat in awe of Hellinger's drinking capabilities. He once remarked, "I got Mark Hellinger so drunk last night that it took three bellboys to put me to bed."

74

"During his later Paramount days," says Ken Englund, "Bill Fields was absolute hell on directors. I worked on one of his pictures, *The Big Broadcast of 1938,* and by that time Bill was so hard to work with that the front office had to devise a way of getting pictures finished in spite of him.

"The main line of the story, which had all the plot and love scenes, was in the hands of Mitch Leisen. Since Mitch was working on a very tightly planned schedule involving all sorts of performers, he simply couldn't be bothered with Bill's various idiosyncrasies— his getting in at all hours, standing around the set and killing time— and his drinking.

"So what they did was to turn all of Bill's comedy stuff over to a second unit, completely separate, and hired Eddie Cline, who was a veteran comedy director, to handle it. Cline and Fields went off and devised all their own comedy hunks, picked up sets somewhere, and made film, working at their own speed. It never bothered Eddie if Fields wasted film, or stood there cursing him out, or went home at lunchtime—he knew how to contain the great man.

"Eventually, in the cutting room, the cutter put together all of Leisen's "A" sequences and the Fields stuff—and Paramount had a picture.

"Of course," adds Englund, "the absolute irony of all this is that thirty years later all that elaborate, star-studded 'main-line' Leisen stuff, done so lavishly, is what today's audience sits and yawns through while they're waiting to see those odd bits and pieces that were picked up by Fields and Eddie Cline in a remote corner of some Paramount sound stage."

SCRIBES AND
PHARISEES

"When not in use, turn off the juice."
SIGN IN WARNER BROS. OFFICES TO DISCOURAGE
WASTE OF ELECTRIC CURRENT, CIRCA 1935

BEN HECHT

Movies were seldom written. In 1927, they were yelled into existence in conferences that kept going in saloons, brothels and all-night poker games. Movie sets roared with arguments and organ music. Sometimes little string orchestras played to help stir up the emotions of the great performers—*"Träumerei"* for Clara Bow and the "Meditation" from *Thaïs* for Adolphe Menjou, the screen's most sophisticated lover.

I was given an office at Paramount. A bit of cardboard with my name inked on it was tacked on the door. A soiree started at once in my office and lasted for several days. Men of letters, bearing gin bottles, arrived. Bob Benchley, hallooing with laughter as if he had come on the land of Punch and Judy, was there; and the owlish-eyed satirist Donald Ogden Stewart, beaming as at a convention of March Hares. One night at a flossy party Don appeared on the dance floor in a long overcoat. "That's silly and showing off, to dance in an overcoat," said the great lady of the films in his arms. "Please take it off." Don did. He had nothing on underneath.

On my fourth day, I was summoned and given an assignment. Producer Bernard Fineman, under Schulberg, presented me with the first "idea" for a movie to smite my ears.

An important industrialist, said he, was shaving one morning. His razor slipped and he cut his chin. He thereupon sent out his butler to buy an alum stick to stop the flow of blood. The butler was slowed up by a traffic jam and the great industrialist, fuming in his onyx bathroom, had to wait fifteen minutes for the alum stick. The movie I was to make up was to show all the things that were affected in the world by this fifteen-minute delay. I recall of the details only that something went wrong with the pearl fisheries. The whole thing ended up with the great industrialist's mistress deserting him, his vast enterprises crashing, and his wife returning to his side to help him build a new life.*

(*from* A CHILD OF THE CENTURY, *by Ben Hecht,*
Simon and Schuster, 1954)

* Mrs. Ben Hecht comments: "Ben did not work on the assignment that had been given him. He and Hollywood were still innocent about 'talking

The Wit and Wisdom of Hollywood

* * *

"I was sitting with Wilson Mizner in the Brown Derby one night," recalls Joe Mankiewicz, "when Rufus Le Maire, a Paramount executive, came in from having attended the premiere of *Morocco*. He was all dressed up and wearing a large Inverness cape. Mizner glanced up at Le Maire as he passed, turned back to me and said, 'That, my boy, sets the Jews back six hundred years.'

"When Jack Warner hired him to write scripts at the studio, Mizner came in to Warner's office with the Los Angeles telephone book, dropped it on his desk and said, 'This might have been good for a picture—except it has too many characters in it.' "

Mizner took a dim view of his boss. "Jack Warner has oilcloth pockets so he can steal soup," he once remarked. Later he was noted for his quip, "Working for Warner Brothers is like fucking a porcupine—it's one hundred pricks against one."

In the days when Mizner was involved in the operation of the Brown Derby restaurant, Norman Krasna remembers one afternoon when the great wit had deigned to sit down with him and his friends. After a few moments' conversation, he got up. "I am intellectually slumming," he said, and left.

Krasna also recalls an incident in which Mizner, somewhat under the influence, told a Warner Brothers producer a story which the producer decided would make a good film. A day or so later there was a meeting at the studio at which Mizner was invited to discuss the story. He could not remember a line of what he'd told the producer.

JOHN CROMWELL

When I first came out to Hollywood, it was at the time when sound was replacing silent films and the place was a complete shambles—around 1928. I'd been in a play called *Gentlemen of the Press*—we opened the week after *The Front Page*—and my contract

---

pictures' and he thought, at the time, that an artist always finds his subject within himself. He went home and wrote a treatment of 68 pages about the Chicago gang wars. He wrote it as well as he knew how and read it to the bosses. It was called *Underworld*.

"They were pleased. He wrote a complete screen play with Art Rosson, but while he was on the train returning to New York, Art Rosson wired him that they had taken his screenplay away from him and given it to Von Sternberg.

"In the following years, he was to learn that the artist in Hollywood doesn't have any control over his material. But that was much later."

with Paramount was contingent on my appearing in the play. After it flopped, I went out to the studio. They rolled out the red carpet for me and Schulberg asked me, "What would you like to do?" I said, "I want to go down to the cutting room and see what that's all about."

I stayed there three months. Then they said, "Now what would you like to do?" and I said, "I want to act in a picture—I want to see what it feels like."

So I acted in one. Now I could see Schulberg was getting nervous and wanted me to get started making a picture.

I found a story that some pretty good writer on the staff had done. I asked where his office was, and when I found out, I went down to this barracks-like building—long halls, little cubbyholes, typewriters clacking away behind doors.

I went into his cubbyhole and I introduced myself and I said, "I like your story. I want to do it as a picture."

He looked up and said, "Oh?"

I said, "Yeah, haven't you heard?"

"Oh," he said, "*We* never hear."

Well, we talked all afternoon. I told him, "There are a lot of things in this you could improve like hell," and he helped me to clarify them—he had a good story mind, very quick and constructive—and when we were finished talking, I asked him, "When do you think you could have these changes made?"

He looked at me and his face was a study in astonishment.

"You mean you want *me* to make them?"

"Who else?" I asked.

"Well," he said, "when we sell a story to the studio, we take the check and kiss the story goodbye. And maybe months and months, or a year later, when we hear that a certain story that smells like it was that one is being previewed, well, we run to the preview and see what the hell they've done with it."

[The film was *Close Harmony* with Buddy Rogers and Nancy Carroll, and the writer was Percy Heath.]

In a script conference, Jerry Wald once began to pontificate on the problems of writing for the screen. Wald, a very successful writer-producer, insisted that good screenwriting could only be done by craftsmen, and that such craftsmen were unable to do a good script alone. "I venture to say that out here in this whole town," he said, "there are only three writers who can do a script alone—Shavelson and Rose, the Hacketts, and the Epstein brothers!"

In the midst of a violent argument over a script, Joe Pasternak cried, "You call this a script? Give me a couple of $5000-a-week writers and I'll write it myself!"

Billy Wilder once created a thirty-second screenplay which epitomizes the plight of the Hollywood writer and his wife.

"The camera dollies toward a house in Brentwood," said Wilder. "It is night. Through the open bedroom window we see a writer and his wife, both sleeping. Suddenly, as if struck by a sublime thought, the writer sits up in bed and claps his hand to his forehead. 'Sarah! Sarah!' he cries.

"The wife wakes up, fearfully embraces her husband. 'What?' she demands.

" 'It just can't be done in flashback!' cries the writer."

NUNNALLY JOHNSON

In the making of a picture, the fellow most unappreciated by the man who wrote the original material is the writer of the screenplay. I must have done a hundred pictures and I don't suppose there's ten men or maybe five who remained a friend or indicated in any way that they forgave me or cared for it. One of them was Steinbeck who was a very good friend—I did two pictures of his books. When I was talking to him about *Grapes of Wrath* he said, "Look, it doesn't matter. You can make a good picture out of it and I hope you do but my statement remains right here, in the book, that's all." I remember we bought *The Moon is Down*, which was on the stage in New York, and when I said, "Look, have you got any suggestions?" he said, "Yeah, tamper with it."

Ernie Lehman did the screenplay for *Who's Afraid of Virginia Woolf?* and Lehman did exactly what he should have done. Nothing. That was the play. He had respect for it. The play was effective and could be just as effective on the screen as it was on the stage. The legend in Hollywood is that Ernie only contributed twenty-seven words, and it says "Screenplay by Ernest Lehman." Albee said, "Twenty-seven words, all bad." Small thanks.

Scribes and Pharisees

*   *   *

Gene Fowler

They appreciate industry out here. A lot of writers who come to Hollywood don't realize that and hold up pictures that should be made fast. Of course, work doesn't come quite as easy here because it is siesta country, and then there are all the Christmas-tree ornaments of the life here that are likely to fool you—the servants, the big houses, the fancy automobiles, the afternoons on the golf course and at the races, the long week-ends in the mountains or on the desert or in boats. When you get believing that you have to have those ornaments, they become too important and it hurts your work.

(*from* WRITERS ON WRITING, *by Robert Van Gelder, Scribner, 1946*)

Eliot Paul

I write the best script that I can manage—it is a fascinating medium with a devil of a lot about it that you can't possibly learn except by experience—and if the producer tells me that it is no good, I say that I'm ready to change it in any way that he likes. That's eccentric. But it's the only way I can do it. I can't use that trick that is so popular there [Hollywood]—the author thinks out the scene about two weeks ahead of the conference but when he is asked what he will do with the scene he says that he doesn't know. No one else knows, of course, but they all have a shot at it, and talk, and get nowhere. Then when he thinks that the time is right the author suddenly leaps up, clenches his fist, pounds the producer's desk and shouts that he's got it. Everyone listens. If he'd said in the first place that he had the answer, they wouldn't have heard him. But when he pounds the desk and shouts—then it's drama. Everyone listens, everyone is relieved to hear a solution, and the author is considered a good and reliable man. The producer is happy because he has had a part in creation. I can't put on such shows, so that makes me a little different, which probably is an advantage, too.

(*from* WRITERS ON WRITING, *by Robert Van Gelder, Scribner, 1946*)

Leonard Spigelgass on Damon Runyon

I first met [Damon Runyon] at Lindy's. That figured. Leonard Lyons arranged it. (Thanks.) Said Damon might be interested in me to do the two stories he'd sold to Universal. Told me to be at Lindy's at twelve and he'd be there with Damon. He was—with Damon, and

Mrs. Runyon, and the Spitzes, and one of the Goldstein brothers, I think Bob, and Chuck Green, and a lot of other people, all of them sitting in the corner on the right as you come in. I was embarrassed and ill at ease, and Damon didn't help any. The dialogue was fast, special, and a little out of my line. I felt I didn't have a chance for the job; and I didn't even think I particularly wanted it. I'm sure he didn't particularly want me either. But we agreed to meet the next afternoon at his apartment at the Parc Vendome.

I waited about half an hour while Damon finished his column, my heels and ears being chewed at by three of the most badly behaved cocker spaniels on record, and then I went into Damon's study, surprised to see that it was Louis XVI and very formal, when I'd expected a cluttered desk, and pictures of Jack Dempsey and Joe Louis. We started off badly. Damon didn't like any of my ideas on *Tight Shoes;* I didn't like any of his. He felt that great pictures had been made out of *Little Miss Marker* and *Lady for a Day,* but he felt that the picture I had produced (sic!), *Princess O'Hara,* was lousy. He was right. It was.

I kept sizing him up, those chilly eyes and that florid complexion, the loud Glen Urquhart plaid suit and the lavish Charvet tie, the gold cigarette case and his cold and incisive voice. The whole thing was not auspicious, until suddenly we got on *Butch Minds the Baby,* and it began to work, and he started a train of thought, and I supplied a topper, and then he topped that, and then I topped him, and then, brother, he topped me, and, before we knew it, we were friends.

I don't know how long ago that was—seven or eight years maybe. But in all that time we've been friends, and I've been on the receiving end. Let me say this right off the bat and get it over with: Damon Runyon was one of the greatest, sweetest, most intelligent men that ever lived. And if that's sentimental, then it's sentimental.

I remember once, after we'd written a treatment of *Little Pinks* in New York (it became *Big Street*) we were returning to RKO on the Coast. Damon hadn't been in Hollywood for a long time. He didn't think he was going to like it. (As a matter of fact, when he finally did come, he didn't go back for two years.) We left on the Century and got to Chicago the following morning. We were met by every sports writer, jockey, prizefighter (champion and broken-down), baseball player, and wise guy in town. They had a gala luncheon for him at the Blackstone and I saw happen there what I'd seen in Lindy's, and at the Yankee Stadium, and in traveling crap games, and in little candy stores where bookies hung out, and at opening nights, and in Washington—the same thing all over again: the adoration

84

of the men and women who looked upon Damon as their best friend, who respected him, told him their secrets openly without equivocation, knowing that their confidences were safe with him. I guess Damon knew more dirt than any man living, and I guess Damon told less.

Anyway, we left Chicago, and his friends loaded the dining car with wild geese, and wild turkey, and pâté, and caviar. And all the way across, whenever we stopped, even at little places like Lamie, New Mexico, guys got on, jockeys who were retired, or ball players who were tubercular, or just characters on the lam, and they looked at him with love, and he looked right back at them with tender eyes and deep understanding. He never condoned crime, understand; he just understood why guys were driven to it.

Literally, he understood more about people than anybody I ever knew. That's why I think he's one of the greatest short-story writers America's ever had. O. Henry, Runyon, Lardner—that's my tally on it. There's no sense my talking about him as a newspaperman. I only knew him in fiction. Because he knew people, and because he was one of the most natural storytellers that God has ever created, he wrote like a demon. I never saw anybody in my life turn out a short story so fast. I never saw anybody so facile at making up plots. Actually, he wasn't making them up at all; he was remodeling things and people he knew, and rearranging them in better order.

That's why he loved the movies. I think he saw every picture ever made. When we worked together in New York, we used to have dinner at the old Lindy's (Clara's) and go to a projection room and see two pictures, and then go to the new Lindy's (Leo's) and talk about the two pictures. He had a canny eye for entertainment, but he hated what he called "message pictures" with a terrible and vindictive hate. He belonged to the die-hard school who said that movies were for fun and jokes and tears; he ruthlessly and systematically tore apart anybody who tried to use them for propaganda. Maybe he was right. Maybe he was wrong. Anyway, that's the way he felt. I'm just reporting it.

He thought screenwriting was one of the hardest jobs in the world, said he could never do it. He never did, either. Best I ever got out of him were occasional lines of dialogue. The rest, I assure you, I stole hook, line and sinker from his stories. He used to wonder how I could imitate him so well. I wasn't imitating him at all; I was stealing his own sentence structure and phrases right and left. He used to say, and I wish he'd written it down, that screenwriting was a special kind of job; it required being a novelist, a playwright, and a civil engineer. Maybe it's because he was a writer himself, but he believed that the story was the most important part of the film, but that you could make a good screenplay out of a bad story. The man said so himself.

He also said a lot of other things that have become part of our language. I once asked him how he made up his words and why, and he explained. He felt that English, unlike Yiddish or even French, had no vocabulary for marginal emotions or marginal characters. For instance, what word is there in English to describe a faded blonde of forty-five trying to be young and not succeeding? Well, since this lady practically always wore a kimono and her hair always looked like a mop, it was easy enough for Damon to decide to call her a "komoppo."

He used to borrow liberally from Yiddish (as a matter of fact, his taste in food began with tomato herring and ended with cheesecake); and from Italian (he once supplied for *Butch Minds the Baby* the astonishing fact that goats are not allowed on the Island of Manhattan and that Italians are always breaking the law over Easter in order properly to observe the holidays); from gamblers (he once took me on a tour of a traveling crap game that started in the garment district and ended in the Bronx); from prizefighters (we used to go up to a gym and case the stables for hours); from baseball players (we climbed to the temporary press box at the top of Ebbetts Field to cover the World Series); from dignitaries (we once spent an evening at the Stork Club with Supreme Court Justice Douglas); from Chuck Green (who is always ordering a "stunning cup of coffee"); from Acey Deucy, from Phil the Weeper, and Butch Towers, and from everybody he met, from everything he saw or heard.

His eyes were always open, his ears were always alert, his senses were always sharp. He became the instrument whereby the core of Broadway was articulated and brought to life. He sat in Lindy's, never in judgment but always in dignity.

Working with him was like a shot in the arm. I suppose I'm the only screenwriter in the world who would get up from his typewriter, go to a restaurant, and be introduced to all his characters personally. The picture we made he liked the most was *The Big Street*. It had a curious ending. He loved it. When he couldn't talk any more last year, he wrote me a note, saying so. And because he did, you get it:

Little Pinks, the busboy, loves a crippled but vicious chorus girl and pushes her wheelchair to Florida. By Runyonesque machinations he gives her a great ball and she dies in his arms. As he carries her off, his two friends, Horsethief and Professor B., discuss it:

TWO SHOT—PROFESSOR B. AND HORSETHIEF
Their eyes are quite wet.

HORSETHIEF

I would like to say as follows: this is pretty silly.

PROFESSOR B.

No. Pinks found what everybody else in the world is looking for.

HORSETHIEF

And lost it.

PROFESSOR B.

It is well known to one and all on Broadway that a citizen never loses what he's got filed away in his ticker.

FADE OUT

(*from* THE SCREEN WRITER)

PENCIL IN THE AIR
by Samuel Hoffenstein

I write a scenario for moving pictures:
I let myself go without any strictures;
My mind works in bright ascensions;
The characters swell and get dimensions;
The heroine rises from Gimbel's basement
To what could be called a magic casement,
By sheer virtue and, call it pluck,
With maybe a reel and a half of luck;
She doesn't use posterior palsy
Or displace so much as a single falsie;
She scorns the usual oo-la-la
And never ruffles a modest bra
(The censor's dream of the cinema),
She doesn't find pearls in common oysters;
She sips a little but never roisters.
The hero's gonads are under wraps,
He never clutches or cuffs or slaps
In heat Vesuvian, or even Stygian—
He acts Oxonian or Cantabrigian
With maybe a soupçon of the South—
Cotton wouldn't melt in his mouth;
The plot could harmlessly beguile
A William Wordsworth honey chile;

87

The Wit and Wisdom of Hollywood

> The Big Shot's hot and the little shotlets
> Wake their wives with contagious hotlets.
> So what happens? The usual factors—
> The studio simply can't get actors,
> Directors, cutters, stagehands, stages,
> Or girls to type the extra pages:
> The way it ends, to put it briefly,
> Is what happens is nothing, chiefly.

(*from* THE NOTEBOOK OF A SCHNOOK, *by Samuel Hoffenstein, Doubleday, 1945*)

At one time in the postwar years Paramount hired several noted *New Yorker* magazine writers to come out West and try their talent at the writing of films. Joseph Wechsberg, St. Clair McKelway and John McNulty took up residence on the legendary third floor of the Writers Building.

It was a friendly coffeehouse atmosphere where much card-playing, coffee-drinking and story-swapping went on—and, remarkably, quite a few good comedy scripts were written as well.

One day McNulty accompanied Jack Rose, another writer, to Hollywood Park. Sitting in Rose's car, basking in the bright sunshine as they drove out to the track, McNulty sighed. "Ah," he said, "it's God's blessing to have a racetrack near one's place of employment."

FRANK SCULLY ON JIM TULLY

He was a red-haired, red-faced Danton of the French Revolution cut down to a California commercial acre—the original hard-boiled Mr. Five by Five of life—but by the time he gave up the ghost and the boutonniered planters of the dead got their hands on him, he was bleached white and down to proportions nearer a sand swept city lot.

In his prime, his magnificent voice could talk your ears off, but for the last two years, he was down to whispers—most of his body paralyzed by Parkinson's disease and arteriosclerosis. . . .

Contrary to general opinion *Emmett Lawler* was not Tully's first piece of creative writing. His fight record was. Boxers normally begin as preliminary boys and work up. Jim Tully began as a semi-finalist by the simple formula of having printed up a record of ten fights which had not taken place yet. They were all knockouts.

88

What he took later in the ring must have left a permanent trauma. He had a perpetually blood-shot eye and his story of a slug-nutty fighter in *The Bruiser* wasn't creative writing in the least. *Black Boy*, a play he wrote for Paul Robeson, also showed how serious he could be about the ring.

Of those fights not in the record books, John Gilbert's was the most hilarious. Upbraided for hitting a matinee idol, Tully said Gilbert was fanning himself to death. "So I put him to sleep for his own protection.". . .

The minister read "The House by the Side of the Road" and similar items hardly culled from *Laughter in Hell*. I thought of a line of Jim's at the Strong Woman's funeral: "The audience looked bored with piety.". . . But Jim's soul wasn't there, anyway, and his body didn't belong there either, because he had received the last rites of the Catholic Church and should have been buried in Calvary, or back in St. Mary's, Ohio, where he was born.

That was where he had his six years of schooling in an orphanage. Blasphemic on most issues, he was forever grateful to the nuns who had given him that much. They taught him to write sentences as short as a prison haircut. He kept them that way.

That he was unique among $1,000-a-week scenario-writers in quitting school at the age of twelve, I doubt. But he was unique in his admittance of how little he contributed to a picture. "All I did for *Trader Horn*," he said, "was to tell Thalberg that animals were afraid of fire." He had a standing offer to become one of Irving Thalberg's writers. He looked on it as a stooge role and refused to do it regularly.

One of the most mixed up men in this town, Rupert Hughes, helped Tully most when a dollar and some guidance made all of the difference. It was Hughes who made possible the completion of *Emmett Lawler*.

Tully raised the lowest form of writing, fan magazines, to its highest level and dragged the writing of novels from the lofty heights of *Lord Fauntleroy* down to the realism of *Shanty Irish*. He was the first Hollywood writer to release an unretouched portrait of a director. That was *Jarnegan* who could be Jack Ford, Jim Cruze, Rex Ingraham or Jim Tully.

For *Beggars of Life, Circus Parade, The Bruiser* and *Shadows of Men* he received a lot of praise. For *Ladies in the Parlor* he got suppressed by Sumner. His books got him listed all over the world as the hobo author, despite the fact that he hadn't been in a boxcar in more than twenty-five years. When I first met him he owned a three-acre, $100,000 estate on Toluca Lake, over the hill from Hollywood. A brick mansion, modeled on the lines of George Borrow's, and hidden among dozens of giant eucalyptus trees, it housed Hollywood's best library. In those days there weren't more than three civilized homes in that land of magnificent mansions, and Jim Tully's was one of the three.

Fifteen miles beyond this retreat which became too hemmed in for him, what with the Crosbys, Powells, Astors, Twelvetrees, Brians, Bruces, Brents, Disneys and other picture personalities building on all sides of him, Tully bought a hundred-acre ranch at Chatsworth so that he might retreat farther from the civilization that attacked him from the west, where he found his fame, and the east, where he had none to lose.

He grew alfalfa on his acres and thought that when the revolution came he could live off his land, because land, in his curiously innocent opinion, is the last thing the revolutionists, whether from left or right, will take. The revolution, to hear him tell it, was just beyond the tenth hill and several leagues this side of the horizon, already.

"Let's have another drink!"

If you didn't let him have another drink, you'd find his wrath swerving from the generality to the particular, and you'd soon be writhing under the lash of his incredible candor. It was a curious mixture of Billingsgate and Shakespeare—a poet pelting you with manure. . . .

He wrote all over the place. In one and the same month he appeared in *Vanity Fair, Scribner's, True Confessions,* the *American Mercury* and *Photoplay.* And if that isn't getting a feel of the public pulse, Lydia Pinkham never had it either.

Nobody has ever been quite so willing to go into dog-houses as Tully, feeling certain he'd bark his way out before dawn. And his bark, more's the pity, was far worse than his bite. He had a compassion for men, which hobbled him at every turn; that compassion, of course, took him out of the running in the Superman Sweepstakes, the Nietzschean dope sheet which drove it's author crazy, Mencken to beer, and Shaw to clowning.

When Mencken sent Tully to San Quentin to report the hanging of a youth, Tully stood by the scaffold and watched the lad's neck pop, then sat down without a quaver of emotion or a break in a line and wrote his most hard-boiled report. Without even one aside, *A California Holiday* remains the most terrible indictment against capital punishment ever written in America. . . .

He used to go to New York twice a year just to see Dempsey, Mencken, Nathan, Winchell, Runyon, and others of the old mob, but after a week or two he began to die every night, waiting for the dawn, and then suddenly he would hop a rattler or a plane and blow for his Hollywood hideaway.

The people he wrote about—hoboes, prize fighters, circus troupers, prostitutes, fugitives from chain gangs, and beggars of life generally—are what the trade knows as money pictures, but Tully's treatment of them was too tough, in the main, for the censors. Producers found it easier to steal his raw material and dress it up as society drama, a seduction on a drawing-room couch being easier to condone, presumably, than one in a boxcar or haymow.

At lunch once with Walter Winchell, he asked the latter for the loan of his column.

"What for?" asked Winchell.

"To keep a road kid from burning," was the answer.

"Okay," said Winchell.

Between the two they saved the kid from the electric chair. He later studied journalism.

"I'm sorry now I didn't let him burn," said Tully.

How he could hold on to the roots of his serious writing in such an atmosphere was the most enigmatic thing about Tully. Writers with as much industry, leaving out entirely the issue of talent, say, to a man, that they can't work in California. Tully on the other hand, swore by Hollywood. He couldn't work in New York.

One of those incredible accidents of history turned him from working to writing for a living. He was twenty-two at the time, and had been sent by Martin Davey, the famous tree surgeon who rose to be governor of Ohio, into the south in command of ten men. His letters to Davey were so interesting the tree surgeon asked him to write something for the company's bulletin.

That was his first published piece, and though he didn't make much money at writing for a long time, he had averaged $80,000 a year between 1926 and 1936.

Wilson Mizner once questioned his talent and became crazed with Tully's own appraisal. Tully claimed he was a better writer than O. Henry.

Mizner's eyes popped. "You—oh God in Heaven, guide me! What do I hear? You digger in the garbage of literature!"

"As you will, Wilson," demurred Jim, "I'm built to go far places."

"On a freight!" Mizner's paunch heaved. "Why, you never took a bath till you were thirty."

"That may be—but anyone'll tell you I can write O. Henry's ears off," insisted Tully.

Mizner's wrath boiled over. "Why, you impudent red-headed cur! You porter in the bawdy house of words. My God!" He rose. "I'm leaving here right now." He walked toward the door but turned to add: "You low rat, you befouler of the great dead, you slime of the underworld, you shady reprehensible rogue."

He paused for breath and added in scorn: "You a better writer than O. Henry! Why, you couldn't sign his tax receipts! You're as illiterate as a publisher. If you had a Roman nose you'd be a courtesan!"

He began to act like bubble gum. He trembled. "I'm leaving your house right now, you damned brainless jazzer of decent English, before you claim you wrote O. Henry's stories."

Tully calmly replied. "No, Wilson, I wouldn't say that."

Mizner, deflated with relief, paused at the door.

"Well," he said, "that's decent of you."

"Not exactly decent," replied the stocky little David to the big fat Goliath, "I'd be ashamed to."

Mizner relapsed. He fell to the rug and crawled toward the door. "Good God in Heaven, deliver me from this lousy literary hobo," he screamed. . . .

(*from* SCULLY ON TULLY, *by Frank Scully,* THE SCREEN WRITER)

After many successful years as a writer in Hollywood, Donald Ogden Stewart evolved a set of rules for survival. "Try to find out who the star of your film will actually be," said Stewart. "It's very disconcerting to have written something for Joan Crawford and find it's Lana Turner who'll be the actual star. Secondly, never tackle a screenplay at the beginning of its development. Let the producer and his other writers mess it up, and then, when they're faced with an actual shooting date, you do the final job. And finally," he added, "you must learn not to let them break your heart."

[Stephen Vincent] Benét knew that there were in Hollywood innumerable men of talent and honesty, for he had worked with some and met others, but it was plain that as a rule they were almost invariably victimized by interference and officious supervision. Once, after a particularly destructive story conference on *Abraham Lincoln*, he phoned a friend who had been in Hollywood for some time. "Aren't there any men of principle in this godamn town?" "No," said the friend, and hung up. . . .

He was interested in the technical problems and he had no patience, then or later, with the thesis that Hollywood and adult movies were somehow absolutely incompatible. "What [Max] Miller has left out of his book," he said in 1936, commenting on Miller's embittered account of his life in the studios, "is the fact that good pictures are made, from Mickey Mouse to *The Informer*."

(*from* STEPHEN VINCENT BENÉT, *by Charles A. Fenton,*
Yale University Press, 1958)

STEPHEN VINCENT BENÉT

This is Wednesday. Let me recount a little about this madhouse. In the first place Hollywood—Los Angeles—Glendale, Pasadena, etc. etc.—is one loud, struggling Main Street, low-roofed, mainly un-skyscrapered town that straggles along for twenty-five miles or so, full of stop & go lights, automobiles, palm-trees, Spanishy & God knows what all houses—orange-drink stands with real orange juice—studios—movie-theatres—everything but bookstores. I am the only person in the entire 25 miles who walks more than 4 blocks, except along Hollywood Boulevard in the evening. There are some swell hotels—up in the hills or between L.A. & Hollywood—& a few night clubs. But in general, everything is dead, deserted at 11:30 P.M. There is the continual sunlight—the advertised palms—coolness the minute the sun sets—and plenty of people with colds. The boys go around without hats. They look like prize ears of corn. The girls, ditto.

Of all the Christbitten places and business[es] on the two hemispheres this one is the last curly kink on the pig's tail. And that's without prejudice to D. W. Griffith. I like him and think he's good. But, Jesus, the movies!

I don't know which makes me vomit worse—the horned toads from the cloak and suit trade, the shanty Irish, or the gentlemen who talk of Screen Art. . . .

I have worked in advertising and with W. A. Brady Sr. But nowhere have I seen such shining waste, stupidity and conceit as in the business and managing end of this industry. Whoopee!

Since arriving, I have written 4 versions of *Abraham Lincoln,* including a good one, playable in their required time. That, of course, is out. Seven people, including myself, are now working in conferences on the 5th one which promises hopefully to be the worst yet. If I don't get out of here soon I am going crazy. Perhaps I am crazy now. I wouldn't be surprised.

At any rate, don't be surprised if you get a wire from me that I have broken my contract, bombed the studio, or been arrested for public gibbering. Don't be surprised at all.

(*from* SELECTED LETTERS OF STEPHEN VINCENT BENÉT, *edited by Charles A. Fenton, Yale University Press, 1960*)

Easily the most quoted Hollywood story about writers during the Thirties concerns William Faulkner and his request to his producer to allow him to work at home. The request having been granted, Faulkner disappeared from sight, and was only found a few days later, at home in Oxford, Mississippi.

"It sound like a press agent's dream," said Leland Hayward, "but the whole thing actually happened, and I ought to know, because I was Bill's agent at the time. I got a call one day from Metro. They were completely confused over there and they wanted to know where in hell was my client, Faulkner! They were pretty sore—nobody was supposed to walk out of Metro without letting the front office know where he'd gone.

"I didn't know where Bill was. He hadn't told me he was going anywhere. I got the office to start making calls all over the damned place, and finally we thought of trying him at his home in Mississippi, and sure enough, there he was. 'What the hell are you doing down *there?*' I yelled on the phone, and he said 'Well, ah asked my producer if ah could work at home, and he said fine, so heah ah am.'"

ALLEN RIVKIN

Winfield Sheehan, a former *New York World* newspaperman and also a former New York City police commissioner, had been hired by William Fox to be production chief of Fox Films in Hollywood and Beverly Hills. For some reason, Sheehan had an enormous respect for writers. But when they got troublesome, he thought there was only one way to punish them: not to let them write! Little did he know. To punish Samson Raphaelson for a minor offense which had irritated him, Sheehan sent orders through Colonel Jason Joy, the story editor, that Rafe must report to the studio at nine and remain there till six, he was to be given no writing assignment, and if he didn't fulfill every last syllable of his contract, it'd be broken.

This was the humiliation routine, a term of punishment to last six months. The writer was supposed to get so frustrated that he would storm into Colonel Joy's office and demand that his contract be torn up.

Not Rafe. He was protecting a huge salary—every cent of which he saved, fortunately—and he was going to be a damned good boy. It was a bit rough, I suppose, when Rafe got orders a little later to keep himself available to conduct visitor tours. But Rafe was willing and worked up a rather fascinating spiel of the wonders of the cinema world and that section of it which was Fox Films, William Fox, president. One day, to his great good fortune, Rafe found that the group he was conducting were all members of the Chase National Bank of New York, the Fox Film angels. He was unusually solicitous of the bankers and they were terribly pleased that this very nice young man was making such a fuss over them and was so literate and enthusiastic in his explanation of the various functions of a huge motion-picture lot. "Yes," said Rafe, feeling a birth of power a writer rarely experiences, "this is all part of the wonderful efficiency with which Mr. Sheehan runs this studio. No ordinary person from publicity conducts tours at Fox, as they do at other lots. Winnie Sheehan wants the best, and he's willing to pay for it. Men, he pays me $3,500 a week to do this!"

What happened to Mr. Sheehan then?

Zanuck took over the studio soon after.

(*from* HELLO, HOLLYWOOD!, *by Allen Rivkin and Laura Kerr, Doubleday, 1960*)

Separately, Ben Hecht and Charles MacArthur were each a top-rank talent. Joined together in the bonds of collaboration, they functioned well and for many years. More importantly, at the end of a day's work, they thoroughly enjoyed each other's company. (As any writer will be only too glad to tell you, collaboration is a much harder and more complicated relationship than anything worked over by Drs. Masters and Johnson. Try going over a script for nine or ten hours a day with another writer, five days a week, and you will soon discover why the landscape is littered with the wreckage of ex-teams.)

The quality of their work is lasting and remains remarkably contemporary. In this humorless era their hilarious comedy The Front Page *recently completed a highly*

95

successful season's revival on Broadway. For an example of their film work, treat yourself to the antics of John Barrymore and Carole Lombard in their Twentieth Century. *They were also capable of turning out such a classic film script as* Wuthering Heights.

Even their failures—and they had quite a few of those —were tinged with savage satire, laughter, and a solid sense of le beau geste.

LELAND HAYWARD

Ben and Charlie were my clients when I was just starting my career as an agent. Ben had rented a large house in Hollywood, and I was living there with him with my first wife. Ben wrote a lot about those days in his books. As always, he needed money, and I went out and got him a job. There was a young guy named Howard Hughes who had a script for a gangster melodrama, and it needed rewriting.

I got in touch with Hughes and he was happy to hire Ben, so I went back to the house and told Ben about the deal, and Ben was very suspicious. He'd never heard of this kid Hughes. Hughes had never made a picture, and Hecht figured him for some kind of a promoter, but he needed dough so he agreed to read the script. Then he said he could rewrite it, but if I was going to be his agent, then I'd have to make a deal with Hughes to get Hecht $1000 a day, in *cash.*

Howard said it was fine by him, so Ben sat down and started working on the script, and every afternoon I'd go over to Hughes' offices and he'd hand me a thousand in cash, and I'd go home to the house and drop nine hundred on the table where Ben was working and keep my commission out.

Ben was so anxious to get the damn thing finished that he worked like a demon, and he finished the script in seven days flat. Seven days—seven thousand—that's what Ben got for doing the rewrite.

That was one time he certainly outsmarted himself. The picture went into production with Paul Muni and George Raft, and it was a big hit. It was called *Scarface,* and it made Hughes an awful lot of money. But Ben only got seven thousand.

Later on in their careers, Ben and Charlie did another rapid-fire job. Nobody believes this, but I know it's the absolute truth—they did the script for *Wuthering Heights* in two weeks flat, for Walter Wanger. That time, however, I got them $50,000 for the job. They didn't bother too much with the Brontë book—they did it from an outline. Wanger sold it to Sam Goldwyn, and Sam made it into a big hit.

Ben was always good at pressure jobs. He worked on *Gone with the Wind* for David Selznick—never read *that,* either. Claimed reading the book would only confuse him, and you know, maybe he was right?

BEN HECHT

In Rome, you do as the Romans. The point is, if you don't fancy Romans, why go there? Why go to work in Hollywood if you think movies are mainly trash, and the bosses who turn them out chiefly muttonheads?

A fair question. I'll answer for both of us. Charlie and I worked together in Hollywood on many scripts. We had the same opinions, although we expressed them differently. I was for broadcasting mine. Charlie said, "Complaints are only a sign you've been hurt. Keep the wounds out of sight."

We argued this point from our earliest meetings. Once, in a speakeasy, Dorothy Parker quoted Hemingway's line that "courage is grace under pressure." I dissented. Charlie agreed. "That's posing for others," I said. Charlie said, "It's posing for yourself."

A number of things used to lead a good writer to Hollywood— when it was Eldorado and not a ghost town. (It'll be a tourist spot like Tombstone, Arizona, before the century's done.) I'll make an honest list of these things.

First, the money. It was easy money. You didn't gamble for it as in the theatre. Or break your back digging for it as in the field of prose. It was money in large sums. Twenty-five- and fifty-thousand-dollar chunks of it fell into your pockets in no time.

You got it sometimes for good work, more often for bad. But there was a law in the studios—hire only the best. As a result, the writer who had written well in some other medium was paid the most. His task was *not* to write as well for the movies. His large salary was a bribe.

The boss liked a superior writer to turn out his kindergarten truck—for a number of reasons, some of them mystic. It was a foolish waste of money, like hiring a cabinetmaker to put up a picket fence. But there was a certain pleasure in it for the boss. The higher the class of talent he could tell what to do and how to do it, the more giddily cultured he could feel himself. A good four-fifths of Hollywood's bosses were money-grabbing nitwits whom movie-making enabled to masquerade as Intellects and Creative Spirits.

97

The boss who hired Dostoyevski to write like Horatio Alger somehow became Feodor's superior.

Not all the talent of a good writer was discarded. A part of it could be used for a script—a dime's worth. And there was an occasional script you could work on with all the stops out. But that wasn't why you came to Hollywood—to do the masterpiece. You came as a pencil for hire, at sums heretofore unheard of for pencils. You brought no plots, dreams or high intentions. If you wrote a good movie it was because you were lucky enough to get on the payroll of a classy boss. Classy or not, the boss called the shots and you did as bid. You were a sort of literary errand boy with an oil magnate's income.

Next to the lure of easy money was the promise of a plush Bohemian vacation. Witty and superior folk abounded. The town was loud with wild hearts and the poetry of success. The wit, superiority, wildness had no place in a movie script. But there was happy room for them in the cafés, drawing rooms and swimming pools.

"You write stinking scripts," said Charlie, "but you meet the people you like to be in a room with."

The other matters that took you to Hollywood had nothing to do with the movies. They had to do with flaws in yourself—flaws of laziness, fear, greed. Being a good writer is no feather bed. Writing is almost as lonely a craft as flagpole sitting (and is becoming almost as passé). You write behind a closed door, and fun is your enemy.

Also, the writer intent on "doing his best" has to expose that best to critical blasts that mow him down, two times out of three. And if he wants to keep serving his art, he and his lacerations must lead a sort of hall-bedroom existence. A writer who goes over a fifteen-thousand-dollar yearly budget has to serve other than Art. The figure may be a little high for the poet, but who considers the poets? Plato long ago threw them out of any ideal republic.

The movies solved such matters. There were no critics to mow him down. The writer of a movie is practically anonymous. The press agents employed by the producers, directors and stars see to that. In the roster of who made the movie, his name is lost among the tailors, hairdressers, sound mixers and other talents that toiled toward its creation. It's a pleasant anonymity.

Writing a good movie brings a writer about as much fame as steering a bicycle. It gets him, however, more jobs. If his movie is bad it will attract only a critical tut-tut for him. The producer, director and stars are the geniuses who get the hosannas when it's a hit. Theirs are also the heads that are mounted on spears when it's a flop.

The movie writer is no stranger to these ups and downs. A man could even brag about being a bad script writer. It was a sign he was possibly a genius who couldn't bend to lowly tasks. Neither Charlie nor I were of this kind, but we met them.

I've written it was easy money—and that's a misstatement, if you examine the deed. Writing cheaply, writing falsely, writing with "less" than you have, is a painful thing. To betray belief is to feel sinful, guilty—and taste bad. Nor is movie writing easier than good writing. It's just as hard to make a toilet seat as it is a castle window. But the view is different.

Charlie's problem in Hollywood was greater than mine. His love of the theatre included anything that required actors. And he had no second speed for writing. He had to write with all he was or not at all. The gift of faking dialogue and pumping up Valentine plots was small in him.

To bring a sense of perfection to Hollywood is to go bagging tigers with a fly swatter. Charlie would rewrite a scene ten times, improving it each time with a phrase, a piece of business, a flash of wit or a more human sound. Likely or not, such scenes were cut out of the script by the boss. Why such sabotage? Because the boss who "edited" and okayed the script had no way of knowing one scene was better written than another. He had never been a writer, or reader; never even earned his keep as a critic.

A boss said to Charlie, "I know less about writing than you do. But so does the audience. My tastes are exactly those of the audience. What I didn't like, the audience won't like."

It was the credo that finally landed Hollywood in the dust bin. But when movies were the only toy on the market, it was the Eleventh Commandment—"Write down."

Once I saw Charlie's boss cut out the first fine sixty pages of his script *I Take This Woman* and turn it from a civilized comedy into a Darkest-Metro soap opera. The boss was Bernie Hyman, successor to Irving Thalberg as producing lord of MGM.

Bernie was a "darling" man, gentle spoken, and with a puppy's eagerness for life. He was devoted to Charlie, imitated as best he could his mannerisms, and annexed him as a traveling companion on trips to Europe and Africa. Yet all this admiration never stayed his boss' hand—the hand, in Hollywood, that knows not what the other is doing, or what it itself is up to.

In his story conferences with other writers Bernie would say,

"Let's make the hero a MacArthur." And he would beam creatively on the room.

"Let's make the hero a MacArthur" was, in fact, one of Holly-wood's more artistic mottoes for many years. I heard it in scores of conferences. It meant let's have a graceful and unpredictable hero, full of off-beat rejoinders; a sort of winsome onlooker at life, no matter how hysterical the plot.

Clark Gable, Spencer Tracy, Cary Grant, George Sanders, Robert Taylor and a dozen others, including Jimmy Durante, "played Mac-Arthur." The trade-mark of the character was that if somebody fired a gun he didn't look up, and if a woman was madly in love with him he amused her by sliding down a banister. . . .

I used to say to Charlie, "Why the hell try so hard? All they want is snappy dialogue and snappy scenes."

Charlie could write badly, but not on purpose. He was also sensitive to criticism, from bosses as well as critics. If his work didn't please the boss, Charlie went into a nose dive. He had valor and tenacity, but he was a man of small defiance.

He knew as well as I that the boss was, rather often, a dreary fellow, incapable of criticizing a waffle. He knew, too, that such criticism was usually the mutter of incompetence, in a position to make its mutterings heard. But it didn't matter. Charlie darkened at its sound.

There are no letters of protest from MacArthur on this gloomy topic. But there was one from F. Scott Fitzgerald, written a few weeks before his "crack-up."

Scotty had toiled on a movie script for four months in the studio. He handed it in proudly to his boss. Like many of his kind, the boss, who had never written anything, had not even sold a he-and-she joke to a newspaper, fancied himself a writer. He redictated the Fitzgerald script in two days, using four stenographers. He changed all the dialogue.

Scotty's letter to this man read, in part, "How could you do this to me? If there's anything I know it's the sound of how my generation has spoken. I've listened to its dialogue for twenty years. I've done little else with my life than listen to it speak—How can you throw me away in this fashion?"

Signature—and crack-up. . . .

Thalberg's reticence as a movie maker was an irritant to his fellow Pharaohs. These were gentlemen given to marching through the world with drums banging and calliopes tooting their wonders.

I wrote about President Woodrow Wilson in conference with our

European allies at Versailles that he was like a virgin trapped in a brothel, calling sturdily for a glass of lemonade. There was about Thalberg a similar out-of-placeness.

"He's too good to last," Charlie said in Irving's heyday. "The lamb doesn't lie down with the lion for long."

The institution, MGM, that Thalberg had built to greatness, rewarded him for his efforts by reshuffling its stock issue, thus wresting voting power from him, and demoting him to a Mayer and Schenck underling. This was done while Thalberg was vacationing in Europe with MacArthur.

"Ten years of sixteen-hours-a-day work had tired him," said Charlie. "He didn't know how to rest, or play, or even breathe without a script in his hands."

On his return from his health-building vacation to which the studio had handsomely blown him, Irving Thalberg learned he had been dethroned in his absence. He caught cold, went to bed, and died.

This was the time of Charlie's disillusionment. Not long afterward, he played a joke on the studio. He was having his car regassed at a Beverly Hills gas station. The young man filling the tank was good looking and spoke with a British accent.

"How much are you getting a week?" Charlie asked.

The young Britisher answered, "Forty dollars."

"Hop in," said Charlie. "I've got a better job for you."

A few hours later, Charlie introduced the well-known English novelist "Kenneth Woollcott" to studio chief Bernie Hyman. It was the good-looking gas-station attendant. The young man had never written a line of anything in his life. "Kenneth is one of the most brilliant and successful young novelists in England," said Charlie, "and has also written a couple of comedies for the theatre that have been hailed as worthy of Bernard Shaw. He's against doing any movie writing because he insists there's no room for any honest creative talent in them. But I've persuaded him to listen to you, Bernie. Maybe you can talk him out of his snobbism."

Bernie did. He succeeded after an hour in persuading young Kenneth, the gas-station attendant, to sign a year's contract as a Metro writer at a thousand dollars a week.

Kenneth Woollcott flourished as a Metro writer for the full year, writing nothing and, coached by MacArthur, making the properly superior faces in conference. Neither Bernie nor any of the dozen directors and producers with whom he "conferred" ever found out that Kenneth was a fake, incapable of composing a postal card.

At the end of the year, Charlie wrote a letter which his protégé signed. It was addressed to L. B. Mayer, Grand Pooh-Bah of Metro since Thalberg's death.

> DEAR MR. MAYER,
>
> I wish to thank you for the privilege of working this year under your wise and talented leadership. I can assure you I have never had more pleasure as a writer.
>
> I think if you will check your studio log you will find that I am the only writer who did not cost the studio a shilling this year beyond his wage. This being the case, would you consider awarding me a bonus for this unique record? I leave the sum to you.
>
> Sincerely,
KENNETH WOOLLCOTT

The bonus was niggardly withheld.

The greatness that was Metro is down the drain. Its captains and its kings have tottered into limbo. Charlie's joke is part of its legendary wonders—wonders that were half mirage and half bad writing.

(from CHARLIE, by Ben Hecht, Harper and Row, 1957)

DESERT ISLE

MARTIN A. RAGAWAY

ANNOUNCER'S VOICE (OS)
Ladies and gentlemen, we bring you a news bulletin from Honolulu. Naval rescue units are still combing the South Pacific for the well-known Hollywood producer Allyn Maxwell, whose yacht foundered last week while he was scouting locations for his new picture. Also missing is his writer, Arnold Freem—or Beam—or something like that. At this moment, hope is waning fast for their safety.

LIGHTS UP on desert isle—a strip of sand, one lone palm tree. The two castaways are there, with torn shirts, looking a trifle ragged and seedy. The WRITER is kneeling against a log, laboriously writing on a small scrap of paper with the stub of a pencil. The PRODUCER stands nearby, holding an empty bottle.

WRITER
   (*with a grunt*):

102

Okay, I think I've got it.

PRODUCER

(*eagerly*):

Let me hear . . .

WRITER

(*reading note*):

"Help!"

(*Producer looks up at sky thoughtfully, mulls it over.*)

PRODUCER

(*finally*):

Read that again.

WRITER

"Help!"

PRODUCER

(*comme-ci comme-ca gesture*):

Will they get it?

WRITER

(*hopefully*):

How about "Help! Help! Help!"?

PRODUCER

(*shrugs*):

Baby, people just don't talk that way. Look, the first thing we have to do is tell 'em where we are.

WRITER

You're right. I figure we're somewhere around—(*Starts to write*) Longitude 47, latitu—

PRODUCER

(*interrupting*):

Oh, come on, baby. *You* understand longitude, *I* understand longitude, but what about the poor slob in Kansas who finds this bottle?

WRITER

Okay, how about—"We are cast away somewhere in the South Pacific. We are starving to death and going mad with thirst. Help!"

PRODUCER

(*grimaces*):

Too much on the nose. (*Thoughtfully*) Couldn't we switch it somehow?

WRITER

(*sarcasm*):

Sure. Having a wonderful time, wish you were here.

PRODUCER
(*brightening*):
You know, that's not bad.

WRITER
(*exploding*):
Oh, come on! We're stranded on this lonely, rotten Godforsaken island in the middle of nowhere—

PRODUCER
Now you're cookin,' baby!

WRITER
(*building hysterically*):
I can't stand it any longer, do you hear? I'm going out of my mind—out of my mind! (*Sinks to his knees, sobbing.*)

PRODUCER
(*heavy sigh*):
If you could only put it on paper. (*Walks over to him.*) Now let's try it again. You can do it, Arnie. You've always come through for me before. (*Arnie kisses Producer's hand.*) No, no, that's not necessary out here. Now remember, we gotta get a hook. Something that'll grab their interest right at the start, or they won't stay for the rest of the note. A little sex, a little glamour. . . .
(*Writer nods, slowly recovers his composure, begins to write.*)

WRITER
"Starry nights . . . moon-drenched palm trees . . . beautiful girls . . . Help!

PRODUCER
They won't hold still for it.

WRITER
(*snaps fingers*):
I got it!

PRODUCER
(*eagerly*):
What?

WRITER
"Heh!"

PRODUCER
(*startled*):
"Heh!"

WRITER
Sure. (*Spells*) H-E-dash-dash . . . like we dropped dead in the middle of the word "Help."

104

(*Producer stares at him a long time, then comes over to him.*)
PRODUCER
(*regretfully*):
Arnie, I like you . . . we've worked together a long time . . .
and I'm truly sorry to say this to you. I'm afraid I'll have to get
somebody else. (*Takes paper, starts tearing it up.*)

BLACKOUT

(*from* POINT OF VIEW)

BEN HECHT

A tired old burro caked with desert dust, his hocks full of burrs,
stumbled up to the curb at 21 W. 52d St. and hung his head. Doorman
Red leaped forward to seize the reins as they fell from the hands of
the tall, hatchet-faced gent in the saddle.

"Hello," said this gent, pronouncing the word slowly like a man
trying out the echoes in a cave, "take care of this animule. And don't
let any ladies pet him. He is a cynic and inclined to snap at their
seats."

Saying this, the hatchet-faced traveler warily removed the silver
saddle from his burro, slung a rope of glittering gold nuggets around
his neck, and hiking up his tattered overalls, strode into the saloon
which is known as 21 because you can't buy anything in it for less
than $21, even a pretzel.

This is a whim of the proprietors based, it is said, on the fact
that they had a favorite uncle who was hanged by a posse containing
21 men.

Entering the emporium, the hatchet-faced traveler cocked his
ear a moment at the click of the roulette balls and the silvery
laughter of the lady croupiers. But with a stern shake of his grizzled
head, he made a bee line for the bar. Addressing Gus, the bartender,
he said:

"My name is Gene Fowler and I'm a stranger in town. I want a
hamburger steak and a bottle of absinthe. Also I got some holes in
my moccasins and I'd relish a new pair, if you have my size in stock."

"What size do you wear?" said Gus.

"I favor a 17 Double C," said the newcomer Fowler, "but, mind
you, without any bead work on them.

"I've had a hell of a trip," went on the Fowler. "My burro gave
out complete in the Grand Canyon. Had to carry him all the way
across Colorado on my shoulders. Ain't spoke to a human soul for

three months. Here, have one of my nuggets. They're worth a fortune, but I like the look of your face, pardner."

"Where you from?" said Gus, pocketing a lump of gold the size of a horseshoe.

"Culver City, Californie, a stone's throw from Hollywood," said the Fowler. "Been working the MGM lode there—the combination gold and diamond mine. Ever heard of it?"

"Yes," said Gus, "run by Louis B. Mayer, ain't it?"

"Well, I don't know who runs it," said the Fowler. "Some folks says it's run by a ghost in a long white beard with a noose around its neck. On the other hand, I've heard tell it's operated by an unhappy fellow who at sundown turns into a timber wolf. Maybe they're both legends—but I don't know. I've seen many a strange thing around the old MGM lode."

"Must be fun digging up all the gold and diamonds," said Gus.

"No, son, it's no fun at all," said the Fowler. "It's a big strain. Look at my hair. It wasn't always white as it is now. You wouldn't believe some of the things I could tell you. For instance, how would you like to spend your nights robbing graves? That, son, is part of the work."

A wild look came into the Fowler eye.

"Every worker in the MGM lode,"—he raised his voice—"has got to have seven corpses in his tent just to show he is not a snob. Well, after you've been sitting around with these grinning cadavers week after week, and the Indians burning up your wagons every night, and no water—not a drop—your tongue gets swollen to the size of a mountain trout. . . . Where was I?" the Fowler voice broke off, "Oh, yes, I was telling you about the bleached skulls that line the corridors of old MGM. Just skulls lying there in the moonlight. And some of them talk. Surprises you at first, but you get used to it. Everybody's mighty kind to them—letting 'em pretend that they're running the outfit and supervising production. Here, I've brought one of them back with me." The Fowler smiled tenderly. "I'm going to make him into a tobacco jar."

He removed a death's head from his jeans and plunked it on the bar.

"I don't know if he'll talk so far away from home," he apologized, "but if you've got a straw I'll feed him a drink. He loves arsenic, if you got any handy."

A goodly crowd had gathered round the newcomer and his tale of marvels—a *potpourri* of writers, painters and slogan makers that lolls about the 21 saloon. Cries began to go up. Poets fell to jostling one another for a look at the nuggets around the Fowler neck.

"Where'd they come from?" the voice of a newly arrived great dramatist rang out.

"Culver City, Californie, a stone's throw from Hollywood," the Fowler answered modestly, "although some geographers now call it Death Valley."

There was a moment of pulsing silence. It was broken suddenly by a strange voice, tender and sepulchral. The bleached skull on the bar had found its tongue.

"Go west, young man," it said, "go west."

There was a rush for the door. Outside Red became busy whistling for conveyances of every sort, including carts, perambulators, motorcycles, scooters and covered wagons. The great gold rush of 1941 was on.

"How about this nugget here?" spoke up Gus after the saloon was empty. "Is that real, Mr. Fowler? I'd like to know."

"Yes," said the Fowler, staring mystically into the empty absinthe bottle. "It is real, son. You can bite it, taste it, hammer it into a napkin ring or a set of beautiful teeth. That gold is real, son, and it is the only real thing that comes out of Culver City, a stone's throw from Hollywood."

(from PM)

MARC CONNELLY

The early thirties at MGM were marked by the importation of authors from every field of writing. Those who proved inept as "constructionists" or dialogue writers did not stay long, but it was said that if anyone could sign his name to a contract he was sure of an annual salary of at least $100,000—for two weeks. Those who were retained were men and women who brought proven talents with them. P. G. Wodehouse was able to write several Jeeves stories while waiting, on salary, almost a year for a studio assignment. Writers noted for their individual creativity were dazed by the material on which they were told to work. Dorothy Parker's biting wit and unsentimental compassion were considered by one producer as ideal assets for adapting that early wave of a flood of soap operas, *Madame X.*

William Faulkner's advent at MGM made an impression long remembered. We had been friends since 1929, when he came to New York for the publication of *The Sound and the Fury.* His speech was always slow, partly because of his natural southern drawl and partly because of a conversational gambit he habitually employed. Before answering a question he would exhale a long, meditative puff from his straight-stemmed pipe; then, as often as not, he would contemplate the bowl for a few seconds more.

When he first met Thalberg, Bill was asked if he was familiar with MGM productions. "Ah don't believe Ah know which pictures are yours," Bill replied. "Do you make the Mickey Mouse brand?"

"No," Thalberg replied icily, "we make some shorts, but we want you to familiarize yourself with our big features and the work of our leading stars."

Bill said he'd be happy to do so. A production room was placed at his disposal where he could privately enjoy the latest masterpieces of Lana Turner and Norma Shearer. Actually he was ignorant of the work of both. Ten minutes after Bill entered the production room he dashed out, almost colliding with another writer. The anguish on Faulkner's face made the latter ask: "What's the matter?"

For once, Bill did not puff on his pipe before pronouncing his impression of MGM epics: "Jesus Christ, it ain't possible!"

Samuel Hoffenstein, press agent and versifier, and Louis Weitzenkorn, author of the highly successful play *Five Star Final*, were also frequenters of the MGM writers' table. One day an unsolicited scenario for a movie was received by the MGM script department. Knowing the difficulty of getting a script read except through a recognized agent, the author had attached this note:

> Don't be too hasty in tossing this story into a waste basket. You will notice that its envelope is postmarked Wilkes-Barre, Pennsylvania. Let me remind you that Wilkes-Barre breeds writers. It gave MGM Herman J. Mankiewicz, Samuel Hoffenstein, and Louis Weitzenkorn.

A few days later the informative author was sent the following:

> Thank you for your note about Wilkes-Barre. We are sending back your script, which we cannot use. We are also returning Herman J. Mankiewicz, Samuel Hoffenstein, and Louis Weitzenkorn.

George [Haight] also sold book matches. For two dollars he would supply you with a carton of them with your name and, if you wished, advertisement on the cover. Harry Kurnitz invested in two cartons. One read: "Scenarios neatly done." The other: "Our hands our only tools."

(*from* VOICES OFFSTAGE, *by Marc Connelly,*
Holt, Rinehart, and Winston, 1968)

When Robert Benchley first went to MGM, someone discovered he never used his office. Another was assigned to him, larger and more luxurious. Still Benchley stayed away. Finally he was prevailed upon just to drop in and look it over. He professed to be delighted. That afternoon he returned with an armful of charts, graphs, maps and blueprints, hung them on the walls, stuck them full of significant pins, and never set foot in the place again.

Julius and Philip Epstein were a very successful team of writers who worked at Warner Brothers for many years, specializing in deft adaptations of Broadway plays.

Warner instituted a strict policy of timeclock-punching for all hands, from the lowest messenger boy on up to the highest-paid writer. Needless to say, the creative types smarted beneath the burden of a nine-to-six regimen.

The Epsteins carried on a constant guerrilla warfare with Warner. At one point he lectured them about their hours. "Executives can come in at nine, railroad presidents can come in at nine, bank presidents can come in at nine, why in hell can't *you* come in at nine?"

A week or so later the Epsteins delivered the first thirty pages of their new screenplay to Warner. Attached to it was a note, which read: "Dear J. L. Have the bank president finish the script."

The argument continued. One evening a new Epstein comedy was taken out for a top-secret preview in one of the neighboring Los Angeles suburbs.

Afterward, as was his custom, Warner held a meeting upstairs in the theatre manager's office. Present were the film's producer and the Epsteins.

"This is a piece of crap!" raved Warner. "Absolutely one of the worst you've ever done!"

"I can't understand it, Jack," said Julie Epstein. "We came in every morning at nine."

109

One evening, the Epsteins attended a showing of Ingrid Bergman in *Joan of Arc*. Emerging from the theatre, someone mentioned dinner.

"What do you think we ought to have?" he asked.

"Nothing barbecued," said Phil.

A L L E N   R I V K I N

John Huston and I were office mates at Warners—shared a secretary between us. One day he came in, tossed a book on my desk, took a stance, pointed a finger at the book and said, "Kid, Warner said if I could get a screenplay out of this Dash Hammett thing, he'll let me direct it."

"He's already made it once," I reminded John.

"Never used the book the first time. You and I—we'll do the screenplay, huh, kid? Read it?" I did. John was right. The first *Maltese Falcon* hadn't touched the story Hammett had written. I went into John's office to give him my reaction. "Let's go," I said, eager for another assignment.

"Fine, kid, fine. But first, before we do that—let's get it broken down. You know, have the secretary recopy the book, only setting it up in shots, scenes and dialogue. Then we'll know where we are. Okay, kid?"

"Fine with me," I said.

About a week later John ambled into my office, looking very puzzled. "Goddamnest thing happened, kid," he said, giving each word a close-up. My eyes asked what. "Something maybe you didn't know," he said. "Everything these secretaries do, a copy's got to go to the department. This *Maltese* thing our secretary was doing, that went there, too."

"That's routine," I said.

"But the department has to send everything to Warner—and he reads it!" John said. The look on his face said that Warner was a Peeping Tom, invading our privacy. "He read this Hammett book we had broken down and he just called me on the phone," John said.

Now I really got worried. "Are we closed out," I asked, "for getting this done without an okay from anybody?" "Closed out, hell!" he boomed. "Warner said he wants me to shoot it—and I start next Monday!"

(from HELLO, HOLLYWOOD!, *by Allen Rivkin and Laura Kerr, Doubleday, 1960)*

Joseph J. Lilley was a musical director at Paramount with a unique and dry gift of self-expression. Cecil B. De Mille was preparing a new picture, and his writers had delivered a sequence dealing with young people. De Mille was not too sure of the current slang, and felt that Lilley was more *au courant*. He had the scenes sent to Lilley with a note, requesting that Lilley rewrite the dialogue using the up-to-date argot of the young. The script, rewritten by Lilley, was sent back a few days later, with an accompanying note which read: "Dear C.B. Here's your scene. Use it fast. This sort of stuff antiquates easy."

Goodman Ace and Arnold Auerbach were preparing a script for Danny Kaye when Kaye was doing his radio show after World War II. In the midst of a script conference, Arnold ad-libbed a comedy line to Ace. "Mm—that sounds very contrived," remarked Ace. "Yes, I know," said Auerbach. "I just sat here and contrived it."

At one time in the palmy days of Metro Goldwyn Mayer, there were so many various Middle Europeans, French and other nationalities represented in the fabled writing department that in desperation Charles Lederer hung a small sign on his doorway which read ENGLISH SPOKEN HERE.

HAIL CAESAR

Possibly the most quoted (and misquoted) of the Hollywood wits of the Thirties was the late Arthur Caesar.

Before he came to Hollywood, Caesar worked for a time as a reporter for the fabled Louis Weitzenkorn, whose newspaper activities became the basis of a Warner film starring Edward G. Robinson, *Five Star Final*. One of the stories Weitzenkorn assigned young Caesar to cover dealt with the so-called justice meted out by the lower New York courts. Several Bowery bums had been arrested for trespassing. They had, it seemed, broken into the church known as St. Mark's-on-the-Bowery.

Caesar took it upon himself to plead their case. He obtained permission from the presiding judge to defend them. He appeared in court wearing an Inverness cape; after a brief conference with the bench, it was agreed by the judge that only one of the bums would stand trial, and his sentence would be meted out to the other defendants as well.

Caesar and his defendant had a short conference and then proceeded to trial. He put the unfortunate wino on the stand as witness for his own defense. "Did you break into St. Mark's?" asked Caesar.

"I did," said his client.

"Why did you do that?" asked Caesar.

As if by rote, the client repeated, "For rest, meditation and prayer."

Caesar turned to the judge, and with a dramatic flourish he produced from beneath his cape a sign which he had removed from the exterior of St. Mark's. "I should like to offer *this* in evidence!" he announced, and held out the sign.

The sign read: ST. MARK'S CHURCH—OPEN FOR REST, MEDITATION AND PRAYER.

"Case dismissed," said the judge.

One of Caesar's New York cronies was young Roger Wolfe Kahn, the son of financier Otto Kahn. Not only was Kahn a dedicated musician who organized his own jazz orchestra, but he was also an expert pilot who owned his own planes, which he kept out in the wilds of Long Island at a private airfield.

One afternoon Kahn persuaded Caesar to drive out to the field with him and join him in a quick spin. Kahn had Caesar strapped into a parachute when suddenly Caesar changed his mind.

"Take this damn thing off!" he demanded.

"What's wrong?" asked Kahn. "My plane is perfectly safe."

"Sure, sure," said Caesar. "And I can just see the headlines if anything happens. OTTO KAHN'S SON AND PASSENGER CRASH! What the hell kind of billing is *that*? Forget it!"

Caesar once wrote a one-act play called *Napoleon's Barber*, which came to the attention of Winfield Sheehan, who bought the screen rights and hired Caesar to come to Hollywood and do the script. The picture was one of Fox's first sound films and was directed by John Ford. From then on, Caesar remained a Californian.

"I used to get all sorts of offers to work in Hollywood," recalls Irving Caesar, Arthur's brother and himself a highly successful song-writer ("Swanee," "I Want to Be Happy," "Tea for Two," and many others), "but I always refused. I'm basically a city boy. To me, north of 57th Street has always been the deep woods.

"When people used to ask my brother Arthur why I wouldn't come out, he always said, 'All Gaul was divided in three parts. But the U.S.A. is divided by we Caesars into two parts. From the Rockies west is mine, from the Rockies east is Irving's.'"

Caesar will always be remembered for his first meeting with Darryl Zanuck. It was on a weekend in Caliente, below the Mexican border, where Hollywood people went during the Depression for rest, meditation and tequila.

Caesar was drinking in a bar with friends. Darryl Zanuck, the youngest production head the Warner Brothers studio had ever had, came in with *his* friends. Caesar examined Zanuck for a few moments and then, without any formal introduction, he went over to Zanuck, who was seated on a bar stool, and gave Darryl a swift kick in the rear.

"Say—what was that for?" asked the startled Zanuck.

"That," said Caesar, referring to one of Zanuck's latest and most pretentious disasters, "is for *Noah's Ark*. From now on, watch it!"

The two men remained friends for almost a quarter of a century thereafter.

Al Lewis, who was a producer at Fox during Caesar's early years there, remembers another time when Caesar became involved with Zoë Akins.

Miss Akins, who later won the Pulitzer Prize for her play *The Old Maid*, came to work at Fox. Although she had been born in Missouri, the lady spoke with a slightly affected English accent. "She was working in the writers' building," says Lewis, "and right next door to her office was Arthur's. When I first showed her the place, she said it was like a prison cell—which was true—but I persuaded her that a truly creative person could function in any atmosphere, and Zoë went to work.

"Arthur was working on *Napoleon's Barber*, but he'd already amassed a huge collection of friends all over the studio. Actors, grips, technicians—everybody would come by his office. He kept open house. Everybody loved to drop in and schmoos with Caesar, maybe have a drink, listen to him talk—he was a brilliant raconteur, and he could go on for hours, never repeating himself.

"One afternoon Miss Akins came in to see me and she started complaining. She told me she couldn't tolerate that office any longer. The walls were very thin and she kept hearing things. 'You know, if

113

there's one thing I cannot stand, it's mace,' she said. 'And there are definitely mace in those walls.'

"I figured out she meant mice, and I decided to go down with one of the maintenance men and check out what was happening. We opened the door to Arthur's office and there he was, on the floor, with three or four grips, and they were shooting craps, tossing the dice against the wall.

" 'What's up?' Arthur asked me.

"I explained the problem that Zoë had raised. Caesar burst out laughing. He got up and went next door and went in. He bowed from the waist."

" 'It's not mace, Miss Akins,' he said. 'It's *dace!*' "

Caesar loved to travel, and he once confided to his good friend George Behrendt the secret of successful traveling. "Wherever you go, especially if you're in a strange town," he said, "you must always find yourself a good whorehouse to stay at—they always serve the best breakfasts. After all, when a staff has been working all night, it stands to reason they'll be very hungry."

One of Caesar's proudest claims was that on his first visit to London, he had decided to go and visit Bernard Shaw at his home. He rang Shaw's doorbell, and when the great author appeared, young Caesar introduced himself as a fellow playwright from America who had come to pay a call. Might he now come in and have a friendly chat? Shaw eyed Caesar. "Go walk around the square a bit until I get used to your face," he said.

On another morning in London, Caesar came calling for Behrendt. He pulled up to the Ritz in a large open touring car, complete with chauffeur and footman. The two men went for a drive through the British countryside.

"Arthur had picked up a long brass hunting horn somewhere," says Behrendt, "and every so often he would instruct the chauffeur to stop the car, at which point he'd stand up in the back, blow a blast on that horn and announce to the people *'Caesar has returned to Gaul!'* "

In the days when Caesar was employed as a writer at the Warner studio, he found some of Warner's rules oppressive. He especially disliked the ukase that all writers must arrive punctually at 9:00, spend a full working day in their offices, and not leave until 6:00.

One afternoon Caesar leaned out of his office window and hailed a passer-by who was headed down the street to the studio gate. "Call my mother, will you please?" he yelled. "Tell her I'm okay— they treat you pretty well here, the food's not bad, the guards are pretty decent—but be sure and ask her if she'll please mail me a carton of cigarettes!"

One afternoon Caesar was invited by his friend Zanuck to sit in on the screening of one of Zanuck's latest productions. When the lights came up in the projection room, Zanuck turned to Caesar. "All right, Arthur," he asked, "what did you think?" "Darryl," said Caesar, "if it were mine, I'd cut it up and sell it for mandolin picks."

There are many legends about the parties which Caesar gave (one of which was for the wives of his good friends, and which took place in the living room of a famous downtown Los Angeles whorehouse, at which Caesar told his assembled lady-friends, 'If we sit and wait here for a bit, I am sure most of your husbands will soon join us'), but the best known of all these stories concerns a costume party of the early Thirties.

Caesar had attended wearing a toga and a laurel wreath. In the early hours of the morning, his car was stopped by a traffic cop.

The cop eyed Caesar with suspicion. "What's your name?" he demanded.

"Caesar," said Arthur cheerfully.

"Don't get wise—*gimme your name*," said the *gendarme*.

"*Caesar*," protested Arthur.

He ended up in a Los Angeles jail.

"Caesar's wit was never directed against little people," says Norman Krasna, who knew him well. "He always took pot shots against the very big boys, the ones who were so smug about their positions and power. They were always willing to laugh at Arthur's cracks, but after a while he found it tougher to get jobs. They'd bring him in for conferences, and he'd take pot shots at everybody, but when it came time to *hire* Arthur, the attitude was always 'Why should I subsidize the guy to make cracks against me?' "

CHARLES BRACKETT
at the funeral of Arthur Caesar, June 23, 1953
Ladies and gentlemen, I come not here to bury Caesar but to praise him. When you've known a man over thirty years, either you

115

don't remember a thing about him, or the things you remember pile up in a rich, untidy heap. Arthur Caesar was a singularly memorable man. I'm going to try to sort out some of the stories and the memories and the legends in chronological order.

The first happened in a cold-water flat on Delancey Street. Arthur took his little brother, Irving, into their parents' room, where hung a picture of their father as a sergeant in the Rumanian army. "You know," he confided to his brother, "there is a King in Rumania, and a Prince. If the King dies, the Prince becomes King. But if the Prince dies, they will have to send to America for Papa, and he will become King and Mama will be Queen and we will be Princes and there will be a parade down Ludlow Street. And as we go along, we will speak to all the humble people, but to the landlord and the butcher and the wholesale candy dealer—not a word."

Somewhat later Arthur built up quite a prestige among the neighborhood kids by telling them about an angel suit he possessed. Every night he would put it on, he said, and fly to the top of the synagogue and tell God what all the kids should get by way of presents. After a while the kids, who'd asked Arthur to transmit some pretty peremptory requests, without any results, began to investigate Arthur's claim. They went to his mother. Arthur's mother stuck by him. It was a habit of Mrs. Caesar's. She indicated a big old European trunk. Arthur's angel suit was at the very bottom of it—she hadn't time to get it out and show it to them just then.

Funds were low, and life was pretty rigorous in that flat of the Caesars in those days. Arthur's imagination did a miraculous job with the situation. He told his brother that the deprivations weren't necessary at all—they were more important than that. They were a kind of Spartan training his father had devised, to give his boys character. It was a shining lie that made it an excitement to endure tough times.

Whatever its physical discomforts, that home never lacked for love or learning. Arthur cut his literary teeth on Walt Whitman's poetry, which was his father's great enthusiasm. He was full grown by the time he was eleven, and the passion for the theatre which was to haunt all his days had begun. He used to hang around lobbies and get intermission passes from drunken customers. It was his boast that in those years he saw the *end* of every show on Broadway.

There's a hiatus in my knowledge now—and suddenly he's graduating from Yale. Getting through Yale at all had been little short of a financial miracle. On Graduation Day the gilded youth in his class were getting fabulous presents—Mercer cars, trips to Europe, power launches. Well, Arthur's mother couldn't manage anything like that. But she wasn't going to let Arthur be without a present. She brought him a dozen white carnations. All the rest of his life, in memory of that gesture of hers, he wore a white carnation in his buttonhole.

Well, not exactly always—for there came a stretch of World War I and a khaki suit with no buttonhole in the lapel. He took the war in the fashion of 1917—romantically. He enlisted and was in a base-hospital unit in France before the draft law was conceived. There his ardor ran into a snag. He was a terrible soldier—sloppy in appearance, utterly lacking in military dexterity, the despair of the unit, a comedy figure. But a call came asking for volunteers who would submit themselves to experiments on trench fever, a disease which was raising havoc with the troops. The medical corps thought it was transmitted by lice, but no one was sure. They needed human guinea pigs.

Arthur was the first to offer himself. In Dijon, where the experiment took place, they put lice on the boy's arm and let them bite; they ground up the insects and injected them under his skin; he had to swallow them. Others who submitted to the experiment died. Arthur accounted for his own survival by saying, "Those were very timid lice. I come from the East Side, where the lice are savage."

Delicate as those insects may have been, they left him with something to remember them by; a partial paralysis in one cheek. I'm glad to say he got another memento: a Distinguished Service Citation, signed by Woodrow Wilson and Black Jack Pershing.

When he got home, he got married and began writing plays. His favorite was a short one called *Napoleon's Barber*. Even more than the Congressional citation, he treasured the fact that he got a word of commendation for this play from George Bernard Shaw. In Hollywood he became one of the figures on our local scene—a big comical man with a white carnation in his buttonhole and rousing love for the good things of life.

People roared at the sign on his desk: "I don't want to be right: I just want to keep on working." His comment on a friend's [Darryl Zanuck's] social achievement, "From Poland to polo in one generation," set the pattern for many a joke.

His screen credits are too numerous to mention. For one piece of work, the story of *Manhattan Melodrama*, he won an Academy Award. But it was as a personality, a wit and a philosopher that he stood forth. His comments on religion became part of his legend.

"It's like a bank. Lots of doors, plenty of tellers—but only one that can okay the check." "We are not punished *for* our sins but *by* them." To a Catholic friend, who considered changing his faith: "Quit trying to play split weeks with religion. God won't be able to find you."

Time passed. He was saying fondly of his wife, "Mrs. Caesar has taken up her option on me for the thirty-first straight year"—and suddenly a terrible physical ailment beset him. He met the horror as was natural to him, with a joke. "All of a sudden my toes began turning red, white and blue," he explained to the doctor, "only nobody was playing the Star-Spangled Banner." "Will you submit to an amputation?" his doctor asked.

"I don't write with my toes. Go ahead." His leg had to be amputated above the knee. "My manicure" was the way he referred to the proceeding. And the amputated leg he dubbed "little Caesar."

To calm any fears he might have about the future, George Behrendt, a noted amputee, not only talked about how little he himself had been hampered by the loss of a leg, but demonstrated it by whirling about the room. Arthur looked up at his visitor with those richly comic eyes. "You make it sound so attractive, George, I'm beginning to be sorry I didn't have it done thirty years ago." [Caesar also remarked to Behrendt, somewhat ruefully, "With my luck, George, I'll get a wooden leg from a tree that has 'John Loves Mary' carved on it."]

He seemed to recover magnificently, became interested in television and was turning out TV scripts with enthusiasm. But the tired body had had too much to take. One can't but feel that after all those years the trench fever experiments exacted their price. The very end was not peaceful—it was better than that—more typical: it was merry. He was chatting gaily in the garden with a friend—one of his younger friends. She was six years old, I believe. And all of a sudden, between a joke and a joke, he just stopped living. And here he lies, under a merited American flag, with a white carnation for remembrance.

You may think I've spoken too frivolously. I've tried to keep it as he would have liked. He left only one instruction for this occasion: "When I die, be sure the services are in the morning, so my friends can get to the track and not lose any time they need for betting."

He had a jaunty mind, a rich humor, and real gusto. I think that somewhere up on top of the synagogue, talking to God, he's asking good things for all of us.

In the days after his leg had been amputated, Caesar was a patient at the Motion Picture Home. Next door to his room, bedridden, was the great Polly Moran, who is best remembered for her comedies with Marie Dressler.

"Polly was fond of delicatessen," said Behrendt, "and she was desperate for the taste of corned beef and pastrami, so, to please her, Arthur arranged for a delicatessen nearby to deliver each night a couple of sandwiches. Arthur had me bring him a fishing rod with a long line. Delicatessen was strictly forbidden Polly, but every night Arthur would drop that fishing line out the window, the delicatessen delivery boy would attach the package to the hook, and then Arthur would reel in Polly's treat and see that the sandwiches got to her.

"She'd devour them. 'Why not?' Arthur would say. 'She's suffering enough, let her have a little enjoyment.'

"But then Polly would have heartburn. We were in his room one night, visiting, and from Polly's room there was a sudden yell. 'Arthur—I'm dying, I'm dying!'

" 'You can't die yet, darling,' Arthur yelled back. 'I haven't written you your last lines!' "

With the advent of Hitler, many European film people had migrated to Hollywood. Among them were a large contingent of Hungarian playwrights. So many of these were employed at Metro-Goldwyn-Mayer that one of the studio wags had a sign made which he hung on his wall: IT IS NOT ENOUGH TO BE HUNGARIAN: YOU HAVE TO HAVE TALENT TOO.

And later, during the dark years of World War II, another anonymous wit offered this official bulletin: OUR B-17'S BOMBED BUDAPEST LAST NIGHT AND DESTROYED THREE PLAYWRITING FACTORIES.

Kyle Crichton, no mean wit himself, reports seeing Dorothy Parker in an automobile parked before a Hollywood supermarket. He leaned in and asked, "How do you like it out here?"

"Oh, it's all right," replied the lady. "You make a little money and get caught up on your debts. We're up to 1912 now . . ."

(*from* TOTAL RECOIL, *by Kyle Crichton, Doubleday, 1960*)

119

The Wit and Wisdom of Hollywood
KEN ENGLUND:

Let us roll up our sleeves and try to scrub some of those cob-webs off our celluloid. To get down to cases: There was a Geneva Convention to outlaw poison gas; can't the members of the Screen Writers' Guild get together to ban and consign to limbo the following which I have tried to categorize?

ROMANTIC DIALOGUE AND LOVE STUFF

"Listen, darling, they're playing *our* song!"

"Violets! Oh, darling, you remembered!"

"Moss roses! You remembered—oh, darling!"

"White orchids with those *same* yellow throats with just a touch of burnt umber! Oh, you're such a darling to remember!"

"Darling—this is *our* place!"

And at "our place" let's send to a Cain's Warehouse for stale characters the genial proprietor Luigi, the musical-comedy Italian who is continually drooling toothily and lasciviously over the Boy and Girl because he "loves lovers" and incidentally wants to pad his part.

While we're still at Luigi's does the Boy always have to carve their initials on a Chianti bottle? Can't it be a Haig and Haig pinch bottle for a change?

THE AQUATIC LOVE SCENE

The springboard the studio bought read: "And in the days that followed they drew closer and closer together. They dined, danced and swam together. . . ." In screenplay the Aquatic Love Scene results:

"Race you to the raft, Freddie!"

So saying, Maureen O'Hara playfully pushes John Payne into the water, dives in, and a gay race ensues. Boy and Girl clamber onto the raft happy as playful porpoises, laughing fit to kill. After they get tired laughing, he gives her a hard, intense, libidinous look and seals her mouth with a very long passionate kiss that holds till the Dissolve so that the screenwriter won't have to think up any dialogue. . . .

THE OUTDOOR OR AIN'T-NATURE-GRAND LOVE SCENE

The Girl in a tight white sweater takes a deep breath and looks around at the other wonders of nature and exclaims (after much coaching): "Oh, Timothy, isn't it beautiful!"

120

Timothy takes a look at her heaving sweater and exclaims back significantly: "Sure is!" and his meaning isn't lost on anyone. I believe we can drop for all time this giddy gambit, along with

THE NIGHT OUTDOOR LOVE SCENE

"Oh, Keith, darling—look—the stars are so close you could reach out and stir them around."

And

THE BAR LOVE SCENE

The Girl (sipping champagne timidly): "Oooohh! The bubbles tickle my nose!"

THE BACKSTAGE MUSICAL

Scene opens with a line of chorus girls in practice clothes practicing. Immediately the Dance Director calls out, "Take five minutes, girls," and they quickly disperse. After extensive research I have discovered that dance directors in "real life" always give the girls at least ten or fifteen minutes, so why can't Larry Parks, Gene Kelly or Dan Dailey do the same? Try and watch these little things, gang, they all add up to perfection.

And can't we do something about the circular iron ladder backstage, and that typical shot of the chorines descending? I know it's a dandy way to catch the backs of the girls' legs, but can't we repaint the ladder or something, or twist the iron the other way? . . .

THE STAR CAN'T GO ON AND THE UNDERSTUDY TAKES HER PLACE

Leo McCarey had the only practical suggestion for a new switch on this chestnut. The Leading Lady gets sick. The Understudy gets her big chance. All her dreams have come true. She runs, puts on her makeup and costume, and then, as she descends the iron ladder, she trips coming down in all her excitement and breaks both legs. The show never opens. . . .

B MUSICALS

Swing versus the Classics! The Long Hairs versus the Crew Cuts! And that malodorous bromide where the kids in the orchestra segue sneakily from Beethoven to Benny Goodman when the hatchet-faced Principal isn't looking! Discovering their audacious prank, she is at first outraged, then starts keeping time to the music. She can't help herself and neither can the helpless audience. If another screenwriter puts this on celluloid, he should be flogged through the Guild.

EPICS, RESTORATION DRAMAS AND PERIOD PIECES

The leading lady is taking a bath in a tub or a rain barrel—a maidservant pouring in hot water. The bather looks up shocked to find that George Sanders has taken the maid's place and is now pouring.

There must be another way to show Paulette Goddard's pretty shoulders in relation to history without always resorting to this prairie bubble bath. Let's dig and maybe put Sanders in the tub and let Goddard pour it on him. But don't get overly particular and ask where she got the bubble-bath preparation in the middle of the great outdoors. There is a branch of Elizabeth Arden's at Fort Sill and the special soap is brought by Pony Express along with the gunpowder, pemmican, firewater to bribe Indians—and comic books for the extras on location.

DOUGLAS FAIRBANKS, JR. (ERROL FLYNN) TYPE PICTURES

In the middle of a duel to the death the two antagonists lock wrists and swap talk, their sweat-drenched faces only an inch apart. "Norman dog! Anglo-Saxon lilies will grow over thy bones ere yon sun sets!" Snarling cheek to cheek, this exchange of insults and plot points goes on for a half hour and finally they are down to saying, "I'll bet my agent can lick your agent," and the impression is created that the age of the actors has given them pause rather than the dictates of the story.

Under the same classification: a murrain seize the writer (or director) who plans a duel that takes the swordsmen through twenty-six rooms. It always appears as though the host was showing his enemy his castle with an eye to renting it rather than the motivation of running him through. Mamoulian staged the best and most realistic movie duel in *Mark of Zorro* in *one* room. The camera was continually on Power and Rathbone and they lost three quarts of blood between them—but it was worth it!

SCREEN BIOGRAPHIES (NON-MUSICAL)

Can't we do without The Tea Scene?

In the dim light of a student lamp Don Ameche is peering into a microscope. A clock wearily strikes three. Bong, bong, bong. Bette Davis enters carrying a tray containing a pot of tea. She says, "Goodness, John—stop a moment and have a cup of tea. You must have some rest. As it is, you'll get little enough thanks for inventing syphilis." He sighs wearily, takes off his glasses and answers: "But, my dear Katrina, *someone* has to do it." He smiles bravely, she smiles bravely. After another brisk exchange of brave smiles, this Tea Scene is interrupted by The Rock-throwing Scene.

As the scientist sips his tea, several rocks come crashing through the study window. Ameche, in spite of his wife's fears for his life, goes out on the balcony and looks below to see a slavering mob of toughs led by Gene Lockhart, the town's leading skeptic. There are angry catcalls, more rocks aimed at the scientist's head, and unkind remarks that all add up to the belief that Ameche is in league with the devil and his dark machinations in the laboratory will bring ruin and the wrath of God down on all the inhabitants of Bad Gaswassar.

The very sight of Gene Lockhart in a biography telegraphs to the audience that he is going to set himself against whatever the hero is trying to perfect, whether it be cellophane or falsies. He has become so immersed in this role of doubting Thomas that his agent tells me it has even affected Lockhart's private life. He has just had the phone taken out of his house, not wanting to risk his life by using the dangerous electrical device of that crackpot Bell! Now when he gets a studio call for a new job as screen skeptic, his agent has to drive over to tell him about it.

BIOGRAPHIES OF GREAT BROADWAY COMPOSERS

"Rita! I think I've got our fourth-act finale—listen!"

And, without a word of warning, the Tin Pan Alley Tschaikowsky leaps to the Steinway and ad-libs what it took Hammerstein and Rodgers six months to compose. The Girl sings the chorus with him, *guessing* the lyrics in advance. They end on a kiss over the piano. Sometimes a playful kitten (on wires manipulated by five stagehands belonging to two warring unions) comes between them for the Dissolve. Or if he's an outdoor composer, the Boy and Girl are on a horse and one of the horses' heads comes between them as they kiss. I'd even settle for the other end just for a change.

THE FIGHTING ROMANCE

"Rosalind Russell is the new Boss Lady of an Advertising Agency, see—but Fred MacMurray, see, *doesn't* KNOW he's working for a WOMAN, *see!*? Because HE HATES WOMEN and he'd never have taken the job in the first place if he knew he was working for a FEMALE! He has a phobia about the opposite sex, SEE, because of a sad experience in his own life—his mother deserted him when he was only forty-two—SEE—but, not knowing Rosalind is his NEW BOSS, he falls in love with her against his will—and that's when the fun begins!" And that's when, if the audience is smart, they'll just tiptoe out on the bickering couple, get into their cars and spend the rest of the evening necking, which is a lot more fun.

A most significant observation as regards the horse opera was made by Sol Siegel's five-year-old child. After his first few trips to the Hitching Post he deduced that the "baddies" wore black hats and the "goodies" wore white hats. Cliché from start to finish, about the only thing that could be done to freshen oaters would be to switch the hats around. Or perhaps have them reblocked—possibly with the actors' heads left in them.

THE DETECTIVE STORY

I make only one plea here—that Sydney Greenstreet stop playing Brahms' "Lullaby" on the piano while he gives Peter Lorre instructions on how to rub out Humphrey Bogart. I also think it incumbent on writers to make clearer just how the poison dart did get lodged in Miss Hush's brain.

It's been awfully plotty out lately, and I've been hoping that someday in desperation Dick Powell would flag down a cab, toss away his cigarette and, hopping into the back seat, order the driver to "Follow that story line!"

ARMY AND NAVY STORIES

"Honest to God, it's moider, fellahs! Is there some law or somethin' that says we gotta have a guy from Brooklyn in every company of the U.S. Army, Navy and Marines who sighs for Moitle, rhapsodizes on the beauties of Prospect Park—ad nauseum?"

Well, I see my time is about up and several of my friends are standing in the wings with baseball bats. But I don't want to get off and take my medicine without trying to make a few constructive suggestions—if I can think of any.

A clue to some Hollywood thinkers' thinking is manifest in a story making the rounds in studio scuttlebutt. The story: When Alfred Hitchcock admitted to a top executive that he didn't see many pictures, the executive, in all seriousness, said, "Then where do you get your ideas?"

(*from* QUICK! BOIL SOME HOT CLICHÉS, *by Ken Englund,* THE SCREEN WRITER)

JOSEPH L. MANKIEWICZ

I had lunch with Norman Krasna one day. He was on his way to New York to see to the production of his play *Small Miracle,* and during the lunch he told me a story he thought would make another good play, and he told me I ought to write it.

I kicked the idea around for a while, and then I got a job at Metro, where they wanted me to be a producer. The idea took shape as a picture story, and I went in to see Louis Mayer, who told me he wanted me to be a producer.

I said I didn't want to produce, I wanted to direct pictures. Mayer wouldn't hear of it. He said, 'No, first you're going to be a producer!'

I said, "I want to write and direct," and Mayer said, "No! You have to produce *first*. You have to *crawl* before you walk"—which is as good a definition of producing as I've ever heard, to this day.

Anyway, I gave in, and I said I'd found a story I wanted to do, mentioning Krasna's story. Mayer screamed at the idea—he hated it, but I yelled back, and finally he gave in. He told me I could make it. I went back to my office, called Sam Marx, who was head of the Metro story department then, and asked him to buy the story from Krasna for me.

Norman called me up the next day, and he said, "Joe, I understand Metro wants to buy that story," and I told him it was true. Norman paused and then he said, "Listen—could you do me a favor? It's been so long since I told it to you, I've forgotten what I said. Would you put it down as you remember it?"

I called in my secretary, dictated ten pages to her, Metro bought the story idea and we made it into a film. It won Norman an Academy Award. The name of the picture was *Fury.*

"Joe is much too modest about this," says Norman Krasna. "He makes the whole thing sound so easy. This was in the middle Thirties when Metro was dedicated to making musicals and fluffy comedies and love stories—pure escapist entertainment. Can you imagine what a hell of a job he must have had to convince Mayer to let him make the first anti-lynching picture—and at *Metro*?" Krasna shakes his head at the recollection of the incident. "It all seems so easy now, when movies are all concerned with social problems and political stuff, but back in those days, Joe must have lain down on the floor and dug in his heels and screamed for a long time before Mayer ever gave in to *Fury*."

George Middleton, a successful Broadway playwright who had been at the forefront of the drive to form the Dramatists' Guild, found himself being wooed to write in Hollywood. It was at the time when Broadway playwrights were much sought after; sound films needed dialogue, and such men as Middleton were considered invaluable.

He went to work at Fox, where his producer was Sol Wurtzel. Middleton brought pages in to Wurtzel, who would read them and then comment, "Where is the menace?"

Middleton would return to his office and revise, edit and continue writing. More pages went to Wurtzel. Again, his only comment was, "Where is the menace?"

Finally, Middleton brought in what he considered to be a completed script. Wurtzel summoned him to a conference. "Middleton," he said, "I've read your script, and I still say, *where is the menace?*"

Middleton stood up. "Mr. Wurtzel," he said, "I can answer that very simply. *You* are the menace."

For several years, Mel Shavelson and Jack Rose functioned as a writing team at Warner Brothers in the era of Jack Warner's implacable edict that all writers, no matter how creative, punch a daily nine-to-five time clock.

Came a production crisis. Work on a film was stopped dead because the star, one of the reigning Warner luminaries, did not like the script. One of the studio executives sought out Mel Shavelson and begged him to use his good offices to persuade the star, his friend, to do the picture.

Mel was agreeable. Where was the star? At a nearby Burbank watering-hole, imbibing heavily. Mel volunteered to go right over and be persuasive. "Wait a minute," said the producer. "You'll have to wait until after five. If Warner finds out you left the lot before then, he'll raise hell with both of us."

"Okay," said Mel. "I'll see him after five."

The producer sighed. "That's not any good. By that time our

pal will be so drunk he won't know who he is—much less you."

"What do we do?" asked Mel.

Desperate times call for desperate measures. "You're going to have to make a break for it," said the producer. He thereupon called for a studio limousine to be brought over to the executive building. Shavelson was led into it and instructed to lie prone on the floor. The studio driver thereupon drove out the Olive Avenue gate, and Shavelson was smuggled out to his rendezvous.

"And that," says Shavelson, "is how I saved the studio."

The friendship of one of America's greatest poets with writer-producer Hal Kanter began when Kanter, then producing a weekly television show starring Milton Berle, persuaded Carl Sandburg to come out to California and make a guest appearance on the show. It was a most unlikely booking, but it proved to be enormously successful; Sandburg, being a born performer, did a poetry reading with his customary dramatic fervor.

During a mid-morning rehearsal break, one of the crew, a young assistant director, approached Sandburg with a volume of poetry and respectfully requested a signature.

Sandburg eyed the volume carefully. "Young man," he said finally, "I see that this is an anthology. Now, I will be happy to sign it *after* you get Alfred, Lord Tennyson, Edgar Allan Poe, Percy Bysshe Shelley, John Keats *and* Edna St. Vincent Millay to sign it. If you want my signature alone, get a volume I *wrote* alone."

At lunchtime the director hurried out to a bookstore and bought a volume of Sandburg's poems, which he brought back to the studio. After rehearsals he re-approached Sandburg. Sandburg turned the signing into something of a ritual. As the crew and studio personnel watched, he sat down at a table. "Now," he asked, "what exactly did this volume cost you?"

"$3.25," said the young man.

"Now there are between these covers," said Sandburg, "some 362 separate poems, which means that each of these poems costs you a little more than one cent—which is undoubtedly the greatest bargain you can get in literature today! I hereby affix my signature thereto."

After the show was taped, Sandburg was in his dressing room backstage, accepting congratulations. Abe Lastfogel, a charming and literate gentleman, then head of the William Morris Agency, came backstage. He was a Sandburg fan from a long way back, and he would deem it an enormous honor if he could meet the poet. He was ushered in to meet Sandburg.

"This is Mr. Abe Lastfogel," said Kanter. "He's very anxious to meet you."

"Lastfogel?" asked Sandburg. The name did not register.

It was explained to him that his visitor was the head of one of the largest talent agencies in show business.

"I'd be pleasured," said Sandburg gracefully.

The two men shook hands and Lastfogel enthusiastically praised Sandburg's poetry, his historical volumes and his performance of this evening.

"Lastfogel," mused Sandburg. "Is that a Swedish name? I don't think so."

"No," said Abe. "It's actually German. Originally, it was Lustvogel—*lust* meaning *prey* and *vogel* meaning *bird*."

"Lustvogel . . . bird of prey . . . bird of prey," mused Sandburg. "What an apt name for a man in your profession."

It was a year or so later that Sandburg returned to California, this time to work with director-producer George Stevens on *The Greatest Story Ever Told*. Several days went by before he called Kanter. He apologized for not having gotten in touch before. "We really must get together, Hal," he intoned, "just as soon as I help Mr. Stevens lick this goddamned Bible story."

After listening to Milton Berle reel off a few moments of his high-intensity comic patter, Sandburg said, with a completely straight face, "Lincoln would have loved him."

Dorothy Parker found herself at a party where an actor, who had been appearing in London for a season, was holding forth. The actor persisted in using various British forms of speech and continually referred to his "shedule." "If you don't mind my saying so," said Miss Parker, "I think you're full of skit."

During the preparation of one of his biggest films, the Irving Berlin musical *White Christmas*, Mike Curtiz attended an emergency story conference at the home of Don Hartman, the film's executive producer.

Danny Kaye had agreed to play the co-starring part opposite Bing Crosby, but one of his stipulations was that Mel Frank and Norman Panama, with whom he had just completed *Knock on Wood,* be brought in to revise the script.

Panama and Frank listened patiently for almost a full hour as Curtiz acted out the entire script for them, complete with pantomime and a grand finale in which the lovers were reunited. "Ve are in Vermont, and de snow is falling, and de music svells, and de lovers are kissing, and it is absolutely beautiful!" said Curtiz as he completed his recital.

Hartman turned to Panama and Frank. "How do you like it?" he asked.

"Is that it?" asked Frank.

Hartman nodded.

"Don," said Frank, "that's the lousiest story I've ever heard."

"Dot's de lousiest story you ever heard?" asked Curtiz.

Both Panama and Frank nodded.

Curtiz turned to Hartman. "If dot's de lousiest story dey ever heard," he said, "den vy am I doing dis picture?"

Robert Emmett Dolan, who actually produced the film for Paramount, supplies the following footnote to Mel Frank's recollection.

"After Panama and Frank agreed to do a complete revision of the script," Dolan recalls, "they locked themselves into an office and went to work at top speed. We had a shooting date staring us in the eye, and we went ahead with the final production details. Pages kept coming down from Panama and Frank. They'd be mimeographed and go over to Mike Curtiz, who was seeing people for casting.

"I was having lunch at Paramount one day when Rosemary Clooney, whom we were considering for one of the female roles, came in. She had been with Mike Curtiz and she seemed very upset."

" 'I was just up with Mr. Curtiz,' she told me, 'and he started to tell me the story of the picture—it was so marvelous—and when he got to a certain point, he was so involved with the story, he actually began to cry a little, and he stopped and said, Excuse me, my dear, I simply cannot go on.' "

"I didn't tell Rosemary," remarks Dolan, "that Mike couldn't go on because Norman and Mel were upstairs and they hadn't sent him the rest of the script yet."

Peter Viertel, the screenwriter, who was a good friend of Ernest Hemingway's, was approached to do the screenplay of that author's

The Old Man and the Sea. He discussed it with Hemingway and asked Hemingway his opinion of possible changes in his work.

"Let me tell you about writing for films," said Hemingway. "You finish your book. Now, you know where the California state line is? Well, you drive right up to that line, take your manuscript and pitch it across— No, on second thought, don't pitch it across. First, let them toss the money over. *Then* you throw it over, pick up the money and get the hell out of there."

Contrary to his own advice, Hemingway did become involved in the filming of *The Old Man and the Sea*, with damage to his personal relationships with cast and producer, and with considerable damage to the novel he had written.

Four years later Viertel met Hemingway again. After both of them had relaxed over a sufficient amount of drink, Viertel summoned up enough courage to ask Hemingway about the debacle. "What about that advice you gave me about pitching the manuscript into California and fleeing with the money?" he asked.

Hemingway shrugged. "I should have listened to myself," he said.

THE LATE MR. HARRY KURNITZ . . .

"Everybody who knew Harry Kurnitz liked him," says Ken Englund. "His humor was never vicious nor spiteful—in fact, more often than not, it was turned on his own quirks.

"I remember there was a time when he signed a contract with Warner Brothers to function as a producer-writer at a very large salary. Weeks and weeks went by, with both H. M. and Jack Warner watching those paychecks go out each Friday, and both of them beginning to chafe over Kurnitz's delay in getting a picture in front of the cameras.

"At last, after a few months, Kurnitz got one started. On the first day of shooting, there sat Harry, chain-smoking, peering through his thick glasses, watching all the activity on the set, nodding as if he really knew what it all was about, and then one of the Warners came down to have a personal look at this miraculous scene.

"Kurnitz spied Warner—it was old H. M., the most dignified and certainly the most humorless of the three brothers—and he waved a cheerful hand in welcome.

" 'Well, Mr. Warner,' he crowed, 'I think I've finally gotten the hang of it!' "

Kurnitz came to work in Hollywood in the late Thirties. Besides films, he was also a detective-story writer, having written such novels as *Fast Company* under the pseudonym of Marco Page. He had spent his early years working in bookstores and antique shops, and he turned that knowledge to good use as the background material for his thrillers. He was also a very serious art collector, and from that avocation there later came his Broadway comedy *Reclining Figure*. Kurnitz was very musical and played the violin; his knowledge of and love for classical music he was later to weave into his comedy *Once More, with Feeling*.

Wherever Harry went, there was always a collection of friends and much conversation. He was an incorrigible coffeehouser and round-table gatherer. "However," says Englund, "when it came to work, he found ways to discipline himself. He told me that when he decided to write *Fast Company*, he took a room at the Hotel Algonquin under an assumed name, and holed in there where nobody could find him. That was the only way he would not be distracted by all his friends calling him up to invite him to various social functions."

"He was an insomniac and a compulsive writer," says George Axelrod. "Harry had this thing about doing a certain amount of writing every day, come hell or high water. Since he didn't sleep well, he'd get up before dawn and write. He told me that once, at Loel Guinness' country house on a weekend, he woke up at five A.M. and decided to work. Only trouble was, there was no writing paper in his bedroom. Harry was so driven to write that he actually pulled out the lining paper from three bureau drawers in the room and wrote four or five scenes on them before breakfast!

"Harry always wrote without making carbons. One weekend he was cruising on somebody's yacht on the Mediterranean—he really enjoyed stuff like that—and he was sitting out on the deck, working on a script, with all the pages on the table. There was a sudden gust of wind and the script blew overboard into the Mediterranean!

"Without a second's hesitation, Harry, fully dressed and wearing his glasses, leaped overboard after it.

"'It was in mid-air,' he told me later, 'that I remembered I could not swim.'

"They pulled Harry and his precious script aboard a few minutes later. I thought it was such a marvelous incident that I wrote it into my picture *Lord Love a Duck*."

"Kurnitz would use any possible excuse to avoid disciplinary pressures," continues Ken Englund. "He got a considerable amount of dough to do the screenplay of *One Touch of Venus* for Universal, but he absolutely refused to go out to work at their studio. Firstly, he loathed studio offices, and, secondly, Harry was already beginning to be something of a social snob. He considered it to be beneath his dignity even to travel from Beverly Hills out to San Fernando Valley, much less to *work* there. So he did the script completely at home and had it delivered by messenger."

"Harry came from a very poor Philadelphia family," said Leland Hayward, who produced the Kurnitz adaptation of the French comedy *A Shot in the Dark*. "At one time, when he was struggling to make a living in New York, he lived in a furnished room on the Lower East Side, near Greenwich Village. Harry told me he was so poor he couldn't possibly afford a pint of whiskey, so in order to get high, he'd save up a few cents each week and buy liquid marijuana from a corner druggist. In those days it was legal—something like extract of cannabis—and Harry'd pour the stuff over a box of cigarettes, let them dry out, and then he'd smoke them and get a mild charge. 'It was all that I could afford in the way of corruption,' he said.

"Of course, later on, when Harry was making a lot of money, he developed elegant tastes to go along with it. I was at a dinner party with him in Palm Springs a couple of years ago, a very big spread at Frank Sinatra's, and the first course was oysters.

"They'd been flown in from the East, and Harry gave us a short lecture on oysters. He was passionate about them, he had researched them, eaten them all over the world, knew all about the different varieties, the French, the Portuguese, English Whitstables, where the best beds were. He reeled off all the varieties you could find up and down the East Coast, and then finally he began to eat his own dozen, with great gusto.

"I thought I'd tease him, and I asked, 'Harry, don't you feel just a bit strange, eating something that's still alive?'

"He peered at me through his glasses and wanted to know since when were oysters alive.

"Well, I explained to him that if oysters *aren't* alive, you simply don't eat them, they're inedible and dangerous. With all he knew about oysters, he didn't know that, and he refused to believe it. So finally I called over the headwaiter and asked *him.* 'Oh, no sir,' said he. 'We only serve live oysters—we could never take the risk of serving dead ones.'

"Harry pushed away his oysters, and then he glared at me. 'I want to thank you, Leland,' he said, 'for destroying my one remaining passion.' And he never, to my knowledge, ate oysters again . . ."

In one of his early screenplay assignments, *Naked City*, Kurnitz and Mark Hellinger, the producer, agreed that Kurnitz should play a bit part, *à la* Hitchcock. He was assigned the role of a candy-store owner on the Lower East Side. "Harry said that was a role in which he could feel comfortable, making his dramatic debut," says George Axelrod. "In the brief scene, the director explained to Harry that as part of his characterization, he should take a couple of bites out of his own candy stock. They wanted him to munch on some halvah, which is a rich almond-paste candy.

" 'I am sorry,' said Harry, 'but I will only eat halvah providing I get stunt-man's pay.' "

In the years when she was beginning her career as an actress, Pat Englund, Ken's daughter, was a steady companion of Harry Kurnitz, both in Hollywood and in New York. "One night we went past the theatre where they were having a big Hollywood-type premiere, and I told Harry I'd love to go, so he went in, spoke to a middle-aged man in the lobby, and we were immediately ushered right into the V.I.P. section inside. I was enormously impressed," she recalls, "and I asked him, 'Harry, who *was* that man?'

" 'Oh,' said Harry, 'that's Harry Cohn's brother Jack. He's sometimes known as Harry Cohn Without Charm.'

"We went to a preview of a musical film, a biography of Chopin, and while the picture was on, Harry leaned over and whispered, 'You know, they sent this script to Art Tatum [the celebrated blind pianist], but he felt it and turned it down.'

"On another evening I went with him to the Stork Club, and we were in the Cub Room when Elliott Roosevelt came in and joined us. It was very heady stuff for me—there we were, sitting with FDR's son, who'd just returned from a trip to Russia on behalf of some magazine, and he'd been received by Stalin, Timoshenko, all the Russian chiefs. He told us how they'd all been very warm toward him, and full of reminiscences about his late father. Elliott paused for a moment, and Harry inquired, 'But Elliott, didn't *my* name come up?'

"And then there was another time, just after I got the part of Ado Annie in *Oklahoma!* on Broadway. Of course I wasn't the original Ado Annie—I was just another one of a procession of ingénues who got their training by playing the part—but, believe me, at the time it was a big deal for me, a real breakthrough in my

133

career. I was absolutely busting with excitement, and Harry took me out to Sardi's for a celebration.

"We were sitting there," says Miss Englund, "and Oscar Hammerstein himself walked in. Harry waved at him, and he came over and sat down with us. Well, you can imagine how nervous I was by then. Harry introduced me to Mr. Hammerstein. 'You must meet Patsy,' he said. 'She's going to do the part of Ado Annie in your show, Oscar.'

"Mr. Hammerstein was very nice. He beamed and said, 'Fine, fine.' I mean, after all, *Oklahoma!* was playing all over the place, and he certainly couldn't keep track of all the girls who were playing Ado Annie, but he behaved as if I were the first who'd ever had the part. And then Harry said, 'Yes, but before she takes over the part, Oscar, Patsy says she's been looking over your book and lyrics, and she's got a few criticisms for you. Now, you don't mind a little honest criticism, do you, Oscar?'

"I couldn't stand it," says Miss Englund. "It was Harry's idea of a funny thing to say—but I actually burst into tears."

Later on, when Miss Englund married Barney Lefferts, a writer whose family origins are from north of Boston, Kurnitz came to dinner at the home of the newly married couple.

"Barney had a few drinks, and he began to show it," Miss Englund recalls. "Harry sat there and listened to Barney and watched him, and then he said, 'I suppose this is what you mean by a New England Boiled Dinner?' "

Larry Adler, the virtuoso harmonica-player, who has for many years lived in London, remembers a time when he was visiting in Hollywood and was asked by his friend Kurnitz to accompany him to a Warner Brothers studio function.

The two men were seated in an audience which was treated to one of Jack Warner's customary speeches, peppered, as usual, with Warner's quips and ad-libs.

"Halfway through Warner's interminable monologue, Harry turned to me," said Adler, "and he whispered, 'I hope Jack finishes up soon—I'm beginning to run out of loyalty laughs.'

"A couple of nights later I remember going with Harry to Ciro's, on Sunset Strip, where Duke Ellington and his orchestra were opening. As we entered the night club, we were hit square in the face with one of Duke's piercing climactic chords—a blast of music played by fourteen men—which absolutely shattered our ears. 'It's their new transcription of *Sheep May Safely Graze,*' Harry cried.

"Harry could drink a lot, but he never really got drunk at all," said Adler. "I gave a party for him one night in London, and as the evening progressed, Harry went on drinking. But instead of passing out, he merely stretched out—right on the living-room floor, directly in front of the door. I'd hired a very proper butler for the party, and he came out of the kitchen carrying a tray of drinks; he looked down and found his access completely blocked by Kurnitz on the floor. The butler looked down at Harry, and Harry looked up at the butler. He blinked and asked, 'Can't you leap?'"

During the mid-Forties, when the nightmarish "blacklist" period descended over the motion-picture industry, Kurnitz became one of the victims.

"Harry was about as much of a Communist as any of the liberals were, which was not much of a Communist at all," remarks a friend. "He certainly wasn't political—in fact, he was a hell of a snob—but his instincts were all decent, he had loads of friends who were liberal, and he kept them, and he didn't give a damn what your politics were as long as you had talent. But back in those rotten days, which were hysterical with fear, the people who drew up the blacklists never gave a damn for truth. They smeared everyone with their same lousy innuendoes—and that's what happened to Kurnitz."

"Harry called me up one day and told me he was leaving Hollywood," remembers Ken Englund. "Said he was going to travel and become a full-time gypsy, a nomad. He'd go wherever the assignments took him. He'd put together a marvelous collection of books and modern paintings. 'What are you going to do with all that stuff?' I asked him.

"'I got rid of everything,' said Harry. 'It's the only way to live—completely unfettered.'

"'You *sold* all those books?' I said, and it hurt me, because I knew how many years he'd spent collecting them. 'I could never do that,' I told him. 'I love my books too much.'

"'Sell 'em,' Harry told me sharply. 'And if you want a book—go to the public library.'"

Kurnitz went into a global orbit, but it was to be always a first-cabin nomadic life. The following years took him to London and to posh English country houses, to the sixteenth *arrondissement* in Paris, for winter weeks in Klosters, and yachting trips on the Mediterranean.

When the Paris edition of an American drugstore opened on the Champs-Elysées, Harry visited it and reported that it could not compare with Schwab's Drugstore on Sunset Boulevard. "Here," he wrote, "they try to give you lunch Hollywood style—a hot dog and vintage wine."

Allan Rivkin and Laura Kerr report that in London Kurnitz was invited to a Thanksgiving dinner which producer Sam Spiegel was giving at his Grosvenor House apartment. When Kurnitz looked around the table, he noticed that all the other guests, like himself, were political exiles from Hollywood. He seized his glass and stood for a toast. "To Sam Spiegel," he said, "a very brave man. Little does he know that there's a thousand dollars on each of your heads."

"Harry was very fond of telling us the story of how he'd gone to see the movie *Genevieve*," said George Axelrod. "Harry had fallen madly in love—as who hadn't?—with its leading lady, the late Kay Kendall. Harry claimed that he'd come into the lobby of the Connaught Hotel and spied Miss Kendall sitting at a table, having tea. Without hesitation, he came over and said, 'Miss Kendall, I am madly in love with you.' Harry said, 'She looked up at me, holding her teacup, and she said, "Move on, my good man, or I shall call the manager—unless, of course, you *are* the manager." '

"Harry had this wonderful reverence for titled people," said Axelrod. "I guess it went all the way back to his early days when he was really poor, back in Philadelphia. When he came to Europe and met them, they were more important to him than anyone else. I was once talking to him here, and he told me he was going to have a golf date with the Duke of Windsor. I said, 'Harry, from all I can gather, the Duke is a nice guy, but he certainly isn't the world's most scintillating conversationalist. Why do you insist on playing golf with *him*?' Harry looked reprovingly at me. 'He was once the *King!*' he snapped.

"One of Harry's absolute passions was gypsy fiddlers," adds Axelrod. "He played the violin himself—not well, but adequately. He always said that after enough champagne he was capable of two good choruses of 'Fascination.' He and I and a girl went to some gypsy restaurant in Paris, and there was champagne, and Harry was weeping—he could get very emotional around gypsy fiddlers— and then a young gypsy flamenco dancer appeared and began that usual foot-stamping gypsy flamenco dance.

"The girl we were with leaned over to Kurnitz, and she asked, 'Do you think she's a real gypsy, Harry?'

" 'Certainly not,' said Harry. 'Orthodox gypsies are not allowed to shave under their arms.' "

There came a time when, in a most unlikely collaboration,

Kurnitz was teamed with Nobel Prize winner William Faulkner to write a screenplay for a monumental (and disastrous) film which was made by Howard Hawks in Egypt and was called *The Land of the Pharaohs*. During the period of Kurnitz's labors on this epic, the Warner studio decided to change the title. As is customary, the front office offered $100 to any interested party who could come up with a likely substitute. Said Kurnitz, "I'll give you $100 if you change the title to *Kurnitz*."

His good friend John Huston, in company with Truman Capote and Humphrey Bogart, produced a suspense film called *Beat the Devil*. The many creative people involved in the production enjoyed themselves hugely during the filming, but when the finished picture was released, it proved nearly incomprehensible. Said Kurnitz, "No matter where you come in during the running, you seem to have missed at least half the picture."

And in a discussion about actress Natalie Wood, Kurnitz remarked, "She is built like a brick dollhouse."

He once had a transitory *affaire d'amour* with a young lady in the South of France. Later, one of his friends inquired as to her general capabilities. Kurnitz thought about it for a moment, and then he remarked, "I have been in Volkswagens smaller than she was."

"He was a sweet man," says Ken Englund, "and underneath that face was the soul of a pixie. I remember a long time ago we threw Harry a surprise birthday party. When it came time to bring out the cake with all the candles, all the women stood around Harry and they said, 'Now, blow out the candles, Harry—make a wish, make a wish!'

"Harry blew out all the candles and then he said, 'Okay, I made a wish.'

"My wife said, 'What did you wish?'

"And Harry looked up at her and said, 'I wish it was my birthday.'"

A short time before he died, Kurnitz came back to Hollywood for a brief visit. He joined Mr. and Mrs. George Axelrod for the annual Screen Writers Guild awards dinner. As they drove downtown to the scene of the banquet, Kurnitz mused, "And now, tonight, we go to meet all the brightest creative minds in Hollywood—and their wives, the girls who looked so good to them twenty years ago on Pitkin Avenue."

137

The Wit and Wisdom of Hollywood

PUSH BUTTON MARKED "DIALOGUE"
by Harry Kurnitz

The Thing happened after the fourth race at Hollywood Park, on July 12, 1964. Eyewitness accounts are scarce nowadays and there is obvious hysteria in some of them, but all agree that it happened either just after the fourth race or just before the fifth.

The tote board had been cleared of the figures compiled on the fourth race and the devotees waited complacently for the great mechanical brain to post the new morning line, opening bids, starting pools. Instead, to the amazement of the crowd, the board flashed:

FADE IN: LONG SHOT. NEW YORK SKYLINE. EXT. DAY. (STOCK)

There were scattered cries of protest and disbelief and thousands of people rushed across the paddocks for a closer look, but by that time the board was already flashing:

CLOSE SHOT. REVOLVING DOOR. INT. DAY. A beautiful clean-limbed girl enters.

The first mechanical screenplay was being written. While a deep hush fell over the grandstand and clubhouse, the apparatus clicked on steadily and at 11:27 P.M. the board flashed the final "fade-out" on what all agreed was a very satisfactory career-girl comedy, *She Married Her Obstetrician:* a typical, punchy box-office vehicle for Fred MacMurray and Rosalind Russell, with strong comedy parts for a number of character people. At 11:28 the loudspeaker announced Professor Waldemar Trigg, of M.I.T., who had adapted the giant electrical brain of the tote board for this purpose. Professor Trigg spoke briefly and to the point. Scripto, as his machine was called, stood ready to deliver screenplays, original stories and additional dialogue to all the producers of Hollywood. Private demonstrations would commence at 9:00 A.M., in the Hollywood-Knickerbocker Hotel.

The next morning a haggard, nervous group of producers and writers, especially the latter, gathered in the ballroom of the Hollywood-Knickerbocker Hotel. Professor Trigg stood before a large electric panel, the size of a standard movie screen, and on a couch, in a lifelike pose, lay Scripto, the mechanical writer. It was about eight feet tall, or long, with three slender stalks of aluminum for legs. On each metal foot was a two-tone calfskin moccasin, and the lower part of each leg wore Argyle hose. Above the stalks was a heavy cylindrical copper "torso" from which protruded a thick cable leading to the control "head." The cable was draped in a Charvet tie.

As producers suggested various characters and story needs,

Professor Trigg pressed appropriate buttons and the electric panel instantly supplied the situation, dialogue (light or dramatic, as indicated), switch, twist, gimmick and tag. All agreed that it was a very impressive demonstration, and for a finish Professor Trigg pressed a button marked "Rewrite" and fed into the machine the script of an old, shelved Republic melodrama, which emerged as a Western, complete with cowboy songs and a chase.

Scripto made heavy inroads right from the start and hundreds of screenwriters were dismissed from their jobs. Some studios, fearful of the new invention, clung to a part of their writing staffs, but that year the Academy Award for the best-written screenplay went to Westinghouse Electric; the best original story was by the Roebling Bridge Company of Trenton, N.J., and the best original screenplay by Youngstown Sheet and Tube, with additional dialogue by The Worthington Pump Company. The next day the panic was on.

In the year that followed, the screenwriter was completely eliminated from the Hollywood studios, except for a few who were kept on as oilers and mechanics. Production and profits in the studios touched all-time peaks and writer-producer relations were never as happy or as congenial. . . .

In 1972 Stark Raving, the last screenwriter left in Hollywood, committed suicide by jumping into the dialogue mixer at Universal-International. Only two inches of tortoise shell from Raving's spectacles were recovered from the giant hopper, and the next day, when this relic was interred at Forest Lawn, only six people showed up. A simple marker, in the form of a marble pencil poised over a pad of limestone, was soon obliterated and that was the last trace of any writer.

In 1973 every single picture produced in Hollywood was written by the machines, and institutional industry advertising featured the slogan "Untouched by Human Hands." Ten engineering concerns, licensed by Professor Trigg, were now in the field, and the original design by Scripto was much improved. There were dozens of brightly colored plastic knobs and dials which a producer could twirl to his heart's content without affecting the quality of the output, and there was a *de luxe* model, at slightly higher cost, which could write forewords and dedications. There was also a special model, called "Gaggo," for comedy routines and other such specialized functions, and another called "Slicko," exclusively for polishing.

It is interesting to note that no machine was ever invented which could duplicate the functions of the producers and directors.

November 1973 became a historic date in the new era. That was the day when Oliver Stritch, an MGM producer, became dissatisfied with the screenplay of *Kiss That Goal,* a college picture being written by one of the machines, and added a second machine to the assignment in the first mechanical collaboration. The dual effort was a huge success and Stritch was hailed as a genius, praise which he modestly disclaimed, giving all the credit to his executive producer. The script produced by the two machines had punch, wit, action, everything, and the picture which resulted from it grossed huge sums.

To be sure, neither machine functioned very well for a time, and Professor Trigg, in an emergency overhaul, determined that they were dissatisfied with the joint-screenplay credit. He warned the producing companies against mechanical collaborations, but his warnings were ignored, and joint efforts of two, three and as many as five machines were produced in that year. Designation of credit was invariably followed by minor work stoppage, slowdowns and curious mechanical breakdowns. Again over Professor Trigg's vehement protests, the studios held credit arbitrations in certain disputes, and for a time this seemed to ease the situation.

In the spring of the following year, however, one of the machines at Twentieth Century-Fox, to the horror of the studio staff, suddenly flashed its signature to a petition urging better treatment of racial minorities, and when the offending device was hastily removed, four other machines got up another petition of protest. A Congressional inquiry revealed no signs of sabotage, or "jamming" by any foreign power, but one machine, despite Professor Trigg's frantic manipulation of its controls, denied the right of the committee to inquire into its private (or short-wave) beliefs. Professor Trigg, in a desperate effort to stem the tide of outraged editorial opinion, demolished the machine in a public ceremony at the base of the Washington Monument.

One week later a tall, stoop-shouldered man named Oliver Wadsworth Venable got off the Super-Space Limited at Burbank and asked the way to the Paramount Studio. An alert reporter interviewed Venable, and the studio shamefacedly admitted that it had hired a writer. Only, it assured the public, as an experiment. Later that day Lancelot Drimmel, the New York playwright, was located at another studio adapting one of his own works for the screen. Venable and Drimmel inevitably met at a dinner party in their first week in Hollywood, and over the coffee one of them murmured, "Say, why wouldn't it be a good idea for us to form a Guild? . . ."

(*from* THE SCREEN WRITER)

SCRIBES AND PHARISEES

AND THE LATE MR. HERMAN J. MANKIEWICZ

Of all the literates who populated Hollywood, one would be hard put to find a wit who left behind him a broader trail of mayhem, deflationary barbs—and laughter—than the late Herman J. Mankiewicz.

"In New York one night," said the always nostalgic Herman, "MacArthur and I were sitting in a stage box at the opening of an Earl Carroll *Vanities*. We had been drinking—drink for drink, nobody loafing. The chorus girls suddenly appeared on the stage dressed as musketeers, nude to the crotch, and carrying weapons. They went into an ooh-la-la fencing dance, crossing swords and doing high kicks. Carried away by the glamour and gallantry of this spectacle, MacArthur leaned out of our box and applauded like an idiot. He kept applauding till he fell out of the box and landed on the stage, where he bowed several times, with ass to the audience, and tottered into the wings. If such a thing had happened to me, all you would have heard the next day was, 'Manky was drunk as a beast last night and fell out of a theatre box—and he is ruining his life.' Well, about MacArthur they said, 'Did you hear about Charlie playing D'Artagnan last night?' "

(from CHARLIE, *by Ben Hecht, Harper and Row, 1957)*

Nunnally Johnson's friendship with Mankiewicz goes back to the days of the Twenties, when both men were journalists in New York. Mankiewicz, the son of an erudite professor, was already making a name for himself as drama critic for *The New York Times* and as a collaborator with George S. Kaufman on a comedy, *The Wild Man of Borneo*. Soon he was to desert Manhattan and his friends at the Algonquin Round Table for the more lucrative siren song of Paramount Pictures.

"Mank was the greatest wit who's never been put down on paper," says Johnson. "Amazing mind, drunk or sober. I remember once I went into Jack & Charlie's. I was with an editor, and there was Mank—at the bar, naturally. I introduced him to the editor, and without a second's hesitation Mank asked him, 'Are you interested in making money?'

"Before the guy could even answer, Mank started talking. Seems he'd just come from spending a couple of nights up at Ben Hecht's house in Nyack. Had insomnia. Couldn't sleep a wink—so finally, on the second night, Ben tried to help out Mank by giving him some sort of a sleeping pill from the local doctor.

141

" 'Now—do you know anything about the trucking industry?' asked Mank, sailing right along. 'Well, their biggest problem is that of keeping their drivers awake while they're out on the highways on night hauls. . . .' I really didn't know what the hell he was getting at, but on he went. 'They need some stuff that will be guaranteed to do that job for them, right? Such an elixir would be worth millions of dollars to them. Now—let's the three of us put some money in this,' said Mank. 'I will get that Nyack doctor's prescription, and we'll go into business with it—because after 4:00 A.M., after taking it, I was not just awake, I was *aggressively* awake! Boys, I tell you, we can make millions!' "

Mankiewicz called up his friend George S. Kaufman a day or so after the successful opening of Marc Connelly's *The Green Pastures*.

"George," he said, "if anyone had come to you a couple of weeks ago and told you Marc Connelly's written a play all by himself, and then they said that this play was all about black people—and do you know where they all are when the play starts? They're up in heaven, having themselves a *fish-fry*. And not only that, George, if they told you that even though he's never done it before, Marc was going to direct the play himself—I wonder, would you have seen any reason why you and I should worry?"

"That," commented Johnson, "was the spirit of the old Algonquin Round Table right there."

A few years later George S. Kaufman and Moss Hart wrote a play called *Merrily We Roll Along*. Unlike their previous collaboration, this Kaufman-Hart work was a serious drama that dealt, in reverse chronology, with the disintegration of a man because of too much success. Mankiewicz went to New York for the opening of his friends' play. The play was a flop—one of the very few flops in the history of the Kaufman-Hart partnership.

Upon his return to Hollywood, Mank was pressed by friends for a description of the play. "It's a problem play," he explained. "It's about this playwright who writes a play, and it's a big success, and then he writes another play, and *that* one is a big success, all his plays are big successes, and all the actresses in them are in love with him, all these beautiful women are in love with him, and he has a yacht, and a beautiful home in the country and a penthouse in town, and a beautiful wife and two beautiful children, and he makes a million dollars. Now," said Mank, "the problem posed by George and Moss is simply this: How did the poor son-of-a-bitch ever get himself into this situation?"

* * *

Early on, Mankiewicz developed a deep thirst. "There was a comedian named Ted Healy," recalls Nunnally. "He was an Irishman who'd been playing in Shubert shows and vaudeville for twenty-five or thirty years. Very funny man. I remember Healy said that when he died he wanted the undertaker to lay him out in the coffin so when people came in, he would be there on his back, with a finger at his lips, indicating 'Shhh.'

"Anyway, he drank with Mankiewicz when Mank was at Paramount, in the early days. They'd go across the street to Lucey's and knock it off. But Mank said to me, 'I never felt Healy and I were really in sync, though we got along very well. Then, one afternoon, when we were having a few, Healy looked at me for a minute, completely illuminated. He said, "I've got it." I said, "What?" Healy said, "I cannot be happy with a fellow until I've got him pegged. Now I've got you pegged." I said, "Well, what is it?" Healy says, "You're an Irish bum." ' "

"Perfect description of Mank," says Johnson. "He was Jewish but he was an Irish bum.

"Groucho Marx told me that 'When we went to Paramount and made those first pictures, Mank was producer. For some reason, we got to talking about our favorite actresses, or women. Mank had conceived a tremendous liking for Barbara Stanwyck, who had just come out, young, charming, beautiful, very easy to talk to, witty. Mank said, "Well, Barbara Stanwyck is my favorite. My God. I could just sit and dream of being married to her, having a little cottage out in the hills, vines around the door. I'd come home from the office, tired, weary, and I'd be met by Barbara, walking through the door, holding an apple pie that she had cooked herself. And wearing no drawers." ' "

"I never knew what bicarbonate of soda was," Mankiewicz said of that period at Paramount, "until I wrote a Marx Brothers picture."

Allan Rivkin and Laura Kerr report that during story conferences none of the Marxes would allow Herman to speak. They continually kept interrupting him with noisy questions that dealt with their characterizations. On this score, it was Groucho who was the most persistent, demanding to know who he would play in the film.

Finally Mankiewicz had had enough. "Groucho," he said, "I have a new character for you. You're going to be a middle-aged Jew with bushy eyebrows, a painted-on mustache—and you smoke a cigar!"

"He was a wonderful, erudite guy," says Sam Jaffe, who was studio manager at Paramount in those days. "But an uncontrollable gambler. He came into my office one Friday afternoon. I'd never met him, but he introduced himself to me and he showed me a studio check for $1,000. He wanted me to cash it for him and give him $900 because he was going out to the track—and I should keep the other $100 as payment for doing him a favor.

"Well, I went ahead and cashed his check, and then he went out to the track. Naturally, he lost all the money. I came in to the studio on Monday and I went over to his office and I said, 'Here's your hundred bucks. I'm giving it back to you now, because I know you'll be going all over town telling people what a bastard I was to keep the hundred—and I want that stopped before it starts.'

"Mank was absolutely amazed that I'd do such a thing—and he and his wife Sara and my wife Mildred and I became very good friends. For many years they'd come to our house. I always felt that Herman enriched my life. His conversation was brilliant, his mind was unbelievable—and then, at the same time, so self-destructive and uncontrolled. He never quit gambling. I remember, toward the end of a week he was short, he owed everybody, and he took one of Sara's rings and pawned it. Monday or Tuesday, Sara found out what he had done. 'But why didn't you tell me about it?' she pleaded. 'Oh, I didn't want to spoil your week-end,' said Herman. . . . She was always known as 'Poor Sara,' " said Jaffe.

"And another time, I remember, when I became an agent and was going through the halls of a building, right near Herman's office. The door opened, an old man in black appeared, and there was Herman, ushering him out. After the old man left, Herman said, 'He's a rabbi, from a very poor congregation, and they needed money badly, and he came to see me.' I knew that Herman was practically broke, he owed money all over town. 'I gave him a check for a thousand,' said Herman, 'they really needed the donation.'

"But the things he said were so vivid," says Jaffe. "One night I asked Herman about a certain scriptwriter, and he said, 'That man is so bad, he shouldn't be left alone in a room with a typewriter!' And there was a director named Lothar Mendes, who could describe magnificent sequences which somehow never came out on the screen as well as he talked them. Now, Frank Tuttle was a director who was a solid, commerical film maker, always brought in his pictures right on schedule, no trouble, but very little imagination in their creation. Mank once said, 'You know, Mendes talks like Lubitsch—and directs like Tuttle.'

"One day I asked him about a certain picture. 'Do you have any idea how bad that picture is?' he said. 'I'll tell you. Stay away from the neighborhood where it's playing—don't even go near that street!

It might rain—you could get caught in the downpour, and to keep dry, you'd have to go inside the theatre!' "

During the stormy period of the Depression, despite obdurate resistance from the producers, Hollywood screenwriters began to organize their own craft union, which was to be the Screen Writers Guild.

At one of the early organizational meetings, impassioned rhetoric echoed through the room as writers pointed out many of the obvious injustices and harsh practices that were rife in the industry. There was repeated mention of the plight of the lowest man on the financial totem pole, the so-called "$75-a-week writer."

But not all the writers who attended were in agreement. One of the more successful film writers of the time stood up and began to rebut. "All this talk about $75-a-week writers," he declaimed. "Who are they?" He turned to Herman Mankiewicz, who was seated next to him. "Tell me—do *you* know any $75-a-week writers?"

"I know lots of them," said Mankiewicz instantly, "but they're all making $1,500 a week."

"Sure, Mank was witty," says Nunnally Johnson, "but his wit took a much more elaborate form than wisecracks. He could improvise in a way that just held you spellbound. It is really shameful of me even to try to quote some of the things that he said. Mank would claim that such-and-such a producer had sent for him once. The producer said, 'Now look, we've got an awfully good beginning for this story. This is it. We open in an office building. Wall Street. Beautiful office. Clearly an old banking firm. This man goes out at five o'clock, gets in his chauffeured car waiting for him, and drives up to an apartment on Park Avenue. He goes into this apartment on Park Avenue, dismisses the limousine. He comes back down, white tie and tails, gets in another limousine. They go way up to the Bronx to a dark street full of black warehouses. He goes and pushes a button, doors open, he goes in, the doors close, and a Hindu bows deeply to him and says, "Master." And he leads him into an enormous chamber lighted by great flambeaux, draped with velvet. There ten or fifteen Nubians bow to him, and he says, "Is the sacrifice ready?" They say, "Yes, Sahib." He goes into a retiring chamber, where he changes into royal raiment of an Arabian character. He's anointed with oil, ointments and so on, and he moves on further into this great hall, like a temple. It is filled with all these Oriental characters, and he is bowed down to like a god, and he goes up in a pulpit. He looks down and he says, "Bring the sacrifice." They go out and they bring back a Circassian slave, blonde, wearing lace. He says, "Kneel," and she kneels.'

" 'And then the fellow stopped,' Mank said.

"Mank said to the producer, 'What else?'

" 'He said, 'Now look. All I want from you is this. What the hell is this son-of-a-bitch up to?" ' "

In the years when Mankiewicz worked at Metro and produced many screenplays, the Metro higher-ups decided to endow a program of training for what were to be known as "junior writers"—i.e., talented young men and women who had as yet not made their mark in the business, but who the studio felt could be nurtured and trained for future successful scripting. It was decided that the junior-writer program needed professional supervision, and to watch over the fledglings, one of the Metro executives selected a writer whom Mankiewicz held in particularly low esteem. "The guy with the biggest clap is running the clinic," said Mankiewicz.

As his good friend Ben Hecht put it, "Herman's wit lashed the new Eldorado, his derisive salvos at Hollywood geniuses kept them writhing and blushing and laughing. A greater phenomenon than Herman's wit was the fact that his victims employed him, at large sums, to write movies he despised for bosses he ridiculed."

He once defined for Hecht the peculiar morality of the motion picture. "I want to point out to you," he said, "that in a novel a hero can lay ten girls and marry a virgin for a finish. In a movie, this is not allowed. The hero, as well as the heroine, has to be a virgin. The villain can lay anybody he wants, have as much fun as he wants cheating and stealing, getting rich and whipping the servants. But you have to shoot him in the end. When he falls with a bullet in his forehead, it is advisable that he clutch at the Gobelin tapestry on the library wall and bring it down over his head like a symbolic shroud. Also, covered by such a tapestry, the actor does not have to hold his breath while he is being photographed as a dead man."

His wit was a gallant one. At a formal dinner at the home of producer Arthur Hornblow, Jr., Mankiewicz had, as on many occasions, had too much to drink before dinner. During the course of the rich meal, his stomach rebelled and he abruptly threw up. He smiled weakly at the host and said apologetically, "Don't worry, Arthur—the white wine came up with the fish."

And then there was *Citizen Kane,* the classic film which Mankiewicz wrote.

About Orson Welles, who directed, produced and acted in the film, Mank remarked, "There, but for the grace of God, goes God."

"I remember Herman telling me about Welles," says Nunnally.

"Orson looked over the credits for the picture. 'Orson Welles, in *Citizen Kane*. Produced by Orson Welles. Directed by Orson Welles. Screenplay by Herman J. Mankiewicz and Orson Welles.' . . . And there was something in that list that seemed wrong to Orson. That other name stuck up there. It didn't matter that Herman had written the script and brought it to Welles—Welles couldn't stand the other name. He actually offered Herman $10,000 if he'd take his name off the picture. And it was tough for Herman, because he always needed dough so badly. Anyway, he anguished over it for a while, and he went to his friend Ben Hecht and asked Ben what the hell to do about Welles' offer. Well, Ben was a realist, as always, and he said, 'Herman, take his money and screw him.' Ben knew what he was doing—because later on the Guild stepped in and upheld the screen credit anyway."

But following the release of the picture, anyone connected with its production was, to say the least, on William Randolph Hearst's *persona magna non grata* list.

"One afternoon, after a lot of cocktails at Romanoff's, Herman got into his car and started up Coldwater Canyon," recalls Sam Jaffe. "Halfway up, he lost control of the car, it jumped the curb, and he ran into a tree, and also accidentally knocked down Mrs. Leonore Gershwin, Ira's wife, who was out on her lawn.

"Hearst was nearby, at Marion Davies' house. He heard the crash below and he sent his butler to find out what had happened. The butler returned to report that a Mr. Mankiewicz had been involved in an auto accident.

"Well, that was all Hearst needed to know. The Hearst newspapers played the story up for all it was worth, and more—big headlines, editorials and all that stuff—and they kept up such a journalistic hue-and-cry that eventually the District Attorney had to bring Herman to trial on various charges, involving drunken driving, reckless driving, and all that stuff.

"The case came to trial and Herman had to hire Jerry Giesler to defend him. The trial dragged on, and finally it ended with a hung jury, so they had a second trial and Giesler made one of his great courtroom speeches—he cited Herman's war record and his good citizenship, and finally he got Herman acquitted. It was a really rough experience to have to go through.

"Would you believe it, a couple of weeks after the second trial, Herman was back at Romanoff's having lunch. He had quite a few, and then he got up and started out. As he got to the door, he pulled the headwaiter to one side and said, 'Listen, would you please call

147

up Mrs. Ira Gershwin and tell her I am leaving this place now, and I'm headed up Coldwater Canyon—and she should look out.' "

BEN HECHT

Nobody has taken the trouble to get the facts straight about the mysterious suppression of Orson Welles's movie, *Citizen Kane.* Nobody ever goes to the trouble of getting anything straight about Hollywood. The ways of that town are, to the press, as dark as the practices of Tibet.

Most of the commentators hired by the nation's editors to cover the studios are a little on the inadequate side. I have seen them for years wandering around the cuckoo-clock vale of art, lollypops in hand and making goo-goo eyes at the famous party-throwing stars. There are a few notable exceptions, but on the whole journalism has never sired so coy a lot of Tom Thumbs.

Concerning the mysterious suppression of the Welles picture there has been infinitely less written than on the heady topic of whose hand Franchot Tone is holding this week. There is, to be fair, a certain hazard for news gatherers in Hollywood. Nobody, not even people being trepanned and bastinadoed by the industry, will ever say anything derogatory to the movie business. Actors, writers, directors and producers all share in this chin-up conspiracy to keep the wonderfully fair name of Hollywood free of smirch and liver crumbs.

Orson, at present hatching out a theatrical production on Broadway, is apparently bitten by this same gentleman-all bug or, as it is known in gangster land, the "nix crackin'." For beyond threatening to sue his good friend and loyal chief, George C. Schaeffer, head of RKO, for failure to release *Citizen Kane,* Orson has kept the silence of an English colonel in the Sudan.

The one fact known about this fancy contretemps is that W. R. Hearst persuaded RKO to withdraw the movie because it contained a supposedly unflattering biographical study of him. How Mr. Hearst accomplished this has been ignored, Chinese fashion, by the commentators.

I can assure you it was not done by Mr. Hearst hollering at Mr. Schaeffer, under whose aegis the movie was made. Nor was it done by Mr. Hearst threatening Mr. Schaeffer with lawsuits plus his journalistic wrath.

Mr. Schaeffer, who hired Orson to do the movie, knew what was in it from the beginning and knew as far as a battery of cold and expert legal talent could assure him that there was nothing libelous in it against Mr. Hearst or anyone else.

Mr. Schaeffer stood up very calmly against all of Mr. Hearst's Fie Fo Fums. For this Schaeffer of RKO is as tough a gentleman to frighten as you will find under any initialed enterprise including that of the RAF.

Mr. Hearst's next move was to seek out a softer and sappier target. This he found in the person of Louis B. Mayer. Mr. Mayer is the grand Poo Bah of Hollywood. He is producing head of Metro-Goldwyn-Mayer and is not only the highest-salaried genius on earth but the oracle to which Hollywood bends its ever deferential ear. It is an ear, by the way, that bends on a well-oiled hinge where Mr. Mayer is concerned.

Mr. Hearst told Mr. Mayer that if the picture was released he, Mr. H., had a medium for offering the country biographical studies of great men every bit as powerful as the screen. This is almost a verbatim quote. It reflects credit on Mr. Hearst not only as a sturdy warrior in behalf of his fancied rights but as a master tactician. For Mr. Mayer became as active as a pool of beavers. Mr. Mayer has nothing to do with the production of *Citizen Kane* and has almost as little to do with the productions put out under his alleged guidance, but he is a Noble Doer of Right and a Great Shepherd. He appealed to the board of directors and to the bankers who are behind the financing of RKO and similar movie-making organizations. He told them that Mr. Hearst, by attacking something called Hollywood, would alienate the public from the movies and everybody would lose money. This is not what Mr. Hearst said. What Mr. Hearst said with Talleyrand cunning was that he would expose Hollywood's "great men" just as he was being exposed, allegedly, in *Citizen Kane* —and do it in his newspapers.

Mr. Mayer, Knight of the Cinema World, won the day for Mr. Hearst. W.R. won't write anything wrong about Mr. Mayer now, or about any of the other sachems of Hollywood. All this must come as a surprise to the many admirers of Mr. Mayer and of his co-moguls. For who would have thought these rajahs had anything to conceal or were afraid of a little literature in the Hearst press? Hollywood's great men taking to a bomb shelter at the sight of Mr. Hearst pointing a cap pistol at them is a baffling spectacle.

Mr. Schaeffer has, however, not joined this rush for immunity. He is still battling for the release of the film he fathered.

To add a last note to the present record of *Citizen Kane*, this movie was not written by Orson Welles. It is the work of Herman J.

Mankiewicz, one of the wittiest of the scenario writers. Herman let me read the script before it was shot.

"Do you think," he asked me, "that Willie Hearst will figure it's about him? I didn't write it about him but about some of our other mutual friends—a sort of compendium."

I told Herman that it had no more to do with W.R. than with Prester John. It didn't occur to me at the time that we were all sitting in a glass house, run by Louis B. Mayer.

(from PM, 1941)

But perhaps the supreme *beau geste* of all Hollywood's history is the story of Herman Mankiewicz's encounter with the tiger, Harry Cohn. Bob Thomas has related it in his biography of Cohn, but it bears repeating in any discussion of the paradoxical wit that was Herman Mankiewicz's.

Having insulted and argued his way out of jobs at practically every studio in town, Mankiewicz was in serious financial trouble. His loyal friends banded together to find him some work. Among them was Leland Hayward, who recalled how he and Phil Berg, another agent, managed to persuade Harry Cohn that to hire Mankiewicz would be a great coup for Columbia Pictures. "We appealed to Cohn's sense of getting a bargain—that he could get Mank, who got at least two grand a week at Metro, to come into Columbia for half that, and Cohn couldn't resist," said Hayward.

"Before we let Herman go over to Columbia, however, we called him in and we read him the riot act. We told him he was to keep his nose absolutely clean, no fooling around—stay strictly at his typewriter, and, above all, he was to stay out of that Columbia executive dining room. It was Cohn's private lunchtime torture chamber, where he sat at the head of a long table and abused everybody who worked for him, and you had to take it or get out. 'If you go in there, Mank, you're *through*,' we said, and he promised to be a good boy.

"Well, Mank was as good as his word, and he reported to his office every morning and wrote, and then at lunch he'd go off the lot, and come back and work all afternoon and go home—which was fine. That went on for a few weeks, and we figured everything was okay.

"And then, finally, he couldn't stand it any longer. I guess he was just too gregarious a guy—there was laughter coming out of the dining room every day, and he wasn't a party to any of it. Well, whatever it was, he came out of his office one lunchtime and he went into the executive dining room and sat down at the end of the table. That was it."

According to witnesses, Cohn spied Mankiewicz at the end of the dining-room table, quietly eating his lunch, and began to bait his new employee. Crudity followed crudity, as Cohn tossed barbed insults at Mankiewicz.

But Mankiewicz valiantly repressed himself. He said nothing, but kept on eating. Almost Christlike in his silence, he endured Cohn's stream of abuse.

Finally Cohn tired of the game and changed the subject. Someone mentioned a new film. Cohn had seen it the night before, and it was, in his opinion, rotten.

Another Columbia executive tried to argue the point, but Cohn would not hear him out. "The picture stank," he said. "And I know." He had, it seemed, an infallible test of a film's success or failure, and it was his own behind. "If it itches," Cohn proclaimed, "the picture stinks. If it doesn't itch, then the picture's going to be a hit."

Silence greeted this ukase, and then Mankiewicz could stand Cohn's arrogance not a moment longer. "I never knew before," he said, "that the entire American motion-picture audience is wired to Harry Cohn's ass."

The dining room burst into laughter.

"Mank got up, left the dining room, and without needing to be told what to do, he went down to his office, cleaned out his desk and departed from Columbia," said Hayward.

BEN HECHT

My friend Herman Mankiewicz died while I was writing this book—and I lost its best reader. But Manky offered me a greater loss. He never wrote a book of his own. What a book that would have been, if only a third of Herman's hilarious and fearsome meditations had gone into it.

I met Herman when he was young, but the doom of unproductivity was already on him. I knew that no one as witty and spontaneous as Herman would ever put himself on paper. A man whose genius is on tap like free lager beer seldom makes literature out of it. In Chicago, the brilliant George Wharton had remained the same sort of unbottled fellow.

I have sat in a room filled with writers of every kind and there was only one to whom we listened—the "non-writer" Mr. Mankiewicz. Beside Manky, the famous people among whom he buzzed all his life like a hornet or gadfly seemed pale-minded.

What did Herman Mankiewicz say? What were his observations, his jokes, his tirades? It is hard to remember. There were too many. They were on every topic. They snarled and lampooned and laid bare sham and roguery. They revealed that all the stupidities of successful people only increased their success, and all the wit of unsuccessful people added only to their failure. They examined the art output of New York and Hollywood, and hundreds of dinner parties quaked as they laughed at Manky's reports.

Manky had no wish to be a funny man. He would have shuddered more at the name "comedian" than he did at any of the others hurled at him by his enemies. (A man cannot hold his world up to caricature for thirty years without a yip out of some of his subject matter.)

Yet most of Manky's utterances, including his deepest philosophic ones, stirred laughter. Even his enemies laughed. He could puncture egos, draw blood from pretenses—and his victims, with souls abashed, still sat and laughed. The swiftness of his thought was by itself a sort of comedy. Never have I known a man with so quick an eye and ear—and tongue—for the strut of fools.

Manky died in his fifties, still writing movie scenarios. That he lasted as long as he did surprised me. To own a mind like Manky's and hamstring and throttle it for twenty-five years in the writing only of movie scenarios is to submit your soul to a nasty strain. Manky wrote good movies. One of them, *Citizen Kane,* won him an Oscar. But all of them put together won him an early death.

When I remember the dull and inane whom Herman enriched by his presence, and his numskull "betters" who tried feebly to echo his observations; when I remember his thrown-away genius, his modesty, his shrug at adversity; when I remember that unlike the lords of success around him he attacked only the strong with his wit and defended always the weak with his heart, I feel proud to have known a man of importance.

(*from* A CHILD OF THE CENTURY, *by Ben Hecht, Simon and Schuster,*
1954)

THE FRONT
OFFICE

"Never let that bastard back in here—unless we need him!"
(ATTRIBUTED L. B. MAYER, HARRY COHN, JACK L. WARNER,
ADOLPH ZUKOR, SAM GOLDWYN, HARRY M. WARNER AND
OTHERS)

*"Great parts make great pictures! Great pictures make
great parts! This girl [Kim Novak] has had five
hit pictures. If you wanna bring me your wife or your
aunt, we'll do the same for them."*
HARRY COHN

RICHARD BROOKS

I'll tell you about those men. They were monsters and pirates and bastards right down to the bottom of their feet, but they *loved* movies. They loved *making* movies, they loved *seeing* movies and they protected the people who worked for them. Some of the jerks running the business now don't even have faces. Not one of them has ever been on the back lot or rummaged through the vaults or walked through their stockpiles to see what they *bought!* I listen to them talk and I don't even know what they're saying. All they want to know is how much did it cost and what will it gross and how much can they dump it for. When we previewed *Key Largo* back in 1948, Jack Warner stood in the lobby talking to everybody who came out and said "Great picture!" and "How did you like it, little lady, it's a powerful picture, don't you think?" before they even got their preview cards filled out. These guys today should be running gas stations.

(*from* THE NEW YORK TIMES, *January 18, 1970*)

At the very bottom of the Depression, with hard times demoralizing the country, the movie business was in just as much trouble as the rest of American industry. Grosses were down, money was tight, and bankruptcy loomed—with no U.S. Cavalry in sight.

An emergency meeting of all the major studio heads was held at the Ambassador Hotel; it was from this conclave that the decision was taken to inflict a 50% cut in salary for all contract executives, performers and creative people still working in the studios. It was an all-day meeting, and it happened that on that very day, Southern California was shaken by a severe earthquake.

"I was young and brash," says Norman Krasna, "and some of us were sitting around joking about the situation. We knew what was going on down at the Ambassador, and it was dreadful, but what else could you do but laugh about it?

"Right after the earthquake, I went to the telephone and asked the operator to put me through to the bungalow where they were all meeting. Somebody there picked up the phone—I think it was Bill Koenig, the Warner studio manager—and he asked 'Who's this?'

" 'This is God calling,' I said, 'and that earthquake will give you an idea how I feel about this cut!' "

When, after many years of being production head of Paramount Pictures, B. P. Schulberg found himself tossed onto the industry's rubbish heap, he took a full-page ad in *Daily Variety* in 1949, to plead for someone to put his manifold talents to use as a producer again. There was little response from the Hollywood titans. (As Sam Goldwyn once said, "It's a dog-eat-dog business, and nobody's going to eat me.")

"I'd known B. P. Schulberg back in the days when he was the production head of Paramount and a real power in the movie business," said Mrs. Ernest Heyn. "When I married Ernie, we took a house down in Florida. Down there we were known as 'the people who read' because we had a bookcase full of our books.

"One afternoon B.P. came to visit us. By that time he'd been retired for years, couldn't get a job, was old and rather sick. I remember how he went over to our bookcase and stood in front of all the books.

"He studied the titles, and I heard him saying, 'I made *that* one, and I made *that* one, and I *bought* that one, and I got that one for the studio.' Actually, it was amazing how many of those books he'd been involved with in his years at Paramount. He went through the whole shelf, and when he turned around, poor dear old Ben, he was crying."

When B. P. Schulberg was having his troubles with the hierarchy of Zukor and Lasky at Paramount, someone chanced to ask Hecht what Mrs. Schulberg was up to. "Ah," said Hecht, "Ad is giving dinner parties and building bridges for Ben to retreat across."

Before Schulberg died, he gave his son Budd a final request. "Put my ashes in a box and tell the messenger to bring them to Louis B. Mayer's office with a farewell message from me. Then, when the messenger gets to Louis' desk, I want him to open the box and blow the ashes in the bastard's face."

(*from* THE MOGULS, *by Norman Zierold, Coward-McCann, 1969*)

* * *

"And then," said Zanuck [at a Screen Producers Guild testimonial dinner in 1953], "I decided to become a genius. Hollywood was full of 'yes men,' so I decided to become a 'no man.' I knocked everything, even Warner pictures. [At the time he was functioning as a writer of scripts for Rin Tin Tin, his output so vast that he wrote under three different names.] One day Jack Warner said he bet I thought I could run the studio better than he did. I told him I was sure I could. The following Monday morning he made me executive producer.

"Now that I had the job of genius, I was going to make the greatest picture of all time. I picked a man who is now one of the finest directors in the business, Mike Curtiz. I got top stars and I made *Noah's Ark*, one of the biggest flops ever turned out. Now Jack Warner and his brothers were certain I was a genius.

"And being a genius, I had to live that way. I took up polo, big-game hunting and skiing. I owe everything to three wonderful men. First, Jack Warner. Second, Joseph M. Schenck. Third, Spyros Skouras. It's great fun being a genius and I am going to continue playing the role."

(*from* THE FIFTY-YEAR DECLINE AND FALL OF HOLLYWOOD, *by Ezra Goodman, Simon and Schuster, 1961*)

George Axelrod was working on his *Seven Year Itch* at 20th Century-Fox with Billy Wilder, who was also preparing *The Spirit of St. Louis* at Warner Brothers studio. Since the Warner dining room was more to his taste, Wilder would repair to Burbank with Axelrod for luncheon each day, and Axelrod would sit amid the Warner executives, none of whom knew who he was, but all taking it for granted that somehow he had a right to be eating with them.

It was at the time of John Huston's disastrous and expensive production of *Moby Dick*, starring Gregory Peck, which the Warners were paying for, and which was being made far away in Ireland. Disaster piled on disaster, and the Warners were in daily communication with Huston.

H. M. Warner began to confide daily in Axelrod. One day he sat down, visibly shaken. "I've just spoken to Huston," he said. "John's a very headstrong, difficult man. I've tried to explain to him, we've had World War I, World War II, and now this Korean War—everywhere in America, in practically every home, there's some family with a veteran who was wounded—so I asked John, *why* does Gregory Peck have to have one leg?"

When Howard Hughes took over the RKO studio, he made a tour of the property and then left. Later the studio head called to ask Hughes what instructions he had for the running of his new acquisition. "Paint it," said Hughes and hung up.

At the time he purchased the studio, Hughes had a huge wooden flying boat under construction in a shed at San Pedro, a project which had consumed months and months of time and millions of dollars. Dick Fleischer, the director, was sitting in Sid Rogell's office at RKO on Christmas Eve when the phone rang. Rogell hung up and said, "Well, boys, Howard Hughes is taking over this studio."

"He'll never get it off the ground," said Fleischer.

Another Hughes story goes back to the early days of TWA, in which venture he was partnered with the legendary Jack Frye. The story goes that one night Frye called Hughes and said, "Howard, we need eight million dollars cash right away, or else we're through."

"Right away?" asked Hughes.

"Eight million dollars—or we have to fold up," vowed Frye.

"Eight million dollars?" asked Hughes. "Do you realize that's a small fortune?"

"I went to a meeting with Howard Hughes one night at his bungalow at the Beverly Hills Hotel," recalls Sam Bischoff. "He met me at the door, wearing dirty Levis and a shirt. We sat down, and he offered me the job of running RKO, which he'd just taken over. We discussed terms, and all the time we talked I kept staring at his feet. I remember he was wearing two sneakers—and only one sock. . . .

"Anyway, we agreed on all the terms, they were very generous, and finally he said he would let me run the place, but he insisted on one proviso—that he have approval of the casting of leading ladies.

"We settled that, too, and then we shook hands on the deal, and I said, 'Mr. Hughes, there's only one thing I want to tell you. You have the reputation for calling people at all hours of the night. Please don't call me up like that—I'm a guy who works hard most of the day, and when I leave the studio at night I'm usually pretty tired, and if I'm going to do a job for you, I'll need my sleep.'

" 'I won't call you,' said Hughes, and we shook on it.

"From that day to this, I've never talked to him again. I made a whole raft of pictures for him, I spent maybe fifteen million dollars of his money—but I never heard directly from Hughes again.

"He never fired me. He never fired anybody. If Hughes wanted to get rid of somebody, he'd merely put somebody else in over the guy."

Harry Cohn was pleased with the job of cutting that Bob Parrish had done on *All the King's Men,* and he called the young man into his office and offered him the job of head cutter at Columbia Pictures. Parrish politely refused, saying that he wanted to be a director, preferably in Europe.

"You don't want to go to Europe," said Cohn. "I've just come from Europe, and there's nothing there." For Cohn, the world began and ended on Gower Street. "What else do you want to do?" he asked.

"I'd like to work on good pictures," said Parrish.

Cohn pressed a buzzer on his desk and sent for three of his top executives, who promptly appeared. "Here's a schmuck cutter who wants to work on only good pictures!" he announced. "It's not bad enough I have writers and producers and actors who give me trouble—now I get it from a cutter!" He waved the executives out.

"Listen, kid," he told Parrish, "I make fifty-two pictures a year here. Every Friday the front door opens on Gower Street and I spit a picture out. A truck picks it up and takes it away to the theatres, and that's the ball game. Now, if that door opens and I spit and nothing comes out, you and everybody else around here is out of work. So let's cut out the crap about only good pictures. How many of those pictures I spit out do you think that *I* think are any good?" He stared belligerently at Parrish.

"Well, Mr. Cohn," said Parrish, "I like to think you think they're all good—"

"Ah, cut the shit!" said Cohn. "I run this place on the basis of making *one* good picture a year. I'll lay everything on the line for that one. I don't care if it's Capra, or Ford, or Riskin, or Milestone— that's the good one. The rest of them I just have to keep spitting out."

Eventually, after a series of rescue jobs on a batch of Columbia pictures and a directorial job for the late Dick Powell, Parrish finally came back to Cohn, who was now receptive to the idea of giving him a directorial job.

At a meeting of studio producers in Cohn's office, Cohn asked Parrish, "What do you want to direct?"

Parrish mentioned a story.

"Tell me about it," ordered Cohn.

Parrish quickly outlined it.

"You like that?" asked Cohn.

"I want to do it," said Parrish.

"Well, I'll tell you what I think," said Cohn. "I think it's a lousy story. And that's the end of that, right?"

Parrish shrugged.

"You're goddamned right that's the end of it," said Cohn, and the meeting moved on to other business.

As the session was breaking up, Cohn went into his private toilet. "Hey, Parrish!" he called. "C'mere."

Parrish joined him inside.

"You really think that story will make a good picture?" asked Cohn quietly.

"Of course I do," said Parrish. "That's why I brought it in."

"Well, I'll buy it for you," said Cohn. "But don't tell any of those bastards out there. If they hear about it, they're liable to buy it first."

When an interviewer doing one of those typical *Cahiers du Cinéma* stories (in depth) on his work asked Alfred Hitchcock why it was that he had always seemed to have an infallible gift for casting beautiful unknowns who became stars later, Hitchcock remarked, "I suppose it's because I was born with two crystal balls."

Reminiscing about Preston Sturges (*The Great McGinty, Sullivan's Travels, The Miracle of Morgan's Creek*), Earl Felton, a screenwriter who had been associated with the writer-director-producer, wrote, "He was too large for this smelly resort, and the big studios were scared to death of him. A man who was a triple threat kept them awake nights, and I'm positive they were waiting for him to fall on his face so they could pounce and devour this terrible threat to their stingy talents. . . . They pounced and they got him, good. But he knew the great days when his can glowed like a port light from their kissing it.

"And he did love his restaurant [Sturges' famous The Players]. It was some place, absolutely a marvel, matchless food, service, decor, etc., but with the serious drawback of Preston usually present, turning baleful eyes on any patron he did not know personally.

. . . He definitely regarded the establishment as his private club, and when it began to fail on account of his massive extravagances (an entire hydraulically propelled stage rising in the midst of bewildered diners with a live show going on, written by himself, naturally) Preston kept pouring more good dough after bad. . . .

"It gradually dwindled from an 'in' spot to one definitely off limits, but none of this slowed his runaway imagination to make it more lavish, adding a hamburger counter on the ground level. [The Players was a three-story operation.] Shortly, this latter extension was all that was left of the grandeur, and Preston, ever the dramatist, used to take perverse delight in wearing his tattered dinner jacket nightly to serve up the greasy concoctions in person, making loud, drunken jokes about how the mighty had fallen. You can easily guess it was . . . sad humor, but he never wept and maintained his haughty, unbearable attitude toward the public right to the finish when the whole masterpiece folded, barber shop, escalating stage, triple kitchens, the works. He didn't bother to lock it up that night. The sheriff had already obliged in that respect. Inside, locked up with some of his treasures, were the memories of those many movie figures, not to forget the personalities themselves, the Bogarts, their hideous quarrels, the royalty of Hollywood, Howard Hughes, the stars and starlets, and the greats and the aspiring, all treated the same . . . Dorothy Parker, Bob Benchley, Marilyn Monroe, well, you name 'em . . . treated with the immense aplomb and icy cool of the man."

EDMUND HARTMAN

If there had been motion pictures in the twelfth century, Preston Sturges would have been a feudal baron and a writer-director in his natural background. He had the grandiose manner, a taste for the exquisite life, a casual acceptance of power and luxury.

One night I joined him for dinner at The Players. It was the night of final foreclosure. The yacht was lost. The mansions were lost. The millions were lost. Now the last asset was going.

He turned to his third, or was she his fourth, wife, young and pregnant . . . his usual baronial, unperturbed self. "Don't worry," he reassured her. "When the last dime is gone, I'll go sit on the curb outside with a pencil and a ten-cent notebook and start the whole thing over again."

*　*　*

One afternoon, as he was finishing his work in a Metro musical, Larry Adler was informed by Henry Koster, the director, that it would be politic if, instead of going home, he would repair to the Metro commissary.

There, in full swing, was a large party; the occasion was the birthday of Mr. L. B. Mayer himself. All the Metro stars were in attendance. One after another, they rose and made speeches praising the virtues of their own beloved L. B.

It became George Jessel's turn to speak. The great toastmaster stood up. Raising his glass, he said, "One thing we got to say about our good friend L. B. Mayer. Believe me—he's no schmuck!"

Jessel left Metro's employ soon after.

Herbert Yates, the boss of Republic studios, was at one time teeing off from a golf game with several of his assorted yes-men as members of the foursome. Yates took a swing at the ball and missed it completely. "Go ahead and take another one, Mr. Yates," said one of his yes-men. "I was busy thinking."

Back at Warner Brothers, as outdoor location costs mounted on *Treasure of the Sierra Madre,* Henry Blanke had a difficult time calming studio brass. One particular sequence in which Bogart searches desperately for water had been four days in production. An unhappy Jack Warner sat through all four days' rushes in the projection room, then turned to Blanke. "If that son of a bitch doesn't find water soon, I'll go broke!" he yelled.

Harry Cohn [head of Columbia Pictures] paid one of his rare morning visits to the studio. He strode into the courtyard around which arose the writers' offices, and he noticed something that disturbed him greatly: silence.

No sound emerged from the tiers of rooms wherein scenarios were produced. The scent of freshly made coffee hovered in the air, adding further evidence of the midmorning lull of activity.

"Where are the writers?" Cohn shouted. "Why aren't they working? I don't hear a sound. I am paying you big salaries and you do nothing. You are stealing my money!"

Suddenly, from a score of windows came the clacking of type-writer keys.

"*Liars!*" Harry Cohn bawled.

And during production of *The Captain Hates the Sea* the director reasoned that John Gilbert would be better controlled at sea, where liquor would be less readily available. He failed to calculate the ingenuity of the rest of the cast, who provided Gilbert with drinks from their own supplies. The cast included such imbibers as Walter Connelly, Victor McLaglen, Walter Catlett and Leon Errol.

Production of the film grew slower. Skies were overcast and Milestone maneuvered the ship about the Southern California waters in search of sun. Often he found some, only to discover the wind too fierce or the actors too drunk for the dialogue to be heard.

Exposed film dribbled into the studio, and Harry Cohn was fuming. In desperation, he fired off a cable to Milestone: HURRY UP. THE COST IS STAGGERING.

Milestone cabled back: SO IS THE CAST.

(*from* KING COHN, *by Bob Thomas, Putnam, 1967*)

Ed Hartmann, employed at Universal, was without a definite assignment. One of the studio producers asked him to take on a "problem" script and see what suggestions he could make for re-writing. Hartmann went home with all the material and went into a conference a few days later.

"I think I've got it," he said. "What you have here is essentially a very old-fashioned story being played against a contemporary background, and it doesn't work. There's really only one way to solve the problem, and that's to take the story and do it in 1810."

"1810?" asked the producer. "When was that?"

"Every director who wanted to do comedies would always go into the projection room and run Leo McCarey's pictures over and over again," said Robert Emmett Dolan. "There were some of his that had been run so often at Paramount that the sprocket holes were worn out.

"There was a time—only once—when De Mille decided to do a comedy—which could never have worked, because De Mille was a completely humorless man who took himself very seriously.

"McCarey told me that De Mille would always ask him for advice

163

on the day's shooting, and he'd go into the projection room and look at the rushes with De Mille. They were sitting there one day when on the screen came a shot De Mille had made of a large crowd of extras all running madly away from the camera.

"McCarey was puzzled. He couldn't place the action at all, and he asked, 'What are *they* supposed to be doing, C.B.?'

" 'Well, I don't really know,' said De Mille. 'But every time I see a comedy, there's always a shot in it like that one—people running—so I thought I'd do one.'

"McCarey didn't know what to say to that—it seemed like such a complete revelation of De Mille's lack of any comedic sense."

"Buddy De Sylva came into Paramount and he did a miraculous job of reviving the studio. Before that," said Henry Ginsberg, "we were running fifth in the industry and everybody knew it. Anyway, the time came when he told the Paramount management that he wanted his own unit, and they gave it to him. That meant that I had to take over as head of production—and he had his own operation.

"Well, right after this happened, one night Buddy went to a party at somebody's house, and a young actress came rushing up to Buddy and she said, 'Hello, Mr. Ginsberg!'

" 'I'm not Mr. Ginsberg,' said Buddy. 'I *used* to be Mr. Ginsberg.' "

BEN HECHT

Many ironic things happen in Hollywood.

Overnight idiots become geniuses and geniuses become idiots, waitresses turn into duchesses and what duchesses turn into won't bear mentioning. Overnight in Hollywood panhandling hams blossom into Coquelins and Lorenzos and vice versa. The boulevards are crowded with royal coaches turning into pumpkins before your eyes.

It's an Aladdin's Lamp of a town, and whichever way you rub it, genii jump out and make sport of the laws of gravity and sanity.

Everybody in Hollywood is used to irony, used to every mirage and monkeyshine of Fate. There is even the irony that people in Hollywood work harder than boilermakers and that this happy land of glamor is a tougher locale for survival than the Yukon. And there is yet the more inscrutable irony that out of this wedding of Jabberwock and the Muses called Hollywood a most astonishing lot of worthy enterprise emerges, full of beauty, wit and high purpose.

But the most ironical of events ever to happen in Hollywood is occurring today in its eastern suburb, the city of New York. It is the trial of Joe Schenck.

Our Government has decided that Joe is a criminal and should be sent to jail. Federal barristers are lambasting the hell out of Joe in open court, charging him with swindles and chicaneries against the income tax laws. And the press of the land is happily focusing its wits and derision on this latest and juiciest of Hollywood scapegoats.

And therein, I assure you, is enough irony to give a hangman a bellyache. For of all the Nabobs and Satraps, Caliphs and Pooh-Bahs who make movies in Hollywood, Joe Schenck is the last man who belongs in a prisoner's dock. It is as ironical a piece of miscasting as was ever indulged in by his own Twentieth Century Company, which, if you saw Tyrone Power in *The Mark of Zorro,* is a considerable statement.

I have never worked for Joe nor any of his companies and none of his silver has ever crossed my palm. Nor am I an intimate of his. I am merely one of the thousands who know Hollywood a little too well and who are looking on wide-eyed at the irony of the pillorying of that town's most humane and gallant gentleman.

Joe's case will never be put into the evidence, however bright his lawyers. He will sit stolidly and take the rap for whatever misdemeanors are accredited to him, and like the classy gambler he has always been he will take his licking without compromising friend or foe.

There will be no evidence of another fact. This is the fact that many of the hundreds of thousands of dollars Joe is accused of having deducted fraudulently in his income tax returns were dollars squandered in secret charities. Joe shelled out a goodly part of his fortune weekly and yearly to hundreds of brokendown hams and glamor girls, to hundreds of one-time jolly people wriggling finally at the bottom of the heap. Joe has been the Santa Claus of the Hollywood and Broadway rubbish heaps. He has supported more burned-out stars and buried more penniless alcoholics, harlots, mimes and scribblers than any gentleman of his time. Joe won't hand in the names of these who have known his largesse as extenuating evidence because that would be against his theory of deportment.

And how the hell is Joe going to get it explained to a jury that his squandering money for entertainment expenses—parties costing from two to four grand a clip—was his honorable way of serving his company and his stockholders?

In these parties Joe created Joe Schenck and, once created, Joe Schenck became a figure of importance in a major if cockeyed industry. In these parties Joe learned wisdom, made friendships, dispensed cheer, consolidated talent deals, eavesdropped on ideas, rhumbaed with starlets and furthered the cause of movie-making as much as any single man connected with it. That the cause is a humpty-dumpty one and that it needs swimming pools and casinos and mixed quartets on the Pacific sands at dawn for furthering is none of Joe's doing. He furthered it for 30 years without making an enemy, turning down a touch, growing a deaf ear or a concrete bosom.

The Press, ever ready to pin its peacock feathers on any big name scapegoat, will see Joe's life as a dizzy and protracted Hollywood orgy. Wine flowed and women laughed and wriggled on divans, poker chips clicked and dress suits dived into swimming pools. But this was no orgy. It was Joe loving life and creating out of his doting not only a humane and gallant gentleman but an industry which brought cheer to millions and great fortune to thousands.

Joe says calmly he is guilty of nothing. But he is modest in his protest. For along with some of his other claims, Joe is also a philosopher.

"My father once told me," he says, "that if you are cold sober and haven't had a drink in weeks and five sane and intelligent people look at you and tell you you are dead drunk, the best thing to do is not to argue but lie down and take a nap for an hour."

Joe is for the present having his little nap. And as Hemingway wrote of another gentleman in trouble, Joe snoozing a bit at his counsel's table "looks pretty good out there."

(from PM, 1941)

L. B. Mayer's Sunday luncheons were legendary. He would invite between twenty and thirty guests, and cast the roster of guests as if it were a well-balanced film—so many Jews, so many Catholics, etc.

"One Sunday," recalled Bebe Daniels, "L.B. got up and made a speech—he was always making speeches, and they were usually about how much money he was earning, or how successful his various projects were—and I remember on this particular October Sunday that L.B. announced, 'I have a confession to make to you.

Between now and January, my accountants tell me I have to get rid of $400,000.'

"There were two priests sitting at the end of the table, and one of them raised his hand to catch Mayer's attention. 'If you really have that problem, Mr. Mayer,' he said, 'then maybe you'll build us a new church?'

"Mayer quickly changed the subject."

"Kate Corbaly was the head of the Metro story department," remembers Joe Mankiewicz, "and one day she sent me a synopsis of a forthcoming book called *Gone with the Wind* as a possible vehicle for Clark Gable and Joan Crawford.

"I read it and I thought it was fine. She said she thought it could be bought for $35,000, so I called Mayer and told him about it, and he said he'd like to hear it. Mayer never read story material—he had it told to him by Kate, who was excellent at doing that.

"We had a meeting in Mayer's office, and she told him the story, and Mayer liked it. He said 'Let's ask Irving,' and in a little while Thalberg came in.

"Kate told the whole story all over again. All the time she was describing it, Thalberg was very impatient. He kept glancing at his watch and fidgeting. When she was finished, he got up and said, 'Louis, forget it. No Civil War picture ever made a nickel.' He had just finished a film called *Operator 13* with Marion Davies, which was about the Civil War, and it had been a financial failure.

"Then he walked out, and Mayer turned to us and said, 'Well, that's it. Irving knows what's right.' "

According to John Cromwell, who made six films for David Selznick (more than any other director), Selznick was never afraid to make long films when other, less venturesome producers would make them short. He would quote Nick Schenck, that veteran showman, who, when asked how long a film should be, would shrug and reply, "How long is it good?"

One day the phone in Leland Hayward's office rang. It was Irving Thalberg, who wished to consult with Hayward, then a successful actors' agent. Thalberg was angry over some aspect of a deal, and he wished it settled by conference, immediately. "Leland,

167

you get over here in fifteen minutes!" he commanded.

"But, Irving—" protested Hayward.

"Don't give me an argument," said Thalberg. "You be here in fifteen minutes!"

"But, Irving—" insisted Hayward.

"You heard what I said!" cried Thalberg, who was not accustomed to being thwarted in anything. "Get yourself over to my office in fifteen minutes!"

"I *can't!*" cried Leland.

"Why *not?*" asked Thalberg ominously.

"Because I'm in *New York*," said Hayward.

PORTRAIT OF A PRODUCER
by Allen Rivkin

He's a small man. His short legs carry him rapidly around his huge modernistic office. His hands are small and so is his head, but not his mind. He thinks big, always in terms of millions. Maybe he will drop ten grand at the Club's crap table, but he's always gambling, on people, on the elements, on time, on national economic conditions, on himself. He has to think big and he has to sell his own judgment and he backs that to the limit. His judgment may make a writer insult him in public, it may make a drunken actor run up and down the lot screaming profane outrages on his head, it may cause a hangnail-minded director to shoot several days' work badly, it may make columnists and magazine writers hurl abuses at his greying temples, it may even make the imaginary New York Office chew fingernails, but it's his own judgment and, when he shows box-office results, that's all that matters.

He's a lonely man; hasn't got a friend in the world. Everyone who is close to him has an angle. His male secretary wants to be a supervisor; his general manager is chiseling with the money men to get his job; his associate producers go home to tell their bridge-fatigued wives what a bastard he is. Withal, he's loyal to the men who have come up with him. He knows they're bad, sometimes he's sure they're stupid; occasionally, even, he is assailed with the horrible thought that perhaps they are knifing him—but they're his pals and, until he has the goods on them, he'll lie for them, steal for them, take raps for them, even loan them money.

But he has very little money. For years—ten, maybe—he's been drawing upwards of two thousand dollars a week, but he can't actually lay his hands on a quarter, unless you give him until tomorrow noon. When his auditor brings him his income tax statement at the March of every year, he sits at his huge desk, tells his secretary he can't be disturbed and looks at those enormous figures. Where did all the money go? What is he working for? Who will take care of his wife and his children and his father and mother, brothers and sisters, in-laws and cousins when he dies, he asks himself.

He's always good for a touch, if you give him a little time on the really big touches. He's a sucker for charity, yet when New York orders him to curtail expenses, he cuts the sixteen-dollar-a-week stenographers first. Let him know that an extra collapsed on the set and had to be rushed to General for an appendectomy, and he immediately has her transferred to Cedars and sends his own personal surgeon to operate.

That's because he's a hypochondriac. Pain drives him crazy and he has an air purifier in his office to drive away the hay fever pollen. He has more sodium bicarb preparations than most diagnosticians know. Every six months or so, he hies himself away to New York to give his ulcers a chance to heal and his colitis breathing space; but he'll never take his doctor's advice about more sleep, less worry, regular food habits and exercise. He gets violent when insurance company statisticians predict for him a nervous breakdown in another year because they know that it's an occupational disease in this industry.

When he gets there, he puts up at the Waldorf or the Warwick or the Sherry, reads the syndicated Hollywood columns daily, gets his *Reporter* by airmail and talks to the studio five times a day. When the floor clerks don't recognize him with the same alacrity he gets from the studio gateman, he feels a bit annoyed, but puts it down to cosmopolitan stupidity and tells jokes on himself and how no one pays any attention to him the minute he leaves Hollywood. He always makes sure to impress his colleagues with the fact that he actually got a rest in New York. But he didn't. He drank too much, saw too many shows, interviewed too many writers and slept with too many actresses. He slept less than he does out here and has no idea what the hell-noise of New York traffic did to his blood pressure.

So he returns to the studio by plane, works twice as hard to get caught up with the work no one else has been able to do in his absence. But it really isn't that his subordinates didn't have the ability to do his work; they simply knew their master.

Although he has a beautiful library—thanks to his wife—he never reads. He knows that twelve Pulitzer Prize authors have inscribed books to him, but what's in them, he doesn't know, and doesn't care. He can't be bothered. When it comes to buying a best-seller property, he calls his salesman-story-editor in to have the synopsis told him. If it listens good and can fit his stars, it's a deal—and he'll move heaven and earth to outbid every other producer in the business to get it, once he wants the property. If they have out-bid him or have reached the author before he has, the story-editor goes in the dog-house, his male secretary tells the associates that he's in bad humor and not to bring in any production idea or casting difficulties till late in the afternoon when usually, due to the pressure of other work, he's forgotten all about his miserable failure. But when the competitor's picture is previewed and it happens to be good, the storm breaks out anew and the scream of "why the hell does every-body get good stories but us?" is heard up and down the ten acres that are his battleground.

He never reads, perhaps, because he's had such brutal luck with writers. He's hired the best in the world and only gotten back affronteries for his gold; and yet he often feels that the nature of screen writing lies in the colleges—and he orders his executives to start a junior writing department at once. It never pans out because no supervisor on the lot will pay any attention to "the kids," but he never knows that; he hasn't got time to investigate.

He's a good showman; his profits prove that; and he usually knows what the public wants. Yet it drives writers and directors to madness when they see him rub the fanny of a white desk elephant to get the missing ending for the story on which they've already spent four valuable days in conference.

He's a bad husband and father, although he loves his wife and kids sincerely. He wants her to have the best, do the best, be the best; he didn't go to college himself, so his kids must go to Harvard, Yale, Princeton or Dartmouth—if he doesn't have too much trouble getting them in. And if he does, he hires a prominent alumnus, may-be donates a sizable sum to their endowment fund, and everything is set. If he does get home for a very extra special dinner party his wife has planned for weeks, it's at nine-thirty and he has a headache. He immediately starts drinking and telling raucous jokes on Goldwyn and Cohn, not realizing that Goldwyn and Cohn are telling similar jokes on him. He really has a good time at his own parties and when he finally crawls into bed, he kisses his wife good-night and tells her they ought to entertain more often. She doesn't argue with him. She's heard that for years. But she loves him dearly because, al-though he isn't thoughtful all the time, he is extremely kind and makes a big fuss over her in public.

When he was young and just starting in show business, he had great plans for himself. He was going to be an important figure in American theatrical history. Now, at forty some odd, he doesn't care anymore. He knows he's a top-notch motion picture producer and he hopes to continue doing a good job of making mass entertainment. Someday, he wants to get enough money just to travel around the world and play, day and night. He'd like so much to get away from conferences, castings, bickerings over contracts, retakes and Hollywood. Hollywood, mostly. He feels that only getting away from Hollywood would fix everything.

But it won't. It can't. He's Hollywood. He'll be here till he dies. He'll have a big funeral too. Everyone will remember the many kindnesses he did, the many fortunes he made, the tremendous showman he was. Everyone will forget all the misery he caused, all the hopes he smashed, all the lives he wrecked, all the pictures he spoiled!

(from THE HOLLYWOOD REPORTER, 1936)

Perhaps one day the documented saga of "quickie" production at Republic Studios will be written, but until that time these few tidbits will have to suffice.

Republic was a mini-conglomerate of small-time independent producers who banded together in the early Thirties and took over the old Mack Sennett studios in the San Fernando Valley. Under the aegis of an energetic producer named Nat Levine, Republic specialized in rapid-fire production of Gene Autry and Roy Rogers Westerns, twelve-chapter serials, detective stories and melodramas, and country-style musicals starring such down-home favorites as the Weaver Brothers and Elviry, and Judy Canova.

Speed and cost-cutting were Levine's specialty. His were the pictures which played the thousands of "neighborhood" theatres all over the country, and which were a staple of Saturday-afternoon kids' matinees.

Jerry Chodorov and Joe Fields, who were to become enormously successful Broadway playrights (*My Sister Eileen, Junior Miss,* etc.), broke into the film-writing business at Republic.

Republic was later taken over by Herbert Yates, a transplanted Yankee, who is best remembered for a series of films he produced starring a lady skater, Vera Hruba Ralston. Broadway producer Cy Feuer, who spent many years as musical director for Republic, is

171

fond of recalling the time when he received orders from Mr. Yates's office to make a recording with the studio orchestra of twenty minutes of soft waltz music. That was the entire specification.

One evening, late, Feuer heard the faint sounds of waltz music coming from a sound stage. He tiptoed up and peered in through a crack in the door. The stage contained an ice-skating rink, and on the ice, arm in arm, Mr. Yates and Miss Ralston were skating to the waltz recording Feuer had made.

One day, Nat Levine announced the production of a melodrama dealing with the Civil War. "What is he going to call it," remarked Joe Fields, *"Lavender and Old Stock Shots?"*

On another occasion, Levine put into work a production called *Hitch-Hike Lady.* "During production," remarked Fields, "everyone will hitch-hike to locations, including the cameraman."

One of Levine's cost-cutting tactics, a story which has become a Hollywood legend, consisted of making a twelve-part serial in which the villain appeared wearing a black velvet hood. Levine hired a well-known character actor for one day's work. The one day's shooting consisted of the climactic sequence of the twelfth episode, in which the forces of law and order trapped the villain and triumphantly unmasked him from his black velvet hood. For these key shots the bewildered character actor received one day's pay— and for one day's pay Levine had a marquee name for his serial!

For another film Republic began to negotiate with Walter Catlett, a noted comedian. There was the customary argument over money, and finally a deal was made for Catlett's services for one week and one week only. After signing, Catlett went to the studio, where he was puzzled over the deal. Only one week in which to make a feature film?

His producer took Catlett into the projection room and showed him several completed sequences in which the character Catlett was to play had been played by a "double" and the scenes had been shot from a distance. "Now we'll match up all those long shots with close-ups of you," explained the producer, "and you'll be finished in a week. Have you got a suit like that?"

"Listen," said Catlett angrily, "you put that s.o.b. in the long shots, not me. So give me *his* suit!"

"But that's Mr. Levine's suit," explained the producer.

"I don't care," said Catlett. "Get me his suit."

"We can't!" complained the producer. "He's wearing it!"

"Then go get it," said Catlett, adamant.

An hour later he was in front of the cameras, wearing Levine's suit, while upstairs in the front office, patiently waiting for Catlett to finish his day's work, Nat Levine worked in his shorts.

Such was the pace of production at Republic that writers were often hard at work on a sound stage, typing dialogue for scenes which were being shot twenty or thirty feet away. "I can remember writing closing lines for a scene," recalls Chodorov, "while the *opening* lines were being rehearsed!"

Chodorov also recalls another cost-cutting ploy of Levine's. "We would finish a shooting script on a Wednesday," he relates, "and that meant we had two days with nothing to do. Late that night a messenger would arrive from Republic and pitch an envelope on our front steps—with a note attached, from Levine, instructing us to read the script by morning and be ready for a rewrite conference at 9:00 A.M. And between midnight and 9:00 we were to have read and digested that script, so that Thursday and Friday we'd be back at work—without an hour being lost to Levine."

One day Levine summoned Chodorov and Fields to his office. He had read a sequence from their latest melodrama, which dealt with "war-torn China." He pointed to a batch of pages. "This hospital sequence," he said. "Take it out. The audience won't like it. Nobody wants to go to a hospital. My own brother is sick in the hospital, and I hate hospitals so much I won't even go to visit him!"

Pat Dane's acting career may not have earned her an Oscar, but the young lady's fame around Metro was widespread; it is based upon the following story.

Miss Dane was a contract player and had been cast in a Metro musical. For several days she had arrived late on the set. Word of this was conveyed by the director to the front office, and Harry Rapf, one of the Metro brass section, was assigned to speak sternly to Miss Dane.

Rapf made his way to the set where Miss Dane was filming, and took the young actress to one side. Peering up at the girl, Rapf inquired, "Miss Dane, do you have any idea how much you cost this company by coming in so late every day?"

Peering down at Mr. Rapf, the young lady unhesitatingly replied, "Mr. Rapf, do you have any idea how much you cost this company by coming in at all?"

One day Rapf was chairing a script meeting with several writers, attempting to solve a problem in their script. He jumped up. "I think I've got it!" he said. He thought over his own idea. "No, no, that isn't it," he said.
Silence.
Then Rapf stood up again. "Say—how about *this*?" he asked. The writers waited for the moment of truth. "Nope, nope," muttered Rapf, and sat down again.
Silence.
"Wait! I think *this* will do it!" he cried, jumping up again. A moment or so later, he shook his head and sighed. "No, that won't work either." He sat down and glared at the silent writers. "Say," he said, "I'm getting plenty of ideas—what about *you* guys?"

It was in 1938 that a Hollywood producer, Walter Wanger, talking with a visitor, mentioned Scott Fitzgerald.
"Why, I thought he was dead," said the visitor [Budd Schulberg].
"If that is so," replied the producer, "I've been paying $1,500 a week to his ghost."

(*from* H. L. MENCKEN, DISTURBER OF THE PEACE,
by William Manchester, Collier Books, 1962)

Of all the offers that came to [Peter Lorre] from American companies, one from Columbia appealed to him most. He still feels that he made the wisest possible choice and regards his association with Columbia as having provided him with the pleasantest working conditions he has known in this country. Things between him and Columbia did not start out very promisingly, however. When a minor executive wanted to give him a part in a "B" picture, Lorre balked, explaining that Harry Cohn, the head of the company, had guaranteed him an important movie. When the executive heard this, he smiled smugly at Lorre. "Do you want to fight *Columbia*?" he said. Lorre was adamant. "You can deport me, you can whip me," he conceded. "But," he added, "you can't make me act. After all, Harry Cohn promised me a big picture." The smug smile came over the executive's face again. "Did he put it in writing?" he asked, almost rhetorically. Lorre admitted that he hadn't. "I'm sorry, then," said the

174

executive. "Harry never remembers anything unless he puts it in writing." At this point, Cohn came into the room and the executive repeated his conversation with Lorre. Cohn listened and then denied flatly that he had promised him an important picture. As Cohn pursued his bland denial, Lorre's eyes, which are certainly the most hypnotic in pictures, stared at him incredulously. Cohn began to fidget under the gaze and finally he could stand it no longer. "All right, all right, I said it," he said helplessly. "Now take your eyes off me." Lorre recalls this without bitterness and maintains that he would rather work for Cohn than any other man in Hollywood.

After mulling over a number of story properties and not finding anything suitable, Lorre decided that he would like to make *Crime and Punishment*. He realized, though, that this presented a problem. *Crime and Punishment* is lengthy and hard going and there seemed little likelihood that he could induce Cohn to read it. Finally he hit upon an idea. "I decided," he says with a good deal of pride, "I'd get the most stupid girl I could find and have her digest the book into a page-and-a-half synopsis." A week or so later he appeared in Cohn's office with the synopsis. "Thanks," said Cohn. "I'll take it home and read it over the week-end." Lorre was dismayed. "But it's only a page and a half, Mr. Cohn," he pleaded. "Read it now and I'll wait." Cohn was about to refuse, but the Lorre eyes were on him and he shrugged resignedly and turned to the outline. As he read, his face began to light up. "Why, this is fine, fine," he said. "But tell me one thing. Has this story got a publisher yet?"

(*from* THE ONE WITH THE MUSTACHE IS COSTELLO,
by George Frazier, Random House, 1957)

A set decorator came into Harry Cohn's office one day with a problem. He wanted approval of more money for the decoration of a set, in which the two leads were to play a love scene. "Lemme tell you something," said Cohn. "If in this whole damn country, when we show that scene, there's one person who'll be looking at your wall—then we're in trouble."

On another occasion Cohn called together all the creative people on the studio payroll. In a fighting mood, he made a brief address. Things weren't going well, and it was time to get down to basics. "Lemme tell you what this business is about. It's *cunt and horses!* . . . Oh, excuse *me*, Miss Caspary," he added, speaking to the one lady writer in the room, whose presence he had just remembered.

The Wit and Wisdom of Hollywood

* * *

According to Harold Clurman in *The Fervent Years*, a studio executive advised Elia Kazan [when he first came to Hollywood] to change his name to the more euphonious "Cézanne." When Kazan pointed out that this was the name of a rather well-known painter, he was told, "You make just one good picture and nobody will ever remember the other guy."

(*from* THE FIFTY-YEAR DECLINE AND FALL OF HOLLYWOOD,
by Ezra Goodman, Simon and Schuster, 1961)

During the Thirties, when biographical films were very big on the Warner Brothers schedule, Hal Wallis was quoted as saying: "Every time Paul Muni parts his beard and looks down a telescope, this company loses two million dollars."

Darryl Zanuck presided over story conferences with writers, dressed in polo outfit and waving a polo mallet to emphasize his story points. Once a pair of writers were stuck on a point involving a wife and a lover and a jealous husband. All sorts of devices had been suggested and tried to produce a proper climactic scene, but nothing was satisfactory.

Finally, Zanuck, in a burst of angry creativity, announced, "This is how it goes. The wife is in bed, see? The lover is there—there's a knock on the door, the husband bursts in! Quick as a flash, she reaches beneath her pillow, pulls out a gun and shoots the husband! And there's your climax—go and write it!"

Silence, and then one of the writers raised a hand. "One question, Mr. Zanuck," he said. "How did the pistol get under her pillow?"

"I *put* it there!" said Zanuck.

Y. Frank Freeman, the boss of Paramount, was holding forth one day in the commissary about blood plasma. A true Southerner, he abhorred the entire concept, claiming that it would mix the races. "Why, if I had one drop of nigra blood in my veins," he insisted, "I'd consider myself a nigra."

Harry Tugend, born in Hannibal, Missouri, but raised up north, could contain himself no longer. "Have you ever been vaccinated, Frank?" he inquired.

"Why, certainly," said Freeman. "Why?"

176

"Then consider yourself part diseased horse," said Tugend.

It was several weeks before Freeman would speak to him.

Later, when Freeman put his son on the staff as a producer and there began to emerge a disastrous version of *Omar Khayyam*, it was Tugend who suggested that the poem be rewritten: "A loaf of bread, a bottle of Coke, and you-all!"

Cecil B. De Mille finished *Samson and Delilah,* and there was to be a showing at Paramount. One of the executives thought of asking Groucho Marx to the screening. Tugend, then a production executive at the studio, warned the publicity boys to stay away from Marx afterward. No quotes from Marx.

When the picture was shown, the publicity boys stayed away, but Groucho was greeted by Mr. Freeman and a group of executives. How had he liked the film? "First picture I've ever seen in which the male lead has bigger tits than the female," said Marx.

Freeman remained true to the South throughout his years in Hollywood. Tugend's first job at Paramount was to adapt the Broadway play *Kiss the Boys Goodbye.* It was no easy job, since most of the political satire in the second half of the play had to be scrapped.

Tugend came up with a first scene, which he suggested to Freeman. Edna May Oliver, as a Southern Lady, would be showing her home to two Northerners, played by Don Ameche and Oscar Levant. At the opening of the scene, she would tell them that she kept a collection of relics of the great General Lee.

"*My* grandmother," Ameche was to say, "showed me relics of General Grant."

"Mostly bottles, I presume," was to be Miss Oliver's answer.

"Tugend—youah just the man for this job!" chortled Y. Frank.

During the preparation of *Gone with the Wind,* the greatest question confronting the country was, of course, who would play Scarlett O'Hara. After years of suspense and screen tests (as well as reams of publicity) Selznick announced to the waiting world that the part would be played by an English unknown, Vivien Leigh.

Mr. and Mrs. Freeman encountered Selznick on a train going to New York. Mrs. Freeman, an even more ardent Southerner than her husband, was incensed at Selznick's betrayal of the South. She bearded the producer in his compartment and pounded away at him to change his mind and hire a Southern girl instead of Miss Leigh.

When she paused to draw breath, Selznick said, "Mrs. Freeman, in these two years I've had my doubts. I've considered Southern girls—but I've been listening to *you* for an hour, and I haven't understood a goddamned word you've said!"

"Brynie" Foy, one of the sons of the great comedian Eddie Foy, was a producer for Warner Brothers. He specialized in making the Warner low-budget films, turning them out at such a fast and furious rate that he was fondly referred to around the Burbank studio as "The Keeper of the B's."

During the Thirties, when Foy was cranking out twenty-odd films a year, Warner assigned the director Joe May to work on a picture with Foy. May had had a long and distinguished career in Germany as a pioneering director for UFA. With the rise of Hitler, he, along with many of his fortunate confrères, managed to escape the Nazis and migrate to Hollywood.

Foy instructed May to browse through the studio literary files and pick out a script which he could then prepare for production. May found a story on the shelf and brought it to Foy, who read it and agreed that it would make a good film. "Who've you got in mind to play the leads?" he asked.

"I think, for the two male leads, I would like Leslie Howard and Errol Flynn," said May. "And for the girl, I see Olivia de Havilland."

Foy nodded. "Good casting," he said, "but I'll tell you who you're going to have. I'll give you Dick Purcell [who was at that time a Warner contract player], Ronnie Reagan and Faye Emerson."

May chose not to argue, but went away with the writers he had been assigned. Working together, he and his writers turned out the screenplay. When he turned in the script, it made its way to Jack Warner's desk. Warner read the script and found it brilliant. He called Foy and informed him that he was taking the script away from the B unit and turning it over to another producer, who would make it as an A.

The next thing May heard about his project was that it would be made by someone else, and that Warner had assigned Leslie Howard, Errol Flynn and Olivia de Havilland to the leads!

May, furious, stormed into Foy's office. "Brynie!" he cried. "You're a Jew, I'm a Jew! How could you have done this to me?"

The extent of Harry Cohn's network of informants has never been better documented than by this incident that took place while

Sam Jaffe was manager of Columbia studios.

Mrs. Jaffe was not fond of her husband's superior, and, being an outspoken lady, she mentioned her dislike of Cohn one evening at a party.

The next morning Cohn called Jaffe into his office and reported he'd been told that Mrs. Jaffe was panning him at a party the night before.

"I'm sorry," said Jaffe, "but that's Mildred's opinion, Harry, and perhaps she shouldn't be so outspoken about it, but I can't stop her from not liking you."

A few days later Cohn called Jaffe in again. "I heard she panned me again last night," he said, aggrieved. "I don't think it's right."

Again Jaffe apologized, but added that he had no intention of censoring his wife's feelings.

A week or so later Mrs. Jaffe went off on a holiday with friends to Honolulu. Cohn called Jaffe into his office. "Damn it!" he exploded. "Now your wife is panning me in Honolulu!"

"Harry," said Jaffe, "I think it's wrong for Mildred to criticize you. I've told her so, but she's a strong-minded woman and she has a right to say what she thinks. So I have a decision to make. I'll either have to divorce you or Mildred. I've thought it over, and I've decided. I'm hereby divorcing *you*."

And with that as his exit speech, Jaffe resigned his job at Columbia and went into the agency business, where he continued to prosper.

It was often difficult to work out the advertising of a really big picture so that all the names who had advertising rights were included. Frank Whitbeck was going over the credits on the main title for *David Copperfield* with a studio executive who was checking to see that all stars received their proper billing, when Whitbeck said, "There's a lot of credit there. But one name that should get credit doesn't."

"Who's that?" demanded the executive.

"Probably the most important of all," Frank said. "The guy who wrote the book, Dickens."

The executive looked up warily. "He's dead, isn't he?"

"Yes," Frank admitted.

"Well," said the executive in relieved tones, "screw him!"

*　*　*

The couch outside Thalberg's office was known as the Million-Dollar Bench. Stars, producers and writers waited endless hours for their meetings with the head of production. S. J. Perelman has chronicled the couch in his much-reprinted piece "And Did You Once See Irving Plain?"

When playwright Moss Hart, who had been called to the Coast from New York, came in one morning for a 10:00 A.M. appointment, the secretary greeted him with the news that Mr. Thalberg was in a meeting and could not be disturbed. At 12:00 Hart was still waiting, and he asked the secretary if he could go to lunch. She gave him a pass to the commissary, where he ate, and then returned to the ante-room and waited until 5:00 P.M. Then he decided to go back to his hotel, and left his telephone number with the secretary. She told him to return the following morning. Hart appeared the next morning, but went through the same routine, with no luck. This went on for five days. Finally, in disgust, he went back to New York. There, a few days later, he related his grievance to friends at the Lambs Club. Another writer, who knew Thalberg and understood how much the producer had to cope with at Metro, said, "I think you were wrong to come back, Moss. If Thalberg said he wanted to see you, he will see you. You better go back."

Hart took a train to the Coast, went to the studio at 9:30 the morning following his arrival. At 10:00 Thalberg walked into the front entrance, saw Hart sitting there, went over, grasped his hand in cordial greeting, and said, "Mr. Hart, I'm Irving Thalberg. I'm so sorry I haven't been able to see you sooner!"

Soon after Thalberg's death, according to Hollywood legend, writer Gene Fowler called on L. B. Mayer in his new white-leather-upholstered office in the shining new four-story Thalberg Building.

"How do you like my new office?" Mayer is said to have exuberantly greeted the sardonic author.

"On the way down," Fowler remarked, thoughtfully, "I saw Thalberg's shoes in the hall and no one has filled them."

(*from* THIS WAS HOLLYWOOD, *by Beth Day, Doubleday, 1960*)

Donald Ogden Stewart also recalls the grim days of the Depression, when he received a summons to Mayer's office. There he was greeted by Mayer, who was upset about the state of the country. "People starving, breadlines." Mayer sighed and began to cry. "I wonder, Don, if you'd agree to take a cut in salary?"

Faced with such an emotional appeal, Stewart readily agreed. It was only later that he discovered that, of all the Metro people, Mayer was the only one whose salary had not been cut.

Before achieving success as director-producer of such films as *The Awful Truth*, *Going My Way*, and *The Bells of St. Mary's*, Leo McCarey got much of his early comedy training working for Hal Roach as a director of Laurel-and-Hardy two-reelers. At that time George Stevens, who was also to achieve greatness as a director, was McCarey's cameraman.

"Those were the days at Roach," McCarey would remark, "when some guy would come in and say, 'Listen—Laurel and Hardy in a cobbler's shop.' I'd say, 'Yes? Then what?' and the guy would say, 'That's it—take over.'

"One day we had a production meeting, and the studio manager got up and made a little speech. He said, 'You know, I've been making a little survey here, and I've noticed that in practically every comedy we turn out, somewhere in it there's a pig. Now, what that means is every time a director yells he needs a pig, I have to go out and rent a pig for him, and I want to tell you, these pig rentals have been crippling us.

'I figured out this was a very unorganized way to handle the pig problem,' said the studio manager, 'so I figured I'll *buy* a pig. I mean, if you own a pig, all you have to do is pay for his food—so it figures that owning this pig is much cheaper than going out and renting one, right?

" 'Well, I want to tell you, it's very frustrating. I've had this pig here for a year now, and not once has this pig been the right size for you directors!' "

McCarey and Buddy De Sylva, who was head of Paramount, had been friends of long standing.

During the shooting of his *Going My Way* there appeared one morning on McCarey's set a quiet man who began to follow him everywhere, watching the director's every move from early morning until the company finished at night.

McCarey became puzzled. "It got so," he told his friend Robert Emmett Dolan, "that I'd finish a shot and I'd say 'Cut,' and then I'd turn to this guy and I'd say, 'Was that all right with you?' and if he nodded, I'd tell them to print it."

Finally, McCarey decided he had to know what was happening,

and he sent an assistant director to find out from the front office the reason for his daily visitor.

The assistant returned with the information that the quiet stranger was Harold Clurman, a New York theatrical director. "They're hoping to have him learn how to direct pictures by having him watch you every day," said the assistant.

McCarey nodded, and thought for a moment. Then he whispered instructions to his assistant.

The following morning, as he did every day, Buddy De Sylva arrived in his executive suite at 10:00 A.M. There, on a couch, was a large and burly type.

"What do you want?" asked De Sylva.

"Mr. McCarey hired me to study you so I can learn how to be a big executive," said the mug. "He says it'll only take me part of one day."

According to Bob Parrish, who worked closely with John Ford on several productions, one of Ford's methods of keeping control of the film was to shoot exactly what he needed in each sequence—no more, no less. "All a cutter had to do with Ford's takes was to cut off the slate number," says Parrish, "and put them together, in sequence. This was Ford's own guarantee against possible butchery by front-office executives or wandering meddlers. Ford left them no extra footage to fool around with."

To illustrate Ford's autocratic attitude toward producers, Parrish recalls the first day of shooting of *The Informer*. Cliff Reid, the RKO producer in charge of the film, appeared on the set, and Ford took him around, introduced him to all the members of the cast and the crew, and then said jovially, "Take a good look at Mr. Reid—because you won't see him again until the picture's over."

And in a projection room at Fox, some years later, Ford ran the final reel of *The Grapes of Wrath* for Darryl Zanuck. When the lights went up, Zanuck profusely congratulated Ford, who nodded and stood up. "Thanks—and try not to spoil it, will you, sonny?"

"When I was a schoolboy," said Billy Wilder, "Von was one of my movie idols." Wilder directed Erich Von Stroheim for the first time in *Five Graves to Cairo* in 1943. He told him then: "It is an honor to direct you. You were ten years ahead of your time."

"No," replied Von Stroheim, who was not given to false modesty.
"Twenty years."

(*from* THE FIFTY-YEAR DECLINE AND FALL OF HOLLYWOOD,
by Ezra Goodman, Simon and Schuster, 1961)

Jack Rose and Mel Shavelson had their own company and made
many successful comedies. But, back in the days of their first script,
a film called *On Moonlight Bay*, they somewhat nervously appeared
on the set for the first day of shooting. The director was Roy Del
Ruth, a veteran of many years of films, both silent and sound.

"Del Ruth was sitting in his chair," recalls Rose. "The script—
our script—was on the floor, and he was turning the pages with
his foot. We stared silently at him. Finally he looked up and was
aware of our presence. 'That's as close as I want to get to the written
word,' he said."

"It's only in the past few years that intellectual critics and film
students have begun to write serious monographs on 'the great old
days of the Hollywood director,'" comments Joe Mankiewicz, who is
in a position to speak with authority, having been a Hollywood
director himself.

"I'd be willing to bet that in all the years I worked at Metro,"
he says, "it would be hard to name a film done by one of the Metro
stable of directors, say Woody Van Dyke, Victor Fleming, Bob
Leonard, Clarence Brown, Jack Conway, and so on, which some
other director didn't complete. People forget. Production in those
days was such an assembly line, with so many films being turned
out, that by the time a film was previewed, the guy who'd originally
directed it would have already gone on to another. After the preview,
there'd always be changes and retakes, and the front office would
assign another director to handle them. Nobody ever thought anything of Sam Wood, who was a fine director, coming in to do the
retakes on a Victor Fleming picture."

One of the most prolific and successful directors of films who
spent most of his career turning out hits for Warner Brothers, Mike
Curtiz came to America from Hungary back in the Twenties. His
ever-present Hungarian accent soon turned this cinematic genius into

183

a master of verbal garblage.

When Vincent Price reported at Warner Brothers studio to play Sir Walter Raleigh in *The Private Lives of Elizabeth and Essex*, he saw signs: CURTIZ SPOKEN HERE.

Among classic Curtizisms was his angry threat to an ineffectual member of his crew, "The next time I send a dumb sonofabitch to do something, I go myself!"

Another case in point is Mike's stage direction to a young starlet: "It is morning and a haystack and lots of sunlight—turn over on your stomach and look sex."

To an actress: "Sit a little more female."

"If you want to become a director, he said to an ambitious prop man, "you should sit on top from the camera and pant like a tiger."

Mike demonstrated that he could defeat almost any effort to help him cope with the perils of English. As Pete Martin recalls, Curtiz was to read from a speech that had been carefully typed out, as a part of the publicity campaign accompanying the opening of *Night and Day*, the biography of Cole Porter, in which he directed Cary Grant. "This man Cole Porter," said Curtiz, "he sticked to purpose of making good music, come hell or hayride." One of the Warner wags remarked about *Night and Day*: "Here's a hell of a script problem. You've got a hero who's born rich, goes to Yale, marries a rich girl, writes songs, has hit after hit on Broadway, and you're supposed to find some drama in his life. The only thing I can suggest is—will the poor son-of-a-bitch make his second million or not?"

Curtiz was also capable of great wisdom. "We are not out here to preaching with pictures, to take political sides, or bring a great message," he told Pete Martin. "We are here to entertain. Moving picture is the cruelest business in the world. You must be like a boxer all the time, with your left hand out. I have a book printed in 1920. It is a blue list of movie greats. Only three men in that book are still working. In Europe, if an actor or director establish himself, he live forever. Here, if he doesn't make dough, they kick him out. Hollywood is money, money, money, and the nuts with everything else. How can any man be conceited when he sees the climb and then the awful nosedive?"

Blake Edwards once gave George Axelrod advice on how to proceed as a director: "Make 'em redecorate your office," he instructed. "That's primary—to make them know where you stand. Then, when you're shooting interior sequences, use your own interior decorator as a set dresser. That way, everything on the set will fit your house when you're finished."

This remark has been credited to several others, but according to Bob Thomas, who wrote *King Cohn,* it was made by comedian Red Skelton on his television show the week following the funeral of the head of Columbia. Remarking on the huge crowd that had turned out for Harry Cohn's last rites, Skelton said, "Well, it only proves what they always say—give the public something they want to see, and they'll come out for it."

Several years ago the noted director George Cukor was giving a talk at U.C.L.A. to an audience of film students. In the audience was Mike Frankovich, then the head of production at Columbia, now a successful independent.

Cukor made reference to Frankovich, reminiscing about the days thirty years earlier when he'd had Frankovich, then an ex-football star, as an actor in one of his pictures. "All he had to say was one line," remarked Cukor, "something like 'Jack, your breakfast is ready,' and he could never get it right."

Frankovich stood up in the audience. "That wasn't the line," he interrupted. "It was 'Your breakfast is ready, *Jack.*' "

"*Now* he remembers the line!" said Cukor.

Leland Hayward reported how he'd encountered Leo Jaffe and some other Columbia Pictures executives at a dinner party in Palm Springs at which the conversation naturally turned to current pictures. Eventually the subject of Richard Brooks came up. Brooks had made *Lord Jim* for Columbia, and one of the stipulations in his contract was that the company could not see the film in any production stage until it was absolutely completed. The picture was a large-scale financial disaster. Brooks then went on to make a picture called *The Professionals* with Burt Lancaster, which proved to be a huge unexpected financial success. "We're a little peeved at Dick," remarked Leo Jaffe. "He never told us how good it was."

Ken Englund reports this from his writer-friend Alden Nash. He was attending a script conference with a producer when that worthy

185

stopped everything cold by demanding, of a jungle sequence, "I want to know one thing—just what is the motivation of the man-eating tiger?"

Producer Sam Spiegel, who cruises the Mediterranean on board his opulent yacht, has become, by default, the last of the legendary tycoon-type pashas of the film industry.

In the summer of 1970, among the guests on Spiegel's yacht for a time was Charles Bluhdorn, the aggressive young financier who in recent years has, through his Gulf & Western conglomerate, taken over control of Paramount Pictures. For an afternoon and an evening, Bluhdorn enjoyed Spiegel's hospitality. Champagne, caviar, haute cuisine, fine cigars; Bluhdorn was plied with Spiegel's finest.

Late that evening, Spiegel sat down next to Bluhdorn and, in front of the rest of his guests, he said, "Charles, I would like to ask you about that interview you gave last month."

"Oh, I never give interviews," said Bluhdorn.

"You did give an interview," said Spiegel. "I read it."

Bluhdorn stubbornly shook his head. "I don't give interviews."

"You were in Amsterdam," said Spiegel. "A *Variety* man spoke to you, and you answered some questions."

"Oh yes, that's true," said Bluhdorn. "But it wasn't *really* an interview . . ."

Spiegel poured Bluhdorn more champagne. "Now, if I recall what you said in that story," he said gently, "you were quoted as saying that what was wrong with the movie business today is that producers are no longer concerned with making films, but they are much more interested in sailing around the ocean in their yachts." Spiegel smiled beatifically. "What I'd like you to tell me, if you would, Charles, is just exactly *which* producer did you have in mind?"

In his nineties, still hale and hearty, Adolph Zukor was walking into the lobby of the New York Paramount home office building when he encountered Arthur Mayer, who was at the time in his early eighties. "My God, Arthur," said Zukor, "are you still around?"

At the entrance hall to the Columbia studio a bronze plaque has been put up which reads:

HARRY COHN

1891   1958

But so all-pervasive is Cohn's spirit over Columbia that one of the executives who remembers him remarked lately to a friend as they passed the plaque, "One of these days I'm going to take a file and remove those last two numbers. *I* don't believe for a minute he's really dead."

Just last spring Jack Warner was interviewed by a New York newspaper, which reported him as "nearing eighty." One of Warner's cronies deprecated the characterization. "What the hell," remarked Warner, "it's a better line than 'Services will be private.' "

IT'S ALL ON CELLULOID

"... Everybody here in Hollywood knows his business,
plus music."
AL NEWMAN

"How do you think a smash hit would go today?"
HARRY RUBY (to a producer)

"No story ever looks as bad as the story you've just bought;
no story ever looks as good as the story the other
fellow just bought!"
IRVING THALBERG

"The picture was so bad they had to do retakes
before they could put it on the shelf."
KING VIDOR

IRVING THALBERG

No picture can be considered a success unless it appeals to the matinee trade. When you've got a picture women want to see, the men will have to go along. But a woman can always keep a man away from a picture that only attracts him.

We should all be very happy that everyone in the world has two businesses, his own and the movies!

If I were a writer I would discipline myself by working on material I know very little about.

[To a lawyer who wanted to get into pictures] If you're the answer to my prayers, then I've only got to send to New York for a dozen lawyers.

It's surprising how few in this business want to make a decision. There should be more, when you consider that a man with the courage of his convictions always keeps the other fellow from knowing if *his* idea would have been a better one!

For the good of the business as a whole, never let your standard be less than great!

(*Quoted by Samuel Marx in* THE HOLLYWOOD REPORTER, 1942)

A Hollywood [publicity] classic has to do with an ingenious publicist at Paramount who, in 1934, devised an unusual publicity stunt for a Mae West movie, *It Ain't No Sin.* He put a platoon of parrots in a room with a phonograph record that kept playing the name of the picture over and over. After a while, the publicist had fifty or so parrots who would say *It Ain't No Sin* on cue. There was just one hitch. At the last minute the studio retitled the picture *I'm No Angel.*

(*from* THE FIFTY-YEAR DECLINE AND FALL OF HOLLYWOOD, *by Ezra Goodman, Simon and Schuster, 1961*)

Sometimes Hollywood films suffered from ambiguous titles, as when a Jean Harlow movie called *The Bombshell* was first released. The public, thinking it another war picture, stayed away in droves.

Later, when the film was shown as *The Blonde Bombshell,* business picked up considerably.

In referring to a certain producer in Burbank whose marriage to the daughter of one of the Warner brothers had projected him with all possible speed into the stewardship of his own production company, Julius Epstein once remarked, after a series of less-than-successful films had emerged from this producer's firm, "He has set the son-in-law business back twenty years."

"The surest sign of depression in the industry is not the cutting-down of stars' salaries or the dropping of contract players or the reductions of work crews. The surest sign is when a major studio begins laying off relatives."

(*from* EXIT LAUGHING, *by Irvin S. Cobb, Bobbs-Merrill, 1941*)

When the magnificent new Thalberg Memorial Building was finished at Metro, offices were assigned to production personnel and writers. An opulent second-floor corner suite, overlooking Washington Boulevard, was assigned to Jerry Mayer, who was L. B. Mayer's brother.

At lunch in the Metro commissary, several writers were speculating on the reason for Jerry Mayer's imposing office suite. His position in the studio did not warrant such lavish quarters.

"You're all wrong," said Irving Brecher. "Mayer has a very important job, and he has to have that particular office. He's supposed to watch Washington Boulevard and warn everybody to evacuate the building if icebergs are spotted coming down the street."

At a gathering, the son-in-law of a studio head heard Levant playing "Lady, Play Your Mandolin," which was one of his popular songs. "That's right, Oscar, play us a medley of your hit," he sneered. Slamming the keyboard, Levant bellowed back, "O.K. Play us a medley of your father-in-law!"

(*from* THE UNIMPORTANCE OF BEING OSCAR, *by Oscar Levant, Putnam, 1968*)

JOSEPH L. MANKIEWICZ

There were many gagmen and wits around in the thirties. My brother Herman, Arthur Caesar, guys like Grover Jones, but I don't think anybody was quite like Bob Hopkins, or 'Hoppy' as everyone called him.

He'd originally come down from the North to peddle leatherwork with burnt designs on it. He drifted into the studios and became a title-writer, and he stayed. Hoppy didn't write—he came up with great ideas for pictures. He feared nobody. Harry Rapf, a Metro executive, had a very large nose. Hoppy said, "Rapf is the only man who can smoke a cigar while taking a shower."

One day he pointed a finger at Bernie Hyman, a Metro producer, and said, "You, Hyman, are the asbestos curtain between the audience and entertainment!"

Hoppy must have smoked ten cartons a week and drunk fifty gallons of coffee. He roamed through the studio, first at Metro, and then at Fox, buttonholing producers and giving them ideas for pictures. He didn't write, he sparked other people. With Hoppy, ideas were like titles—a story had to be told in ten obscene words, or less.

We were sitting in Bernie Hyman's office one day, Hyman, Gottfried Reinhardt and I—I guess we were discussing *The Great Waltz* —when the door was thrown open and Hoppy came in. He pointed a finger at Hyman. *"Hyman!"* he barked. "Jeanette MacDonald is a whore. Gable is a gambler, and her pimp. Spencer Tracy is a priest. They all get caught in the fucking San Francisco earthquake. Call it *San Francisco* and you're *in*—you're a great producer, Hyman!" He walked out, and does anybody need to be reminded of the picture Hyman made from that suggestion?

Hoppy had absolutely no fear of Zanuck. Darryl has two large front teeth, and Hoppy once remarked, "Zanuck is the only man who can eat a tomato through a tennis racket and not spill a drop."

One day, during the early years of the Second World War, Hoppy walked up to Zanuck, stuck a finger into Zanuck's shoulder and said, "Zanuck! Tyrone Power—*a Yank in the R.A.F.!* Zanuck— I've made ya!" He walked away. Zanuck made it into one of his most successful pictures.

Another one of Hoppy's choice phrases flickered out of a Zanuck story conference. (According to Beth Day, the transcriptions of Zanuck's story conferences were bound and then sent around to everyone who had attended.) During one of these summit meetings, while Zanuck was lost in thought, Hoppy became bored with the ponderous silence and began whispering to the man sitting next to him.

Zanuck's secretary was immediately reproving. "Quiet, Mr. Hopkins!"

"Hell!" snorted Hoppy. "It's so quiet in here now you can hear a mouse peeing on a blotter."

At one point, Leo McCarey was filming a picture with Irene Dunne and Charles Boyer, and, as was his custom, was working on the screenplay barely a day or so ahead of the cameras.

Boyer was very upset. "I don't know if I'm to be the hero or the villain," he complained, "and McCarey won't tell me."

A Hollywood joke which sprang forth in the De Mille era dealt with Pharaoh and his daughter. She brought the infant Moses in to her father for his approval. Pharaoh glanced at the baby and said "My God—what an absolutely ugly kid! Where'd you get *him?*"

"I can't understand it." His daughter sighed. "He looked so good in the rushes."

Writers Nat Perrin and Arthur Sheekman did a small service for one of their employers without charging a fee. In gratitude, the producer sent them both expensive watches. "From now on," sighed Perrin, "we're going to have to call up our agent every hour and give him the time."

Sir Cedric Hardwicke deplored "The madness of the Hollywood preview system, by which a multimillion-dollar picture costing the time and talent of thousands over a period of perhaps a year or more, is 'sneaked' unheralded onto the screen of some out-of-the way movie house in Pasadena or Glendale. There it faces its ordeal by comment card, known otherwise as death by a thousand cuts. Let one dim-witted adolescent schoolboy scrawl *Lousy* on his card, and the entire studio may be stampeded the following morning in executive meeting to discuss slicing and revising the picture to shreds. On Hollywood's theory that the customer must know best, the schoolboy's *Lousy* is regarded as the last word in dramatic criticism."

(from A VICTORIAN IN ORBIT, *by Sir Cedric Hardwicke, Doubleday, 1961)*

* * *

In her early years at MGM, Garbo once turned down a story that had been offered her by the studio brass. To punish the obstinate star, L. B. Mayer cast her opposite Colonel Tim McCoy in a low-budget Western. When Lionel Barrymore, who was also at the studio, heard what had happened, he remarked, "That's like cutting Tolstoy's beard so he wouldn't write any revolutionary novels."

Jackie Cooper, an ex-child star himself, is fond of telling the story of the afternoon when a sudden crisis took place during the shooting of a Lassie picture. There on a raft in the river, along with the small boy actor, was Lassie. The current was too swift, and without warning the raft went rapidly down the river, bearing its precious burden. On the shore the camera crew and director stood and watched—but not Rudd Weatherwax, Lassie's trainer. "He tore off his jacket," says Cooper, "leaped into the water, swam out to the raft, and pulled Lassie off! The kid he left to fend for himself!"

JOE E. BROWN

Jack Warner gave me a big build-up. "All the principal actors in the studio are going to be in this picture [*A Midsummer Night's Dream*]. "Dick Powell, Jean Muir, Olivia de Havilland, James Cagney, Arthur Treacher, Ian Keith, Anita Louise, Victor Jory, Mickey Rooney, they're all going to be in it and we've brought Max Reinhardt over to direct it." Then he talked at length about Reinhardt and about his great success in Germany and what a fine director he was. "It's a wonderful opportunity for you, Joe. Why don't you go talk to Reinhardt?"

So I met the great Reinhardt and I liked him right away. He was an artist, you could sense that immediately. His accent was pretty bad, but I understood him. He said he wanted me to play the part of Flute. I said I didn't know much about Shakespeare. He waved that aside. The first time he saw me, he said, was in the Vendome Restaurant. He had never met me but he recognized me and nodded. "Und den Brown nodded to me und schmiled—und ven he schmiled Brown faded oudt und Flute faded in." That was his way of telling me I was a perfect Flute.

After a half hour of this, I went back to Jack Warner's office. I still was not convinced. And after another half hour with Warner, Ivan [Kahn], and Hal Wallis all working on me I agreed to think it over. Then Ivan said, "Is this to be one of Joe's regular pictures or is it an extra? And how much will he get?"

Wallis said, well, it was not to be one of my contracted pictures. They weren't thinking in terms of money. Everyone in the studio would be in it, sort of a big family party so to speak. Nice chance for everyone and we thought Joe would want to be in it. He's one of the oldest on the lot in point of service, and so on. Ivan interrupted him. "Hal," he said, "he isn't to get paid?"

"Well, no, not exactly."

"You mean he won't get any money?" Ivan was incredulous.

Wallis and Jack Warner acted as if the point were of no consequence. But Ivan was persistent.

"You mean he's to do this whole thing and not get any money? You won't give him anything at all?" Ivan's incredulity was now tinged with scorn.

"Oh," said Jack, "we'll probably give him a present of some kind."

"For instance?" asked Ivan doggedly.

"Well, perhaps a Packard car or a Cadillac or something like that."

Ivan said, "A Packard? A Cadillac? And Jack, what would my commission be, a bicycle?"

(from LAUGHTER IS A WONDERFUL THING, *by Joe E. Brown,*
Barnes, 1956)

BEN HECHT

I remember a phone call to Nyack from the MGM Studio in Hollywood. Bernie Hyman, then the studio head, wished my help on a plot problem that had arisen in a two-million-dollar movie being prepared for shooting.

"I won't tell you the plot," he said. "I'll just give you what we're up against. The hero and heroine fall madly in love with each other —as soon as they meet. What we need is some gimmick that keeps them from going to bed right away. Not a physical gimmick like arrest or getting run over and having to go to the hospital. But a purely psychological one. Now what reasons do you know that would keep a healthy pair of lovers from hitting the hay in Reel Two?"

I answered that frequently a girl has moral concepts that keep her virtuous until after a trip to the altar. And that there are men also who prefer to wait for coitus until after they have married the girl they adore.

"Wonderful!" said the Metro head of production. "We'll try it."

(from A CHILD OF THE CENTURY, *by Ben Hecht,*
Simon and Schuster, 1954)

* * *

Dmitri Tiomkin, a Russian-born composer, has scored many great films, including the classic *High Noon*, for which he composed the title song. He is justifiably famous for his Academy Award speech, in which he insisted on thanking Beethoven, Brahms, Bach, Mozart, Shostakovitch, *et al.*

Once, at a studio recording session where Constantine Bakaleinikoff was conducting the studio orchestra in a performance of one of Tiomkin's scores, Tiomkin sat in the booth with the engineer. The orchestra had played a few bars when Tiomkin interrupted through the monitor.

"Who is playing first violin?"

"Who wants to know who is playing first violin?" snapped the irritated Bakaleinikoff.

"I want to know," replied Tiomkin, with authority.

"And why do you want to know?" demanded the conductor.

"Because," said Tiomkin, "I wish to tell him that in my opinion he stinks."

"Well, in my opinion," replied the outraged Bakaleinikoff, "your opinion stinks!"

At another Tiomkin session he was conducting a studio orchestra himself, along with a full choir of children, in a highly patriotic finish to a new film. Suddenly Tiomkin stopped and rapped for attention. In his thick Russian accent he cried, "Shildren, shildren! Votch de diction! It's *swit lend of liaybertay!*"

JOHN FORD

There was this obnoxious little character—I think he was the son of some big shot. He said, "You're way behind schedule." He'd been pestering me for days, so I tore out ten pages of script and said, "Now we're three days *ahead* of schedule. Are you happy?"

JOSEPH M. SCHENCK

In the wave of economy that studios generally have when they get desperate, they drop a few hundred-dollar-a-week employees and then hire a four-thousand-a-week executive.

"Harpo Marx was making a movie that required a lot of dogs," says Arthur Sheekman. "So the front office hired two groups of

197

dogs. Each group came from a different rental outfit, with its own trainer. The director got all the dogs together and he instructed the trainers to have all the dogs bark when he gave the signal.

" 'Now!' yelled the director, and all the dogs barked, on signal, and there was bedlam.

"The director waved for silence, and the trainers shut up their dogs. 'Too loud,' said the director. He pointed to one trainer and said, 'When I give the signal, I want just your dogs to bark.'

"Just exactly like a stage mother, the second trainer stood there, looking pained while he listened to the rival trainer's dogs barking.

"When the barking was finished, the second trainer sniffed. 'You call that a bark?' he demanded."

When Billy Wilder was shooting *Sunset Boulevard*, he told cameraman John Seitz: "Johnny, keep it out of focus. I want to win the foreign-picture award."

In the same picture, Gloria Swanson was lying in bed in one scene with slashed wrists. Seitz asked Wilder what kind of a camera setup he wanted. "Johnny, it's the usual slashed-wrist shot," Wilder said.

There was a dead chimpanzee in *Sunset Boulevard*. Seitz again asked Wilder about the camera setup. "Johnny, it's the usual dead-chimpanzee setup," Wilder said.

(*from* THE FIFTY-YEAR DECLINE AND FALL OF HOLLYWOOD,
by Ezra Goodman, Simon and Schuster, 1961)

RALPH BELLAMY

I did a horror picture at Universal. . . . We finished a scene, and [the director] said to Cedric Hardwicke and me, "We have to go down to the backlot for a staircase, to shoot a silent shot. Why don't you sit here and relax?"

So Cedric and I had a pleasant hour, two hours, and finally decided to go down to see how they were doing. There was a lot of hollering and running around, and the assistant director finally went to this little director and said, "We're ready." He picked up the megaphone and almost bumped the assistant as he turned it around. He said, "Get Evelyn Ankers at the top of the stairway." He started to pace back and forth, with the megaphone, and said, "Now, Evelyn, you're all alone in this dim, dark, dank, dingy, ancient, oozing, slimy castle, at four o'clock in the morning. Your mother's been carried off by the Frankenstein monster, your father's been killed by the wolf-man, the servants have fled, your lover is being chased across the moors by the dogs. I want to get the feeling from you, as you come down this stairway, that you're fed up with it all!"

Anytime Cedric and I saw each other anywhere in the world after that—and it was a lot of places—we'd say, "You fed up with it all?"

(from FILM FAN MONTHLY, September 1970)

Chaplin was working on one of his late films, Monsieur Verdoux. Bob Parrish, who at this time in his career was a cutter, was invited by Chaplin to see some of his rushes.

The scene was a simple one. Chaplin's cameraman, Rollie Totheroh, shot from above a flight of stairs. Chaplin, as Verdoux, came to the bottom of the stairs, smiled at an imaginary lady who had gone up, and then followed her.

There were five "takes" of the scene. In the third, following Chaplin's movements, Totheroh's camera had inadvertently panned and caught a glimpse of an electrician standing by his light. The rest were all fine.

When the lights came up, Chaplin turned to Parrish. "Which one did you like the best?" he asked.

"I thought the fourth was the best one," said Parrish.

"What about the third one?" asked Chaplin.

"Well, in that one I saw the electrician—" said Parrish.

"What were you looking at him for?" snapped Chaplin.

At one point, during the production of a film called Pursued, Milton Sperling had Ted Allan, the writer, working for him on another script. "I don't like people to yes me," said Sperling. "Whatever you actually feel, I want to hear about it, do you understand?" Allan agreed to provide his honest opinion, when and if it was requested.

Several days later Sperling asked him into a projection room to witness some screen tests that had been made of unknown leading players. Sperling needed a young cowboy type for Pursued, and his casting people had come up with two possibilities.

The first test was run off. Several of Sperling's staff were enthusiastic about the young actor's potential. "I can get him for very little money on a long-term deal," said Sperling to Allan. "What did you think?" Allan shrugged. "A good actor," he said, "but I'd say

199

he'd do better in sophisticated roles. He's really not the cowboy type."

Sperling nodded. The lights went down, and the second test was run off. Again the staff was enthusiastic about the actor's potential. "I can get *him* cheap for a nice long-term contract too," said Sperling. "What did you think, Ted?" Again Allan was negative. "He's much more of the city type, I'd say," he mused. "Also not a cowboy. If you ask me, neither of them is right for the part." Sperling nodded, and the projection-room session ended. "Thanks for your advice, Ted," he said. "I appreciate your honesty."

About two years later Allan, having finished his contract, was living in a New York suburb. One day the phone rang. It was Milton Sperling, arrived in the East. Would Allan join him today? "Meet me in Times Square, at the corner of 44th and Broadway," he instructed.

Allan made the trip into town, hurried to Times Square, and there, at the appointed hour, he met Sperling. Without a word of greeting, Sperling took him by the arm and turned Allan around so that he could see a large billboard. "Read *that!*" he instructed. Allan made out an announcement of a new Western film starring Kirk Douglas. "*He* was one of the two guys we tested!" snapped Sperling —"the one you said wasn't a cowboy. He's a cowboy!"

He pulled Allan about so that the writer was now facing a second huge billboard, on the opposite side of Times Square. "There's the second guy you didn't like!" said Sperling. The sign heralded the film *Red River,* and in huge bold letters was the name of Montgomery Clift. "He was the *other* guy!" said Sperling. "And *he's* a cowboy!" He glared at the hapless Allan.

"Who told you to listen to *me?*" pleaded Allan.

One of the more colorful executives at Metro was Billy Grady, head of the Casting Department. Prior to coming to Hollywood, Grady had a long career as a vaudeville booking agent, and one of his best friends was W. C. Fields.

Grady was once in a long and involved casting conference with a Metro producer and his aides. The problem revolved about the choice of a leading man for the producer's next film. The producer insisted on using Jimmy Stewart. Grady kept suggesting alternatives. The producer was adamant; only Stewart was ideal casting for the part. On and on went the wrangle, and finally Grady excused himself to check on Stewart's availability.

He came back a few moments later. "I've just gotten terrible news," he said sadly. "Jimmy was in an auto accident this morning and the poor bastard's dead."

The room became silent. Stunned, the men digested the horrible shock. A few minutes later, after a pause for fond reminiscence about the late star, the producer sighed. "We'd better get back to our problem," he said. "Life has to go on."

The conference thereupon returned to the primary problem, casting the picture. Various alternative names were suggested for the lead. Grady scribbled notes. Finally, when a list of possible leading men had been agreed upon, the conference came to an end.

"All right," said Grady, rising, "now I have to tell you. Jimmy Stewart wasn't in any accident. I made up the whole thing. The guy's fine."

"What the hell did you pull such a crazy stunt for?" demanded the angry producer.

"I just wanted to prove that Stewart wasn't the only one who could play this part," said Grady. "And I did."

Possibly the most quoted remark ever attributed to Jack Warner was purported to have been made when he returned from Europe, during the Sixties, to be informed by a friend that Ronald Reagan, who had been a Warner contract player for many long years, had been nominated to run for Governor of California.

Warner is supposed to have shaken his head. "No, *no*," he said. "*Jimmy Stewart* for governor—Reagan for his best friend!"

Prior to the production of *Exodus*, Otto Preminger held a pow-wow with his press agents to discuss the presentation and billing of the picture. "I see it as Otto Preminger's *Exodus*," he told the assembled flacks, in a spirit of the highest dedication. "But, Otto," hazarded one drumbeater, "that's just what a lot of people are waiting for." Needless to say, the press agent is no longer with Preminger.

(*from* THE FIFTY-YEAR DECLINE AND FALL OF HOLLYWOOD,
by Ezra Goodman, Simon and Schuster, 1961)

There have been many legends surrounding the filming of *The African Queen*, which starred Katharine Hepburn and Humphrey Bogart, but none of them is as charming as producer Sam Spiegel's recollection of the first day of shooting. (And proponents of the *auteur* school of film-making, who insist on setting the importance of the director above and beyond all other elements in film production, should pay special attention.)

"We were established in what was then the Belgian Congo," recalls Spiegel. "We had built our own camp—and for four long weeks we were inundated by endless rain. We had not made a single foot of film. We sat knee deep in mud in our camp, pestered by insects, and by the end of four weeks you can imagine how demoralized we all were. Not Huston. The weather did not bother him—he found a native hunter and went off into the jungle each day. Once in a while Katie Hepburn would accompany him, but Bogey and his wife would have nothing to do with Huston's hunting.

"One morning we woke up at six and were greeted by brilliant sunshine. It was like a rebirth. We got the cameras out, the equipment and the lights, and we hurried down to the river to set up our first shot. And then we discovered Huston was missing! He was out somewhere in the jungle with his hunter, still hunting.

"The native drums began to beat out a message to Huston's hunter. Meanwhile, Jack Cardiff, our cameraman, set up the cameras for the first shot. He positioned the actors, and just as he was about to start, Huston and his hunter appeared at the edge of the clearing. He dashed down to the cameras, and without even taking a look at Cardiff's set-up, John yelled, "Camera—action!"

During the summer of 1968 Blake Edwards was shooting sequences for *Darling Lili* on location in Ireland. The film, which at last reckoning had cost something more than twenty million dollars, was a World War I spy story and starred Rock Hudson and Julie Andrews.

In Ireland, Edwards spent several months shooting aerial sequences with a huge crew of technicians and actors, running up costs at an alarming rate.

Charles Bluhdorn, head of the conglomerate Gulf & Western (and of Paramount as well), decided he would take a trip to Ireland to survey how Paramount's money was being spent.

One sunny afternoon Bluhdorn arrived at the location site. He got out of his limousine and was startled to see the entire *Darling Lili* company stretched out on the green Irish sod, basking in brilliant sunshine. Extras, technicians and expensive actors were all relaxed; not a single sign of film-making was evident, not a camera was turning.

Bluhdorn strode over to Blake Edwards, who was also dozing in the sunlight. "For God's sake, Blake!" he yelled. "What's going on here? Don't you know what this is costing? Why aren't you people making film?"

"Sorry," said Edwards yawning, "but we can't."

"What are you talking about?" asked Bluhdorn.

"Well, everything we've shot so far is the usual cloudy Irish sky," said Edwards. "It's a problem of matching. We're waiting for this goddamned sun to go away."

ANYTHING FOR A LAUGH

*"Some say, What is the salvation of the movies?
I say run 'em backwards. It can't hurt 'em
and it's worth a trial."*
WILL ROGERS

BEFORE *Animal Crackers* was made into a film, it had been a successful Broadway musical comedy with a score by Bert Kalmar and Harry Ruby, and starring the four Marx Brothers.

"We tried out in Philadelphia," recalls Ruby. "After the opening night Bert and I had a party in our suite at the Warwick Hotel, which overlooked a garage in the courtyard. Lots of food and drinks, and everybody came.

"After Groucho and Chico finished eating, they tossed their plates out the window of the suite. 'Why should some poor guy have to wash dishes all night?' asked Groucho, and he went around the room collecting crockery and tossing it out. Pretty soon they'd tossed practically everything out the window—and then Harpo came in. He took one look at what was going on, and went for the upright piano in the corner—and he and the boys started hoisting it out the window! It was all we could do to hold on to the piano—after all, we needed it. We were writing songs on it.

"Next morning, after we'd gotten everybody cleared out, I went downstairs and the manager stopped me. He said that one of the guests in the hotel, a manufacturer, had been complaining about all the racket from our suite, and if it continued, he'd take his business elsewhere. I promised him we'd be more careful.

"The following morning the manager met me, and he was really upset. The manufacturer had really raised hell and said we were destroying his sleep. He'd made a big scene in the lobby and said he was moving to another hotel.

"Well, I knew we hadn't made a sound, and I got suspicious. I asked the manager what this guy looked like—and, sure enough, he described a thin guy with glasses and a big nose.

"'You poor guy!' I told him, and I was laughing. 'That guy who was complaining about all the noise the Marxes were making was *Groucho!*' He refused to believe me until he spotted Groucho coming in that night from the theatre.

"They'd do anything for a laugh," says Ruby fondly.

During the late Thirties, Ben Hecht and Charles MacArthur organized their own chamber-music society, known as The Ben Hecht

Symphonietta. As recalled by the composer George Antheil, who served as the group's pianist, Hecht played first violin, MacArthur essayed the "clarinet in B flat major," and the other musicians included Charlie Lederer and the gifted harpist H. Marx. In an interview, Mr. Hecht deplored "the general crass and low level of Hollywood musical taste" and announced that his Symphonietta had been organized solely to remedy that appalling cultural lack.

The first rehersal took place in a small room on the second floor of Hecht's rented manse. The personnel gathered and began to play. In the midst of the music, the door was suddenly thrown open and Groucho Marx yelled, "Quite, please!"

"Groucho is jealous," remarked Harpo.

"I wonder what the hell he's up to," mused Hecht. "I've been hearing our front door open and close all evening."

"He's jealous because we wouldn't let him join the group," said Harpo.

"But he only plays the mandolin," remarked one of the other members. "How do you fit a mandolin into chamber music?"

The mystery remained a mystery until the rehearsal-room door opened again and Groucho again cried, "Quiet! You lousy amateurs!" He left the door open and stamped his angry way downstairs.

After a moment, there came a sound which raised Hecht's rented rafters—the *Tannhäuser* Overture, played by a full symphony orchestra. The Symphonietta rushed to the stairs, and "There," recalled Antheil, "was Groucho, directing, with great batlike gestures, the Los Angeles Symphony Orchestra. At least one hundred men had been squeezed into the Hecht living room."

Hecht capitulated and welcomed Groucho into the Symphonietta, mustache, mandolin and all.

KING VIDOR

At one point in my career, while directing Miriam Hopkins, I became infatuated with the soft Southern talk of the Georgia queen. One evening we had a dinner engagement which was known only to the two of us. Miss Hopkins told me she had been sent a new script by Ernst Lubitsch with the request that she give an answer on the following day. She asked if I would help her decide whether she should play the part. She read straight through, and we were both elated with Miriam's part and with the sharp humor of the story. As Miriam read the final lines on the last page of the manuscript, her eyes fell on a scribbled notation at the bottom of the page. It read:

"King—Any little changes you would like, I will be happy to make them. Ernst." The Lubitsch touch had exploded our secret world.

(from A TREE IS A TREE, by King Vidor, Harcourt, Brace, 1952)

Benchley was not a man given to practical jokes, but once in Hollywood he was the author of one which is still talked about. Among the varied and assorted people who were his friends there was a doctor who although called a quack by the critical was to the sympathetic Benchley merely experimental. And earnest. In his experiments with the common cold, hangovers, headaches, flea bites and such, Benchley was his willing guinea pig. He swallowed pills for him and allowed himself to be studied for results. The doctor branched out once, however. He invented a pill which he believed would cure lost manhood, and wanted to try it out. His guinea pig felt this was going too far. He took the pills but when the doctor called on him the next day for the check-up, Benchley was ready for him.

No, he reported, there had been no change in temperature. No, he had remained exceedingly calm. No, he had felt no warmth or flutter. He had been excited only by a Rex Stout murder story he had read all night. Yes, he had taken the full dose. The doctor scratched his head and protested that there must have been some kind of change, somewhere, somehow.

"Nothing at all," said Benchley, "except maybe this." He dropped his pajama pants and showed him the base of his spine. On it, with the painstaking help of his friend Roland Young, he had glued a small but graphic sprouting of rooster tail feathers.

(from MERELY COLOSSAL, by Arthur L. Mayer, Simon and Schuster, 1953)

According to Bennett Cerf, Robert Benchley and Donald Ogden Stewart were one time guests at the home of Robert Lovett, who was an important figure in banking circles in the early Thirties. Lovett was called to the telephone during the course of the evening, and his guests heard him saying, "Why, yes—let Austria have eight million dollars." The following day Stewart sent Lovett a telegram which read: YOU HAVE MADE ME THE HAPPIEST LITTLE COUNTRY IN THE WORLD, and was signed: AUSTRIA.

* * *

In the early Thirties, both Deanna Durbin and Judy Garland—then in their early teens—were placed under contract at MGM, and made a musical short together. Louis B. Mayer decided that it was Durbin who had star potential; Garland did not inspire him at all. He decided to let Judy go and keep Deanna, but his plan misfired. Mayer went on one of his European buying trips, and while he was away from Culver City, the studio allowed Deanna's contract to lapse. In a matter of days Universal, searching for a young girl singer to play the lead in *Three Smart Girls,* snapped up Deanna.

When L.B. returned, to find that he had lost his teen-aged canary, he lost his temper. His wrath resounded through the executive halls. From his scorn no one was spared. Finally, an anonymous practical joker took over. In his private bathroom one morning, Mayer discovered the face of Deanna Durbin printed on every sheet of toilet paper.

ARTHUR SHEEKMAN

I can remember some of the savage practical jokes that used to happen around Warners in the early days. Some poor writer got a note one afternoon with Jack Warner's name signed to it, which said "We're considering doing *War and Peace*—we'd like to have an answer on it by morning. Would you please read it and get in touch with me?"

The guy sat up all night reading. Then he burst into Warner's office—if it's at all possible to burst, after sitting up reading *War and Peace* in one night—and he said to Warner, "Is it really necessary for me to do you an outline?"

And later on, after Barbara Hutton had divorced Cary Grant, there was a young actor working in a picture with Cary who was also named Hutton. Someone came to him and said "Look, Mr. Warner would like you to change your name because it's embarrassing to Cary Grant—they had a miserable time together, and your name constantly reminds him of her."

The actor thought about it and he finally said, "What would you suggest?" And the wag said, "Mr. Warner feels we've had enough pretty names in pictures and he'd like someone with an earthy name that anyone might have. This is a country created by immigrants. He'd like, if you don't object, a name like Tomashefsky. It has a European kind of flavor, and at the same time it has a quality—it could be you or it might be me. I realize it's kind of an odd name for a movie actor, but when you become a star, you'll make it a fine name."

The actor asked if he could think about it. He was getting married, and he said, "I don't know how my girl will feel about it." "Oh, come on," said the guy, "it isn't up to *her* whether you change your name, now, is it?"

The actor went home, and the next day he came by and said, "You mean, I won't have the part if I don't use that name?" "Well, Mr. Warner really *likes* that name," said the joker. And he kept on nagging the poor guy for days—until finally they let the actor know it was a gag.

Max Gordon, the Broadway producer, made his debut as a film-maker with a version of Robert E. Sherwood's *Abe Lincoln in Illinois*. The film was far from a financial success, and the failure depressed Gordon.

Shortly thereafter his fortunes took a drastic turn for the better when Jerry Chodorov and Joe Fields did their adaptation of Ruth McKenney's *My Sister Eileen* and brought it to him. Under Gordon's aegis, the comedy opened on Broadway to become a smash hit.

Gordon, basking in the glow of success, took a trip to Hollywood, the scene of his late failure. Aboard the Chief, he received a wire from Joe Fields inviting him to Fields's home for a sumptuous dinner —he was to go there directly upon arriving in Los Angeles. The menu was listed in detail, and Gordon, who loves good eating, looked forward to the dinner all the way West from Albuquerque.

When he arrived in Los Angeles, he hurried to the Fields home. He was ushered into the dining room. There, seated around the table, were seven of his friends. They had all prepared for the evening by going to a studio make-up man, who had equipped them with moles and chin whiskers, and all seven, including Chodorov and Fields, were attired in Lincolnian frock coats, shawls and stove-pipe hats.

Gordon stood in the doorway and stared moodily at the costumed guests. "Hmph," he said. "I suppose you guys think Lincoln is funny!"

But perhaps the most famous anecdote concerning Gordon's ill-fated film production of *Abe Lincoln in Illinois* is the tale of the special screening which was held at the White House for President Roosevelt. When the lights in the White House theatre went up, Gordon politely inquired, "How did you like it, Mr. President?"

F.D.R. beamed. "It's a beautiful picture, Mr. Gordon."

"Yeah," sighed Gordon, "but will it make a quarter?"

It was also after Gordon produced *Abe Lincoln in Illinois* that Lou Holtz said to him, "I can't understand it, Max—Lincoln was so kind to everyone but you!"

Gene Towne and Graham Baker were a very successful pair of writers whose irreverent antics were always imbued with a fine lunatic tinge.

Somewhere on a used-car lot Towne and Baker found an old ambulance, which they immediately purchased. It was refurbished, and they drove it everywhere, day and night. In the back were ample supplies of liquor, and wherever they went, the ambulance provided the setting for an instant party.

While working on a film for Samuel Goldwyn, Towne and Baker were called one morning by Goldwyn's secretary and informed that after lunch their boss would be bringing some guests down to the Writers Building for a visit. He wished to drop by their office and show his guests where and how his writers worked.

At the appointed hour Goldwyn appeared in the building, his guests in tow, looking for Towne and Baker. He was directed down the hall to the Men's Room. Upon opening its door, Goldwyn discovered two desks, two chairs, typewriters, Towne, Baker and their secretaries, all hard at work.

Robert Emmett Dolan

I think the most elaborate practical joke I ever heard of was the one Victor Young played on Max Steiner. And for sheer intricacy, it was marvelous.

Victor and Max and a lot of other Hollywood composers used to play cards once a week, usually at Victor's house. Max had very bad eyesight and he'd given up driving, so Victor would go over to Warner Brothers and pick Max up and bring him to his house—that was the kind of thoughtful, sweet man Victor was.

One particular week Max was scoring a picture—I believe it was *Now, Voyager*—and he was on the stage when Victor arrived. Victor got inside the first stage door, and then the red lights went on, so Victor stood there, between the doors, listening to Max's music. The orchestra had just come to the love theme Max had written for the picture, a great, sweeping, typically Max Steinerish theme.

Victor stood there, and he got an idea. He listened to the music, pulled out a piece of paper and jotted down the notes of Max's new theme. Then he went inside, picked Max up and took him to his house for the card game.

The next day Victor was scoring a picture at Paramount, and he took the Steiner theme to one of his arrangers, who did a quick orchestral scoring of it. Then Victor took it down to his recording session, and in five minutes he had the Paramount orchestra make a full recording of it.

Then he took the recording home. Victor loved gadgets—he had all sorts of equipment and speakers there—so he made a special recording of Steiner's theme, cutting it into a recording he'd already made of a local Los Angeles news program. Then he was ready.

The following week Steiner arrived, and the game proceeded. At about 11:00, one of the players suggested they turn on the news, and on it went. Over the speakers came the voice of the local announcer, presenting the local program, and then the full orchestration of Max Steiner's *Now, Voyager* theme.

Max jumped up as if he'd been stabbed. "Listen to that!" he yelled. "That's *my theme!*"

"Oh don't be silly," said Victor, dead-panned. "Deal the cards."

"Listen to them—they've stolen my music!" yelled Steiner.

"How could they steal your music?" said Victor. "That's a program that's been on five times a week, fifty-two weeks a year, for years and years, and they've used that signature ever since they first went on the radio."

"It *can't* be!" howled Steiner. "I *just wrote it!*"

He was about to go into hysterics when Victor started laughing and finally revealed what he'd done.

The absolute nadir of the great Buster Keaton's career must be the period in the late Thirties when he was placed on the Metro payroll, at a very small weekly salary, to be a "comedy consultant."

A short decade before, Keaton had been one of Metro's biggest and most commercially successful stars; now, through a series of unfortunate circumstances, he was reduced to a humiliating role, accepting a form of L. B. Mayer's weekly dole.

It is even more ironic to consider that one of Keaton's primary jobs was to assist Red Skelton in working up comedy "bits" in a series of films which were all remakes of Keaton's own previous Metro successes.

"Buster never complained," recalls Jerry Bresler, who was a Metro shorts producer at that time. "He went about his business, and always tried to be helpful if anyone needed his considerable talent. The only sign you'd ever have of how Buster felt about the position he was in was down in his office. He had a ratty little room down at the end of a studio alley, and when you went inside, there was a huge machine on his desk, which he'd constructed out of a couple of Erector sets. When you pressed the button, wheels began to turn, arms moved, stuff went up and down—it was a real Rube Goldberg contraption—except that it had one Keaton embellishment. At the end of the performance a little curtain was pulled aside to reveal a picture of Louis B. Mayer."

Charlie MacArthur fancied himself a rather expert chess player. During the Thirties some friends told him they'd run into a Spanish type named José Rodriguez, a perfect chess pigeon, who was looking for a match. Would MacArthur oblige? At the appointed time, in the presence of quite a large group of his friends, Rodriguez appeared, ready to play chess with MacArthur. José Rodriguez was actually Capablanco, the world's leading chess champion. MacArthur, it is said, did not catch on to his opponent's identity for quite a while.

[Peter Lorre] used to take high glee in puncturing the vanity of his employers. All in all, he succeeded remarkably well, but he feels his masterpiece was played one afternoon a few years ago when Harry Warner was conducting a delegation from the Iranian Air Force on a tour of the studio. Stepping up to the proud Warner and his gaudily uniformed guests, Lorre feigned almost uncontrollable indignation. "Listen, you creeps," he said, addressing the Iranians by his favorite term, "get those uniforms the hell back to wardrobe in a hurry."

(*from* THE ONE WITH THE MUSTACHE IS COSTELLO,
by George Frazier, Random House, 1957)

William Wellman, the director, went on location with a Metro epic entitled *Westward the Women*. His film was sent back to Metro, where it was run off for producer Dore Schary and his entourage.

The first rushes were ostensibly a rollcall of pioneer wagon-train casualties. The sound track pronounced the name of each deceased lady, as the camera panned down to a close-up of an actress, with fatal Indian arrows protruding from her anatomy.

In the middle of this visual inventory of casualties, the camera suddenly focused on a plump female, her torso liberally studded with arrows. In the corpse's hand was a copy of the Los Angeles *Examiner*. The sound-track voice intoned the name of Louella Parsons, and then another voice—familiar to millions of radio listeners—uttered the words: "My last exclusive."

At the halfway point in the writing of the script for *Moby Dick*, John Huston came in one afternoon looking grave. He handed writer Ray Bradbury a telegram which read: CANNOT PROCEED WITH FILM UNLESS SEXY FEMALE ROLE ADDED. It was signed: JACK WARNER.

"Has the man gone insane?" Bradbury shouted. "This is terrible! We can't stick a woman on board! My God, he can't be serious!"

Huston shook his head. "That's Hollywood, Ray. Warners is paying the bill, and if they want love interest, we'll just have to get it in somehow. Maybe Ahab could have an affair with Gina Lollobrigida as a disguised stowaway."

Furiously, Bradbury crumpled up the telegram and threw it to the floor. Then he looked over at Huston. "John was doubled up on the couch, laughing like a big monkey," he says. "That's when I knew *he'd* sent the thing. I was so relieved I couldn't get sore."

Both Abe Burrows and Arthur Laurents, the playwright, were patients of a California analyst, Dr. Jud Marmor. When they discovered their kinship, they both agreed to play a practical joke on their analyst. They concocted an elaborate "dream" and then both arranged to tell it to him on the same day.

First Burrows told the "dream." Then, several hours later, Laurents recounted it, word for word. The analyst nodded soberly when Laurents finished. "That's remarkable," he said. "You're the third person who's told me that same dream today."

LIFE IN FILMLAND

"Hollywood is a sewer—with service from the Ritz-Carlton."
WILSON MIZNER

"The Garden of Allah apartments is the sort of place
you expect to find down the rabbit hole."
ALEXANDER WOOLLCOTT

"Hollywood is a carnival where there are no concessions."
WILSON MIZNER

"I'm not a real movie star—I still got the same wife
I started out with nearly twenty-eight years ago."
WILL ROGERS

"It's a great place to live—if you're an orange."
FRED ALLEN

"Hollywood impresses me as being ten million dollars'
worth of intricate and highly ingenious machinery
functioning elaborately to put skin on baloney."
GEORGE JEAN NATHAN

I N the golden era of Hollywood, back in the early Twenties, it was nothing for a picture to run for a year or more, especially at a theater where Sid Grauman (aptly called "The Ziegfeld of the West") put on the premiere. So spectacular were his live-talent prologues that the audience became completely enamored with all the glamour, and no matter what the quality of the picture—good, bad, or indifferent—everyone left the theater declaring it the greatest ever filmed.

At one such premiere, the most talked-about arrival was not one of the lavishly jeweled, furred, and satined movie queens, but a plain, ordinary writer. Oh, he had plenty of movie credits and was co-author of the famous play *Alias Jimmy Valentine*, but he was definitely no Don Juan. Old-timers, however, will recall him as the wittiest wit of Hollywood. His name was Wilson Mizner. At that particular premiere, fans were screaming, oohing, and ahing over each luxurious limousine as it pulled up to the theater. Suddenly there was a shocked silence, broken only by the sound of a badly missing motor in a broken-down Ford car. The crowd craned to look and listen as the driver, faultlessly dressed in evening clothes, stepped out and handed the keys to the parking attendant, who looked haughtily at the old Ford.

"What shall I do with it?" the attendant asked.

"Keep it," said Mizner and walked blithely into the theater.

(*from* AS I REMEMBER THEM, *by Eddie Cantor, Prentice-Hall, 1960*)

"I remember my first Hollywood party," recalls Dagmar Godowsky, who was for many years a reigning silent star. "The actress Dorothy Wallace gave it, and I almost gave it back. She had a beautiful estate. To reach it, I had to walk through her lovely gardens. This was difficult. It was necessary to climb over the drunken, half-dressed bodies of Mary Pickford, Douglas Fairbanks, Thomas Meighan, Wally Reid, Gloria Swanson and sweet little Mae Marsh. They were all lying along the path in classic attitudes. It was like an obstacle race. My vamp's face remained inscrutable, but my ingénue's heart was pounding. It almost stopped when I entered the drawing room. All the stars I had just seen in the bushes were chatting very correctly and in most proper dress. Please! Dummies had been placed out there to shock the guests. This party was different."

(*from* FIRST PERSON PLURAL, *by Dagmar Godowsky, Viking, 1958*)

Harold Lloyd bought acreage in Benedict Canyon and as his film career blossomed into success, continued to add to his holdings. Eventually he had twenty acres of prime property.

According to the late Hedda Hopper, when Lloyd married Mildred Davis, his leading lady in *Grandma's Boy*, in 1923, he built himself and his bride an opulent residence—forty rooms, with two elevators, a theatre which seated a hundred guests, and a four-room dollhouse complete with electric lights, plumbing and grand piano. Around the house, which is still the Lloyd residence in 1970, he built kennels for his Great Danes, a swimming pool with a fountain, two reflecting pools and a Greek temple.

Mrs. Lloyd loved it all, then took a second look at the front door and burst into tears. What was the matter? "No keyhole!" she sobbed.

Perhaps apocryphal, but more than likely not, is the story of the Metro producer who was conducting a story conference with a pair of writers during the Rooseveltian era. "I want this to be the story of a typical American family," he said. "Just simple, ordinary people —the kind you meet every day on the street. Typical, see—the father makes about twenty thousand a year."

"I believe that God felt sorry for actors," said Sir Cedric Hardwicke, "so He created Hollywood to give them a place in the sun and a swimming pool. The price they had to pay was to surrender their talent."

(*from* A VICTORIAN IN ORBIT, *by Sir Cedric Hardwicke, Doubleday, 1961*)

Hollywood is the worst of the dope peddlers because it sells its opium under a false label. Its customers pull at the pipe in the belief that it is harmless and, when finally they give it up, find that they are still helplessly dreaming the former delusions.

(*from* THE THEATRE BOOK OF THE YEAR, 1948–49, *by George Jean Nathan, Knopf, 1949*)

HARRY RUBY

My partner Bert Kalmar and I came out here to work in Hollywood in the early Thirties, and maybe it's nostalgia, but the place was so much more fun to live and work in then. There were so many guys around who all liked each other and enjoyed drinking and talking and pulling crazy gags—Bob Benchley, Charlie Butterworth, Marc Connelly, Harpo and Groucho, and guys like that.

I remember one day Bert and I were hard at work in my house on Canon Drive. Al Newman, the conductor and musical director, had just moved into a new house up the block. He was throwing a big party that night.

We were in the middle of doing a title song for a picture at RKO when there was a knock at the door. Bert opened it, and some moving men came in. They started taking out my furniture. I was so busy working I didn't notice what was going on until the living room was almost empty. Then I jumped up and yelled, "Hey, what is this?"

Bert calmed me down. He explained that Newman was in a spot —he was giving this big party and he didn't have any furniture, so Bert had gone ahead and told him he could borrow *mine*. Well, what the hell, Al was an old friend, so I let them have the stuff. Then they started to take out the piano, and I started yelling again, "How the hell are we going to finish this song without a piano?"

"Let me see whether Al needs a piano or not," said Bert, and he called Al. Then he came back. "It's okay—we can keep the piano," he said. "Al's got a piano."

So we stayed there, in that empty room, working on the song. And Newman gave a hell of a good party—with *my* furniture."

"It *was* a hell of a party," recalls Bobby Dolan. "Newman had called up Charlie Butterworth, who lived across the street, and borrowed a couch. When the party broke up, about two in the morning, we all figured the decent thing to do would be to return Charlie's couch. So we all picked it up and started out with it, across Newman's lawn and down to Canon Drive—Harry Ruby, Bob Benchley, Marc Connelly, Butterworth and me, among others. It was a big heavy couch, and we started across Canon Drive, and then we all got bushed, so we put the thing down, and sat on it and started swapping

221

jokes and having laughs—right in the middle of the street. We could've all been killed!

"A couple of minutes later some guy in a car came up, and when his headlights picked us up, he jammed on the brakes—and started yelling at us. Can you imagine what we must have looked like, lounging on a couch in the middle of Canon Drive?

"That's when Marc Connelly turned to me and said, 'You people here in California sure know how to live.' "

"Never in my life," Nick Schenck observed once, after a walk around his Metro-Goldwyn-Mayer studio, "have I seen so many unhappy men making a hundred thousand dollars a year."

Jesse Lasky was far from being an expert golfer but he played the game with zest, especially when the stakes were high. He loved to bet on each hole with more expert players.

One afternoon he made a foursome with three good players at the Hillcrest Country Club. They teed off on the tenth hole. Instead of getting to the green, Lasky's ball flew over the fence, across the street, and onto a smaller adjoining course, the Rancho Country Club.

Lasky and his caddy trudged off the Hillcrest links, across the street, and over to Rancho, where he examined his ball. He turned to the caddy. "What kind of club should I use?" he asked.

"Mr. Lasky," said the caddy, "you tell me which course you're playing and I'll tell you what club to use."

In the great tradition of Waugh's *The Loved One*—and perhaps inspirational to that author—is the story of Paul Bern's funeral at Forest Lawn.

Bern had recently married Jean Harlow, and his death was officially called a suicide, although to this day the actual circumstances are the subject of controversy.

"I always hated funerals," recalls Donald Ogden Stewart. "And especially at Forest Lawn, where there was usually an element of bad taste involved. But John Gilbert and I went out to pay Paul our last respects.

"Everything went along quite well until the very end of the services, at which point one of the undertakers stood up and said, 'Before you all leave, I'm happy to say that you will now have an opportunity to say goodbye to your friend Paul.' With that as a signal, and aided by some piece of electrical machinery, the coffin swung around, tilted up until it was facing the crowd, and then the top of the coffin slid away, to reveal Paul Bern staring at us.

"We went out and got awfully drunk after that," adds Stewart.

There was a crowd in our bungalow at the Garden of Allah one afternoon when Don Stewart arrived in a new spring outfit, looking very elegant. To the roar of welcome and congratulations, Don replied by patting the lapel of his new coat humbly and saying, in an apologetic voice, "This spot belongs to another suit."

(*from* TOTAL RECOIL, *by Kyle Crichton, Doubleday, 1960*)

Many years ago, a *Time* senior editor was going out to Hollywood and called the Time-Life bureau chief there and said he wanted to meet a starlet at his bungalow at the Beverly Hills Hotel. The bureau chief called Harry Brand [head of publicity] at Fox and Brand said he'd get a $100-a-night girl and he'd pick up the tab. Brand kept getting a $100 tab every day, three of them. Brand called the bureau chief. The bureau chief called the senior editor at the Beverly Hills Hotel and the editor said, "It looks, the way things are going, I think in another day or two I'm gonna be able to lay her."

(*from* THE FIFTY-YEAR DECLINE AND FALL OF HOLLYWOOD, *by Ezra Goodman, Simon and Schuster, 1961*)

Harry Ruby, whose dedication to the game of baseball is well known, was holding forth at a Metro commissary table one day about the game.

Joe Mankiewicz, who had heard Ruby on the subject for many months, finally decided to test the songwriter's devotion to baseball. "Let's assume something," he said. "You're driving along a mountain road, high up. You see a precipitous cliff, with a sheer 600-foot drop to the ravine below. You look over, and you see two pairs of hands on the edge of the cliff. Two men are hanging there. They are both desperate. One of them is Joe Di Maggio, the other is your father. You have only time to save *one* of them. Which one do you save?"

"Are you kidding?" replied Ruby. "My father never hit over .218 in his life!"

* * *

"As everybody knows who's ever lived here," said Mrs. Arthur Sheekman, who was Gloria Stuart before she married the screenwriter, "all little children in Beverly Hills are constantly being given lessons.

"I remember one day when George Burns' little boy came over to visit Harpo and Susan Marx's children. They were all out in the back yard, and Alex Marx started to climb up the big tree that stood out there. George's little boy stood at the bottom, and when Alex came down, he asked, 'Who's your climbing teacher?' "

It is not generally known to those outside, but during the Thirties and the Forties, within Hollywood, there flourished a thriving and active underground press. Its equipment consisted mainly of one typewriter, a stack of carbon and typing paper, and the fertile wit of Mr. Gene Fowler.

Fowler is known to the upper world as the author of Good Night, Sweet Prince, *the biography of his good friend John Barrymore;* Schnozzola, *the life story of Durante;* Timber Line, *the saga of his first employers, Bonfils and Tammen, the owners of the* Denver Post; Beau James, *the chronicle of Mayor James J. Walker; and his autobiography,* A Solo in Tom-Toms, *as well as many other works. As a word-shaper in the celluloid factories he wrote screenplays for* Beau James, The Earl of Chicago, Billy the Kid, *and other first-rate films.*

But it is as the author of a sporadic series of unpublished classics in verse that Mr. Fowler is truly cherished by his aficionados. Retyped, mimeographed, passed from hand to hand over lunch tables, mailed from Los Angeles to New York, tucked away for safe-keeping in desk drawers, Fowler's anonymous broadsides told it like it really was—in rhyme, with satire, and with style. They were even more precious because they emanated from a walled town where honesty was always the worst policy.

Here is an example of vintage Fowler.

TESTAMENT OF A DYING HAM
by Gene Fowler

On the eve of his self-immolation—
By means of a rafter and strand—

A Hollywood mime of a happier time
Wrote his will with a resolute hand.

To the fair-weather Leeches who bled me,
Who helped me to scatter and spend,
Who flattered and licked me, but soon enough kicked me,
Who fleeced me while calling me friend . . .

To the wenches who trumped up a passion
And held a first lien on my cot,
To the simpering starlets and glee-ridden harlots
Whose sables were masking their rot . . .

To the preeners who haunt drab parties,
To the crackpots in snobbish undress,
To those bogus upstarters who flip off their garters
To pay for a puff in the Press . . .

To those impotent, credit-mad authors
Whose skulls with manure are be-crammed,
To those clap-trap extollers and stinking log-rollers
Who mince in the waltz of the damned . . .

To the venomous merchants of slander—
A conclave of pandering gnomes—
Whose seedy portmanteaus are bulging with cantos,
To poison the air of your homes . . .

To the parasite rabble of agents,
Who nibble like rats at the yield,
To those scavenging cravens, the ten-percent ravens,
Who croak o'er a gilt battlefield . . .

To the poseurs who simulate talent—
The nances, the Lesbian corps,
The cultists, the fadists, the blustering sadists,
The slime of the celluloid shore . . .

To the mountebank clan of producers,
Who hang their dull stars in the skies,
Who rifle the pockets and gouge the eye-sockets,
But never look higher than thighs . . .

Witness:
I leave them the curse of the dying;
I leave them their own fetid crowd;
I leave them the voices of midnight;
I leave them the hope of a shroud;
I leave them the groans of the fallen;
I leave them the culture of swine . . .
All this, but another—bear witness, good brother—
I leave them the fate that was mine.

Victor Saville, the British director, was assigned by Metro to direct Errol Flynn in a film version of Rudyard Kipling's *Kim,* which would be shot in India. A farewell dinner was arranged by various Hollywood performers for the director. As a fellow Englishman, Sir Cedric Hardwicke was asked to introduce Saville to the assembled guests. He was also cautioned to keep his speech short, simple and dignified. "I am delighted to be here," began Hardwicke, "to pay tribute to Victor Saville, who is leaving for India—for *Kim.*" There were no further speeches.

HOLLYWOOD JABBERWOCKY
by I. A. L. Diamond

'Twas ciros, and the cinelords
Were lollyparsing with their babes:
All goldwyns were acadawards
But demille ruled the nabes.

"Beware the Jarthurank, my lad!
The lion's claw, the eagle's wing!
And when U-I his pix, be glad
That DOS dos everything!"

He took his johnston code in hand:
Long time the ranksome foe he sought—
So rested he by the schary tree,
And stood awhile in thought.

And as in quota-quotes he stood,
The Jarthurank, of happy breed,

Came boulting through the korda wood
And caroled on his reed!

For sin! For shame! On cleavaged dame
The censor shears went flicker-flack!
He scarred the Bard, and coward marred
Went gallupolling back.

"And hast thou haysed the Jarthurank?
Come to my arms, my breenish boy!
O date and day! Elate! L.A.!"
He xenophobed with joy.

'Twas ciros, and the cinelords
Were lollyparsing with their babes:
All goldwyns were acadawards
But demille ruled the nabes.

(*from* THE SCREEN WRITER)

The late William Goetz was an art collector and, as such, became
involved in a controversy over a Van Gogh painting of doubtful
authenticity which he brought from Europe. Out of the immense
publicity given to this painting sprang one of Goetz's most anguished
remarks.

He was invited to an advance showing of *Lust for Life,* in which
Kirk Douglas played the role of Van Gogh. When the picture ended,
Vincente Minnelli, the director, asked Goetz what he thought of its
commercial possibilities. "You've got nothing to worry about," Goetz
remarked wryly. "If everybody who owns a Van Gogh goes to see the
picture, it should be very successful."

WALTER PIDGEON

I was like a kept woman during my twenty-one years at MGM.
Hollywood was like an expensive, beautifully run club. You didn't
need to carry money. Your face was your credit card—all over the
world.

(*from* CONFESSIONS OF A HOLLYWOOD COLUMNIST,
by Sheilah Graham, Morrow, 1969)

The Wit and Wisdom of Hollywood
TODAY'S EFFUSION
by Robert Benchley

A careful perusal of the effusions of Hollywood press-agents would indicate that the members of the movie colony lead strangely similar lives, think strangely similar thoughts, and are moved by strangely similar instinct. Following are examples of what the press-agents seem to feel is the Full Life in Hollywood.

Funny coincidence on the way to the studio the other day on the part of Cleo Klieg. She was driving along when a little boy ran right in the path of her car and stole a front tire. Cleo stopped (she is crazy about kids) and although she was already ten minutes late on account of having had to take her mother to task, she asked the little shaver what his name was. "Cleo Klieg," was the instant reply. "That's funny," said Cleo, "that's my name too." . . . And it was.

Nothing seems to upset Margate Lemming. Although she has been working at Screeno Studios for three years, she didn't recognize the gateman when she drove in the other morning, and he had to go to the Front Office to get identified before *she* would let *him* let *her* through the gate.

Nice gesture on the part of Ralph Ralph, sending his hairdresser to finishing school. . . . Great fun on the set of *How's My Ankle?* the other day. George Thrin didn't show up. George is an ardent Victory gardener. . . . Nice gesture on the part of Thelma Olay, paying every cent of her income tax for 1940. . . . According to Bill Bortsch, the way to a man's mouth is through his stomach. Bill, by the way, has nine Victory gardens. . . . Bob Benchley is going to drive East in a Stanley Steamer with five midgets. . . . Nice gesture on the part of Mansard Mann, leaving home. . . . If you believe Anderson Ord, the way to a man's mouth is through his stomach.

Two years ago Marion Merk, who was then modeling seams in New York, was approached by a nondescript tattooed man who asked her for carfare to go to Hollywood to do camouflage work. She gave it to him and forgot the incident, except that she had an IOU for $140 signed: "Joe Indeldorf." A year later Marion came out to Hollywood herself to get some rain for her sinus trouble. Last month, while sitting on a stool in a drugstore, a man came up to her and asked her if she would like to go into pictures. She thought that he looked vaguely familiar, but gave the matter no thought until he handed her his card and told her to look him up at Superdupe. The name on the card was Arthur J. Wash!

Nice gesture on the part of Teal Wringer, helping the crew of his picture *I Saw Double* to get off early Saturday afternoon by collapsing on the set. . . . When Martin Drag was a kid, he always wanted to be a lawyer. Now that he is set in pictures, he is being sued, and gets a great kick out of it. . . . Lila Lint believes that the way to a man's mouth is through his stomach. . . .

Life's a funny proposition after all, according to Andy Beestring. The other day when the gateman at the studio didn't recognize him, he took a train for New York and is now in the importing business.

Funny coincidence on the part of Bea Vospich the other day. A group of autograph hounds rushed up and wanted to sign their names on her back. One of them looked vaguely familiar to her and she asked his name. "Joe Indeldorf," he said, the very same Joe Indeldorf who had borrowed railway fare from Marion Merk about three paragraphs above.

Nice gesture on the part of Bob Benchley, writing this column for Edith Gwynn on his way East in a Stanley Steamer with five midgets. Bob claims that the way to a man's mouth is through his stomach.

(from THE HOLLYWOOD REPORTER, 1943)

Frances and Albert Hackett are a highly successful married pair of writers who have functioned as well on Broadway as they have in writing for the screen. One evening in Hollywood they were dinner guests at an elaborate party at which other guests included the late Erich Wolfgang Korngold, the composer, and his wife. The following day Mrs. Hackett called to thank her hostess and they chatted. "How did you like the Korngolds?" asked the hostess. "Oh, they were delicious," said Frances.

"Everybody kisses everybody else in this crummy business all the time," said Ava Gardner. "It's the kissiest business in the world. You *have* to keep kissing people when you're penned up and working together the way we are. If people making a movie didn't keep kissing, they'd be at each other's throats."

George Jessel once described Romanoff's as "the place where a man can take his family and have a lovely seven-course dinner for $3,400."

* * *

Martin Ragaway is a comedy writer and wit who has labored long in the West Coast vineyards. One day an Eastern friend showed up, preparatory to moving to L.A. permanently, and Ragaway took it upon himself to show his old friend the town. Later as they sat drinking and enjoying the local fleshpots, Marty nodded soberly at his friend, who was having himself a time. "You know something?" he remarked. "You'll never know how dull this town is until you move here with your wife and kids."

Gene Fowler was with a small group of intimate friends of the late Lionel Barrymore, waiting for the actor's funeral services to commence, when he suddenly grasped Red Skelton's leg just as the comedian was about to stomp a spider. "Don't!" Fowler whispered in a spectral voice. "It might be Lionel!"

(*from* THIS WAS HOLLYWOOD, *by Beth Day, Doubleday, 1960*)

Ken Murray once defined Hollywood as a place where you spend more than you make, on things you don't need, to impress people you don't like.

One day at the Paramount commissary, Irving Brecher was at a table with some friends when they were joined by Y. Frank Freeman, the genial Southern gentleman then in charge of the studio.

Brecher was recounting the good luck he and his wife had had in employing a housekeeper. Traveling from New York on the Super Chief, he had got into conversation with his dining-car waiter, who had recommended his wife as an excellent housekeeper. Subsequently the Brechers had hired her, and she had proved to be a jewel. A few months later the dining-car waiter had retired from railroad service and had come to work for the Brechers as a live-in butler.

"He must give you marvelous service," remarked Freeman.

"Absolutely marvelous," said Brecher, deadpan, "but with one small drawback. He never flushes the toilet while our house is standing still."

Harry Tugend was asked how he had managed to stay happily married to his wife, Jean, for more than forty years. "It's a matter of compatibility," said Tugend. "We both love to fight."

230

*   *   *

On his CBS television show Danny Kaye worked with another golfer, a director named Foster, who during the war had been a paratrooper. The TV schedule allowed them only Sunday for golf, so Kaye and Foster worked out a schedule. Early Sunday morning they drove to the Burbank airport, got into Kaye's plane and flew a brief half-hour down to Palm Springs. Foster, wearing his parachute and golf bag, dropped from Kaye's plane onto the course, hurried over to the clubhouse and signed the pair up for early tee-off.

One Sunday morning Kaye dropped Foster, but the wind blew the parachute slightly off course and Foster found himself dropping down directly in the path of a nice old gentleman playing through the hole. He yelled from above, but the old gentleman (deaf, as it turned out) paid no attention and concentrated on his swing. When he looked up to see a man with a golf bag, parachuting down on him, the Sabbath golfer fainted.

Sonja Henie was emerging as an extravagant hostess. At a gathering for two hundred at her Bel Air estate, with the tent breezing atop the boarded-over swimming pool, sculptured ice dripping all over the place, and Hoagy Carmichael at the piano, the ex-ice queen announced dinner in rhyme, in her excruciating accent. When an old-timer at the party talked about the good old days of Pickfair parties, Jack Warner reprimanded him. "My boy, *these* are the good old days."

During the late Sixties when Shirley Temple, the child star of the Thirties, was running for office in California, political posters appeared which consisted of large blow-ups of ten-year-old Shirley beaming out at the populace. Underneath were the words: IF YOU DON'T VOTE FOR ME, I'LL HOLD MY BREATH.

POLITICS, RELIGION AND CENSORS

HOLLYWOOD is every public man's pigeon. There is no editorial writer so dull that he can't straighten out the movies on an average of four times a year. There is no preacher who can't get at least three rousing sermons annually out of Hollywood. There is not even a Congressman so benighted that he can't speak with confidence on what ought to be done about that business out there. Surely someone ought to talk back.

Not that this situation itself hasn't its usefulness. A man in Opelika, Alabama, goes out into the barn and throws a stout rope over a scantling. He is a failure. Life has finally licked him but good. He can't make a living, he can't keep a wife, he isn't even competent enough to be elected to public office. If he could even think of one subject, no matter how small or insignificant, of which he could feel he was master. But no, he's gone over his list time and time again, and he knows now that he knows literally from nothing. He is a complete and indisputable cipher.

Then, with the noose already tightening around his gullet, he suddenly remembers Hollywood. Removing the rope, he gets down off the barrel and walks out into the world again, a new man with new strength. There is one subject on which he is prepared to speak with authority! So, as long as Hollywood stands, no freeborn American need surrender to an inferiority complex. It is the greatest boon to psychiatrists since sex. Hollywood never gets the credit due it.

NUNNALLY JOHNSON

Leo McCarey, who was responsible for *Going My Way* and *The Bells of St. Mary's,* was a Catholic. One day he was being questioned by a persistent interviewer, who turned the conversation to the subject of the religious tinge in McCarey's films.

"Tell me why it is," asked the interviewer, "that Hollywood is so concerned with subjects involving Catholics. Why doesn't anyone ever make a film about a Jewish rabbi or a Protestant minister?"

McCarey pondered the question.

"Hollywood *did* make a picture about a minister," he replied. *"Rain."*

* * *

235

The Wit and Wisdom of Hollywood

During his years as a highly successful screenwriter, Donald Ogden Stewart worked on many Metro-Goldwyn-Mayer films and won an Academy Award for his adaptation of Philip Barry's *The Philadelphia Story.*

Stewart saw nothing untoward in holding leftist political views. Conversely, so long as his films turned a good profit, his Republican boss, L. B. Mayer, saw no reason to dispense with Stewart's services.

Stewart did a screenplay called *Keeper of the Flame,* which was made with Katharine Hepburn and Spencer Tracy, and in it were embodied some strong anti-fascist statements. For some reason Mayer had not seen the picture during production and did not attend a screening of it until he got to New York, where it was showing, to packed houses, at the Radio City Music Hall.

"L.B. was so angry at that picture," recalls Stewart, "that he got up in the middle of it and stamped out of the Music Hall."

During the Congressional hearings, some writers, rather than take the Fifth Amendment, testified to their knowledge of so-called "Communist" infiltration. At Warner Brothers, some of those same writers ended up with jobs. Perhaps it was a payoff on the part of management. Whatever it was, a sign appeared in the Warner commissary one day: IT IS NOT ENOUGH TO HAVE INFORMED—YOU MUST ALSO HAVE TALENT.

The practice of blacklisted writers using pseudonyms produced ludicrous situations. "Bob Rogers" had done a script for one producer. A few weeks later, as "Dick Jones," he was called in to confer with a second producer. This producer had just acquired a script which needed rewrites. Would "Dick" be interested? He passed over a screenplay written by "Bob Rogers." ("Bob Rogers" and "Dick Jones" were Walter Bernstein.)

At a time when the industry was being harassed by Congressional hearings, and was very sensitive to political pressure, Jerry Wald insisted that he would continue to make pictures that said something valid. He showed *Johnny Belinda,* with Jane Wyman, at the Warner home office, and when it was over he approached one of the New

Yorkers. "Bold and fearless, right?" he demanded. "Can't say I don't have guts, can you?"

"No, Jerry," said the New Yorker. "You certainly came out flat-footedly against deafness."

As the omnipresent Billy Wilder said, "Blacklist, schmacklist, as long as they're all working." And he added: ". . . of the Unfriendly Ten only two have talent—the other eight are just unfriendly."
(*from* THE FIFTY-YEAR DECLINE AND FALL OF HOLLYWOOD, *by Ezra Goodman, Simon and Schuster, 1961*)

Apocryphal or no, this is the story. In the late Forties, when the political clouds were lowering over various liberal and left-wing writers and the Thomas committee hearings were threatening, a writer friend of George Raft asked him to help in the raising of a defense fund. "These guys are getting a bum rap, George," he insisted. "It's up to us to take a stand against government harassment, political censorship and blacklisting. These guys need your help!" Raft's eyes narrowed, and then slowly he remarked, "Yeah? So where were they when Bugsy [Siegel] was in trouble?"

Dorothy Parker squelched a drunk, who nagged her in a bar during the unpleasant period of her blacklisting in the late Forties: "With the crown of thorns I wear, why should I be bothered with a prick like you?"

While directing *Heaven Knows, Mr. Allison* on Tobago, John Huston was informed that an official studio representative was headed for the island in order to check out any remaining elements in the script which might prove censorable. Huston immediately set up a scene for him to witness. "We've added this new sequence to the film," Huston told the man upon his arrival. "Thought you'd enjoy watching us shoot it."

The censor seemed pleased at the opportunity, but as the sequence progressed, he began to turn pale. "Great Scott!" he whispered to Huston. "Mr. Mitchum is *seducing* the nun! This is absolutely horrible! You can't allow—" Huston told him to be quiet,

237

that it was too late now to make any further script changes. What the sweating censor didn't know was that Huston was directing the scene behind an empty camera.

In commenting on taboos imposed on movies "by organized pressure groups or else by unorganized but highly vocal minorities with a taste for outsize fig leaves," Wolcott Gibbs observed: "This makes it impracticable to name political philosophies or explain what they stand for, to discuss religion in any terms conceivably startling to the inmates of a parochial school or a Baptist seminary, to speak disparagingly of any specific business, except, perhaps, dope-running or the white-slave trade, or to deal with sex in any way that might indicate that minor irregularities are not necessarily punishable by a lifetime of social ostracism and a lonely and untended grave."
(*from* THE FIFTY-YEAR DECLINE AND FALL OF HOLLYWOOD, *by Ezra Goodman, Simon and Schuster, 1961*)

GENE FOWLER'S TEN COMMANDMENTS FOR THE MOTION PICTURE INDUSTRY (1936)

1st Commandment

Thou shalt not photograph a lady and gentleman in bed together, even though said lady and gentleman have been properly introduced, one to the other. Thou mayst try it but thou wilt get thyself into one hell of a jam. In the wicked city of Chicago, minions of the law did break in and find one buckaroo in such aforesaid state with two ladies of blonde extraction and he did cry out that he learned such trick from the movies. To wit that such scenes are hereby decreed subversive of the public morals.

2nd Commandment

Thou shalt avoid rape as the pestilence and shalt not show the villain having his foul way with the fair of our land, lest it giveth idea to the gentler sex and causeth consternation in the American scene.

3rd Commandment

Thou shalt not photograph the wiggling belly, the gleaming thigh or the winking navel, especially to music, as goings-on of this ilk sorely troubleth the little boys of our land and so crammeth the theatres with adolescence that papa cannot find a seat.

4th Commandment

Have not thy little dramas in the house of prostitution, the bawdy house or the place of call, for thou givest thereby free advertising to another industry and wilt, anyway, find thyself in the clutch of the law.

5th Commandment

Thou shalt not have thy hero smack a lady in the puss, as these acts of violence giveth idea to the husband and disturbeth the American family.

6th Commandment

Eschew the gangster picture as thou wouldst the plague, nor display the profits of crime by having the tough guys flash a roll. If thou bumpest off one mug too many, thou'll find thy shekels wasting away from the coffers and thy studio in the hock shop.

7th Commandment

Thou shalt not have thy gentry kick each other's teeth out, nor fill the belly full of lead—not burn nor torture thy victims, lest it giveth the more delicate soul to puke and ruineth valuable theatre equipment.

8th Commandment

If thou givest thy audience a stick-up, thou'll be damn careful, for thou art giving idea to the immature dope, with which our fair land aboundeth in plenty, and thou'll find thyself up the creek in New York and Pennsylvania—places of money.

9th Commandment

Thou shalt not give tongue to vulgar expressions, to wit, "Nuts," for such invective hath a peculiar significance to the spinsters of this world and is held by them as having a biological import.

10th Commandment

Love thy foreign brother as thyself and call him not Chink nor Wop nor Greaseball—lest thou findst thy country at war and thy studio up for sale by the Marshal.

* * *

The Wit and Wisdom of Hollywood
HOLLWOOD'S 23RD PSALM
by Gene Fowler

Will Hays is my shepherd, I shall not want.

He maketh me to lie down in clean postures.

He purgeth me with bilge-waters.

He forecloseth my soul. He leadeth me in the paths of self-righteousness, for the game's sake.

Yea, though I walk through the alley of the shadow of debt, I will fear no drivel; for the Purity Seal is with me; Will's prod and Will's gaff, they confound me.

He prepareth a fable before me in the presence of my betters; He anointeth my head with banana oil; my heels runneth over.

Surely mediocrity and pelf shall follow me all the days of my life; and I will smell in the house of art forever.

As writer-producer Claude Binyon said, "Hollywood must never permit censorship to collapse—it's far too good for the box office!"

GENE FOWLER

Now that the Ulysses of Mr. Joyce has been anointed with judicial oils, it would appear that something can be done to garrote censorship in general. The wit-nit babblings, stale violet fancies and imbecile-antics of censors have been negatived somewhat in the so-called literary field. Just why the motion picture industry has not tweaked the indigo noses of the censorial eunuchs is not clear.

The press wears a chastity belt by constitutional right, and any newspaper unincumbered by corporate control or other corrupt leanings may move virtuously and breathe legally. The editor, functioning within the sphere of his publisher's policy, guards against such libels as might threaten his economic structure and rules out such obscenities as might alienate his readers. While amenable to all manner of one-horse laws, the more modern purveyors of information, propaganda and entertainment—the cinema and the radio— have no specific and firm foundation assuring them a decent freedom of expression. This condition directly hampers the writers of pictures, confronting them with such monumental problems as: "How much of Harlow's leg may we show in Kansas?"

Whenever anyone makes a plea for freedom of any sort, the bible-benders and thyroidic hymnsters set up a yammer. Guided by their own strangled preferences—were they free to act and had the necessary vigor of gland—they cry that license, not liberty, is the pole star of the petitioner. Yet, in a script, the very stifling of convincing dialogue or honest situation leads to a condition far more deplorable than the presentation of an open effect openly arrived at.

The producer, director and writer, shackled like a troupe of rheumatic Houdinis, connive, scheme and risk mental hernia to circumvent the censor. Resultant scenes ofttimes are so dizzy that they offend discerning spectators and drive morons into the park to swing little girls.

I remember a scene in which Mr. Somebody suddenly carried Miss Somebody Else into another room for purposes which presumably were giddy and gay. This was allowed—the scene I am speaking of—provided no beds were shown and no dialogue was used to identify the chamber of horrors. Still, I don't think anyone looking on and drooling the while, believed the lad and lassie were bent upon counting their beads. The scene following was a masterpiece of censorial evasion. The ostermoor arena was DARK. But there were subdued noises, such as are identified with biological well-being. And then we saw two small lights—indicating a pair of cigarettes—being waved like the batons of weary orchestra leaders. Of course, we of bawdy minds never once dreamed that anybody was in bed—or on the floor—smoking those cigarettes. We all thought we were glimpsing the nuptial zooming of fireflies.

A confection such as cited above does not strike me as an important contribution to the arts or sciences. It merely confuses one's sense of honest taste, or compels the less sturdy of our kind to reach over and pinch Mrs. McGillicuddy's bustle. Monsieur Rosenblatt should interview the ushers on this phase of national fun.

So long as a movie creator indulges in a hundred-yard dash of innuendo, a few furlongs of double entendre, depicts his hero and heroine in coats of mail while hanging from pretzel-shaped trapezes, he is permitted to put over the idea that a shot-gun wedding is in the cards.

The animalistic embrace is allowable and certifiable only on the following conditions:

1. If a lot of mumbo-jumbo words are said over the grappling twain, attesting to matrimony.
2. If the senor and senorita are blindfolded and riding back-to-back on a wild horse about to go over a cliff.
3. If accompanied by the magic words: "Come up and see me sometime."

241

Every writer should endeavor to kick this picayune censorship directly in the groin. Presumably the producers won't, or can't, do anything about it. Armed with the greatest publicity weapon of all time—the picture—the moguls do not realize what opportunity is theirs in the field of militant propaganda and for sound causes.

What would happen if a choir of pelvic jailors were to censor the newspapers? A political blast such as would change Congressional seats and drive the hecklers back to the Black Forest. What would happen if the picture people were to boycott the penny ante politicians, keeping their mugs out of the newsreels (else showing their noses in Technicolor), unleashing films of the *Gabriel Over the White House* variety, exposing the sham and insincerity of the moral guardians?

Of course we have a few boys here, who—without a checkrein—would go on a rowdy spree. This is evidenced by the tendency to overdo each new and arresting word that comes to the screen. I am thinking of the still unburied and timesome slang, such as the word "Scram" and the constantly recurring "Nuts." Perhaps I am too naive, but I was fourteen years old before I realized that nuts grew on trees.

The broad views on censorship as held in the gallant state of California have not demoralized anyone. Of a certainty, those views—like so many other paternalistic slants—were fostered by a pecuniary desire to pamper local industry. But the result is the important thing to consider.

If writers continue to be bludgeoned and hamstrung by censorship, pictures will continue to be dull and misleading. How to cope with all the verbotens that make Burgomaster Hays' headquarters look like the dead letter office is beyond the ken of any author. Gulliver is held by Liliputian strings.

Inane censorship is one reason a writer goes back to New York feeling as useless as the male udder. Of course, there are other reasons, but why say "boo" to the firing squad?

(*from* THE HOLLYWOOD REPORTER, *1934*)

Mark Hellinger, the columnist and producer, was fond of the remark made by Laurette Taylor about Frank Fay, the comedian. In his later years Fay became violently reactionary, and was voluble in calling some actors anti-Catholic Communists. "For years they've been looking for the Holy Grail," the actress said, "and all this time Frank Fay's been drinking out of it."

* * *

Once a year, show business breaks out with a collective rash, symptomatic of awards fever. In Hollywood, it's the Academy Awards—all those golden Oscars which serve to bolster box-office grosses and egos. In New York, producers are holding their breath to see which play, which performer, which playwright will carry home a Tony. Latterly, both coasts join electronic hands to celebrate the bounties of the past television season with Emmy Awards.

Tony, Oscar, Emmy—all of the attendant rituals that go along with their bestowal have been properly televised to an anxiously waiting world. Those precious Prince Waterhouse envelopes are torn open, there are the de rigueur *gasps, the tears, the firm handclasps—and that set speech in which the temporarily humble winner thanks everyone who helped, up to and including his mother's midwife. There are the not-so-gracious quips by emcees, and, of course, brief pauses for messages from sponsors, somewhat redundantly urging the world outside to capture this precious moment on film.*

But the outside spectator has never, alas, been party to the best awards dinner. It's the annual Writers Guild of America banquet, at which film writers, those usually anonymous gallery slaves without whom there never would have been any Oscars at all, gather to honor their own.

Two tickets to the WGA awards banquet are harder to come by than a pair to Broadway's Tony winner. It's not the food nor the company that draws the packed house—it's the after-dinner show, written and produced by Hollywood's brightest (and often most frustrated) minds. Sketches, musical numbers and blackouts are performed by a cast of top-drawer stars, who for one show at least are guaranteed good material. So scathing and sharp and ribald are the satiric slings and arrows hurled at the audience that no TV network would dare to put this ninety-minute show on a home screen.

It was at the dinner in 1967 that Groucho Marx (with a written assist from Hal Kanter) remarked: "I can't understand why some Easterners think it's unusual that California elected Reagan. After all, the state is just going along with the political trend. One of our major industries is motion pictures, so our Governor is an actor. In New York, the

243

nation's financial center, their Governor is a multi-millionaire financier. In Michigan, the home of the automobile industry, their Governor is a car manufacturer. In Georgia, the state that grows the bulk of our nation's papershell pecans, they elected a nut. I wouldn't be surprised if the next Governor of Florida is a grapefruit."

It was in the same Writers Guild awards show that Mary Tyler Moore and Shelley Berman performed a piece of material by Jay Livingstone and Ray Evans, a top-rank songwriting team, entitled "The Rabbi and The Nun." Here, with the kind permission of its authors, is the first reprinting of their somewhat anti-clerical-rabbinicae musical-comedy broadside, the definitive R.I.P. to Hollywood's "religious films."

THE RABBI AND THE NUN

by Jay Livingstone and Ray Evans

Nun: Mary Tyler Moore; Rabbi: Shelley Berman.

NUN: Hosannah and hail,
A new era has begun.
A brand-new career
Is waiting for ev'ry nun.
For now that *The Sound of Music*
Is making the box office pay,
I get more offers than Doris Day does
And G.A.C.
Is looking out for me
And I'm on—my—way!
The hills are alive
With the sound of music,
And each singing nun
Is a brand-new star!

RABBI (*Interrupting*): Wait, I'd like to say a few words on behalf of . . . What do you mean—every singing nun is a brand-new star? I protest! The Jews are taking over show business. Is there a Jew in the orchestra? (*Orchestra reacts.*) Give me an intro.
Us rabbis ain't done bad,
We're now what folks prefer;
Since *Fiddler on the Roof*

Was blessed by Walter Kerr!
And when they make *The Fiddler on the Roof*,
Oh what a fancy movie,
What a bofferoo!
And on the way to picking up my Oscar
I will tip my hat to you!

NUN: I beg your pardon, Father.

RABBI: Father?

NUN: I've been in show business for over a year now, and I know what audiences want.

RABBI: You do? Tell me.

NUN: Candles, cathedrals, and Joseph and Mary,
Nuns who play baseball and Leo McCarey;
Mike Conn'lly's column and angels with wings—
These are a few of their favorite things!

RABBI: I beg *your* pardon, sister. My people have been in show business for five thousand years. *We* know what audiences want!
Tallises, temples, and cantors and knishes,
Doctors and lawyers and two sets of dishes;
Joyous Bar Mitzvahs where George Jessel sings—
These are a few of their favorite things!

NUN: Excuse me, sir. Are you aware that in the current movie *The Sound of Music*, the expected gross is $23,643,982.51 domestic . . . fourteen mil American and nine mil European . . . and in addition to expecting return on the negative cost within the first three months, it also received a smash review and had a boff opening?

RABBI: This is what they learn in a convent? Look, listen to me. I'm a wise old man.

NUN: I don't mean to be disrespectful . . . I know this wonderful priest who has taught for many, many years, and if you don't mind my saying so, a priest is much smarter than a rabbi.

RABBI: He should be, you tell him everything.

NUN: Anything you can do, I can do better;
I can do anything better than you!

RABBI: No you can't!

NUN: Yes I can!

RABBI: No you can't!

NUN: Yes I can!

RABBI: No you can't!

NUN: Yes I can! Yes I can!

RABBI: Anything?

NUN: Anything.

RABBI: I need a *donation* from somebody. We need a new wing for the temple. Tell me, madame, have you ever officiated at a bris?

I

NUN: Oh Mr. Rabbi, Oh Mr. Rabbi,
They will make more movies 'bout my kind of folks;
We're the kind the Legion likes
As they try to stem the dikes
'Gainst the nudie pictures and the naughty jokes!

RABBI: Oh Sainted Sister, Oh Sainted Sister,
In the world of show biz we have just begun;
Have you heard the latest dope?
We've been pardoned by the Pope!

NUN: Absolutely, Mr. Rabbi?

RABBI: Positively, Mrs. Nun!

II

NUN: Oh Mr. Rabbi, Oh Mr. Rabbi,
We love pictures in a strong religious vein;
Everything inside us glows
When the Holy Water flows!

RABBI: We can get that feeling with a two-cents plain!
Oh Sainted Sister, Oh Sainted Sister,
I'll be such a ruddy hit with everyone
They'll invite me to the pub
At the L.A. Country Club!

NUN: Do you mean it, Mr. Rabbi?

RABBI: Hallelujah, Mrs. Nun!

III

NUN: Oh Mr. Rabbi, Oh Mr. Rabbi,
We can finance all our pictures on our own;
Rome has ev'ry cent we need
And the source is guaranteed!

RABBI: *We* just have to call Bart Lytton on the phone!
Oh Sainted Sister, Oh Sainted Sister,
We know how to do a show that has a run;
We'll do stories that are new,
We'll make Irene Dunne a Jew!

NUN: Hardly likely, Mr. Rabbi!

RABBI: Don't be chicken, Mrs. Nun!

(DANCE)

IV

NUN: Oh Mr. Rabbi,

RABBI: Oh Sainted Sister,

NUN: Oh Mr. Rabbi,

RABBI: Oh Sainted Sister,

NUN: We have Bing and Dennis Day to guard our forts;

RABBI: Sammy Davis is our boy,
Mrs. Burton we enjoy,
Not to mention Milton Berle and Bernie Schwartz!

NUN: Oh Mr. Rabbi,

RABBI: Oh Sainted Sister,

NUN: Oh Mr. Rabbi,

RABBI: Oh Sainted Sister,

NUN: How can you compete with everything we've done?
We have Churches like Saint Pat's,

RABBI: We have Balaban and Katz!

NUN: We have men like Bishop Sheen,

RABBI: We have Mirisch and Leveen!

NUN: We look saintly in our hoods!

RABBI: But we sold you the goods!

NUN: (*Pondering a moment*) Absolutely, Mr. Rabbi?

RABBI: At a rebate, Mrs. Nun!
Join us . . . join us, sister . . . do you hear me? Everything, everything in show business is Jewish . . . Jewish.

NUN: Everything in show business is Jewish?

RABBI: Everything. Writers . . . all the writers are Jewish.

NUN: All the writers are Jewish?

RABBI: All the good ones.

NUN: Excuse me, sir. George Bernard Shaw . . . a Jew?

RABBI: You saw his beard? Everything . . . etc.

NUN: What about the directors?

RABBI: Jews . . . Jews . . . all of them.

NUN: Excuse me, sir, John Ford is Jewish?

RABBI: You saw his latest picture, *Chayam Autumn*? But who is this Dominique you're always singing about?

NUN: Who's Bernie Schwartz?

RABBI: Bernie Schwartz? That's Tony Curtis.

NUN: Now wait just a minute. Tony's an Italian name.

247

RABBI: *Forget it!* Do you know that Kirk Douglas . . .

NUN: Him too?

RABBI: I could give you names . . . I'll name some Jews. I'll show you who's better.

NUN: Frank Capra . . .

RABBI: Otto Preminger . . .

NUN: Leo McCarey . . .

RABBI: George Sidney . . . and he takes pictures too.

NUN: David Lean . . .

RABBI: (*A beat*) Sidney Miller . . .

NUN: Mervyn Leroy . . .

RABBI: Him you can have.

NUN: Tallulah Bankhead . . .

RABBI: Sylvia Sidney . . .

NUN: Katharine Hepburn . . .

RABBI: Leo Fuchs . . .

NUN: Shelley Winters . . .

RABBI: Him you can have too.

NUN: Mary Martin . . .

RABBI: Julie Andrews . . .

NUN: Julie Andrews? Audrey Hepburn I know, but Julie Andrews? (*Groping*) Lucky Luciano . . .

RABBI: A reformed Jew.

NUN: Dr. Schweitzer . . .

RABBI: A doctor?

NUN: Cardinal Spellman . . .

RABBI: Sam Spellman from Boston.

NUN: Oh . . . the next thing you'll be saying . . . our Beloved . . . (*she looks up*)

RABBI: The first one.

BOTH: Let's do everything we can
For the brotherhood of man!
Absolutely, Mr. Rabbi!

NUN: It's funny, you don't *look* Jewish—

RABBI: Positively, Mrs. Nun!

(from WGAw NEWS, 1966)

Barney Dean was a vaudevillian who became a gag-writer. He was a diminutive, cheerful man with a droll sense of humor, gifted with the ability to ad-lib. Most of his days were spent on the set of Bob Hope or Bing Crosby pictures, where he stood by, ready to toss lines when they were needed for a particular scene.

On the set of *The Bells of Saint Mary's*, the Leo McCarey picture in which Bing Crosby was co-starring with Ingrid Bergman, Barney was standing next to Crosby when Miss Bergman, radiant in her nun's habit, made her first appearance on the sound stage.

In an undertone, Crosby said to Dean, who was Jewish, "Hey, Barney, could you roll in the hay with her if she were a real nun?"

"Bing," sighed Dean, "I'd roll in the hay with her if she were a real rabbi."

THE BUSBYS OF BERKELEY

by Jay Livingston and Ray Evans

ANNOUNCER

At this time we take great pride in presenting a remake of one of the great musicals of 1928. Naturally, colleges have changed a little bit and we had to make a few alterations. Ladies and gentlemen, the Writers Guild presents the first college musical of 1967—*The Busbys of Berkeley.*

We open on a rousing chorus of college students, all in modern dress. They are all singing.

ALL:

C'llegiate, c'llegiate,
Yes we are collegiate,
Nothing intermejut,
No ma'am!
We're so active
And we're quite attractive,
It's so satisfactive,
Yes ma'am!

3 GIRLS:

Mommy, Daddy,
They don't understand:

3 BOYS:

They're the finks who just elected Ronnie Reagan!

ALL:

Never quiet,
Protest is our diet,

BOY:

Got an "A" in riot!

249

ALL:
We're collegiate, rah rah rah!

SQUARE:
(*Wearing a raccoon coat and a beanie and carrying a pennant that says, "Busby—1927." Whether he has dropped out of a time tunnel to our modern-day musical or is here for an alumni reunion or is still going to school, heaven only knows.*)

Hey, gang, let's all go down to the Sugar Bowl and have a strawberry malt.

1ST BOY:
Man, have you flipped? Let's grab our chicks and have a little groovy togetherness.

2ND BOY:
Great idea, Ollie. Where'll we go?

1ST BOY:
Where'll we go? Where else?

ALL:
Down the old Ox Road,

SQUARE:
Yesterday we used to take her there
And kisses we'd steal,

BOY:
But today the proposition's like a real-estate deal;
We pick out our private plot
And like as not the little coed will be
Soon e-scrowed

ALL:
Down the old Ox Road!

GIRLS:
Yes sir, there's no baby,
Take that pill,
Don't say maybe,
Yes sir,
There's no baby now!

SQUARE:
Hey, gang, let's all go over to the Dean's house and swallow his goldfish.

GIRL:
Goldfish? Ycch! I got a better idea. Let's leave the scene and fly to a happier world.

BOY:
Whatcha got in mind?

250

ALL:

Maybe a pill, maybe some pot,
Candy it ain't,
Tobacco it's not,

BOY:

That's the way to get that
Varsity Jag—

GIRL:

Check with your druggist!

ALL:

Hire a house, hire a hall,
Take off your clothes,
Climb up the wall,
That's the way to do the
Varsity Jag!

SQUARE:

The moon belongs to everyone,
But the best things in life are

2 BOYS, 2 GIRLS:

Tea for two
And two for tea;
A puff for you,
A puff for me!

ALL:

'Cause
Everything is
Psychedelic,
Ain't we got fun?
When you wanna
Be rebel-ic,
Join in the fun.

BOY:

I'm feelin' weary,
I'd like to get high;

SQUARE:

Call Dr. Leary

STUDENTS:

And learn how to fly!

SQUARE AND STUDENTS:

Votie-oatie,

STUDENTS:

Try peyote
And make the scene;

SQUARE AND STUDENTS:

Poopie-doopie,

STUDENTS:

Join the groupie

For mescaline!

BOY:

There's nothin' sweeter

Than the intercollegiate Dolce Vita!

SQUARE AND STUDENTS:

Everything is

Psychedelic,

Ain't we got fun!

SQUARE:

Hey, gang, I think I'm catchin' on. What you want me to do is get turned on at a freakout. Or is it freaked on at a turnout?

BOY:

You were right the first time, fella. C'mon, grab your steady date and let's go!

SQUARE:

(He looks closely at two people with very long hair)

I will if I can!

Who's my little whoozis?

Who's my turtle dove?

Which of you is female,

Which do I love?

Student enters carrying his own platform. Standing on it, he says:

STUDENTS:

I was an exchange student for the CIA.

(Then he sings plaintively)

Ma, they made a spy of me!!

He immediately steps down and a girl speaker takes his place.

GIRL:

Is it our fault? Did we make this mess!? Did we ask to be born? ONE WORLD! Forty worlds is more like it.

As the group takes up song. She continues her harangue, but she is just mouthing words.

SQUARE:

Three cheers for Betty!

ALL:

(Raising fists in Communist salute)

Hip hip hooray!

Hip hip hooray!
Hip hip hooray!

Betty Coed has lips of red for Moscow
Betty Coed just hates the p'liceman's blue;
Betty Coed can handle prose that's purple
And lie across the road when troops are due.
Betty Coed knows how to get arrested,
How to get pushed and hit upon the head;
Wouldn't you like to leave your books
And cares behind
And shack up in a cell with Betty Coed!

SQUARE:
Gosh, I do love her so!

The girl of my dreams
Is the sweetest girl
With her party banners high;
She is Castro's gal,
She is Ho Chih Minh's pal,
She's the sweetheart of Chou En-Lai!

SQUARE:
Hey, gang, let's all go over to the frat house and do the Black
Bottom.

BOY:
Shh. We just call it the Bottom now.

GIRL:
I know a dance that'll *really* turn you on.

SQUARE:
How do you do it?

GIRL:
We'll show you.

GIRL:
First you wave a sign 'bout a civil right,

BOY:
Then you go to Mississippi and start a fight

GIRL:
You let a sheriff grab you and hold you tight,

SQUARE:
Then you twist around and twist around
With all your might!

ALL:
Right!

253

Come from all the cities and all the farms,
Sing "We Shall Overcome" as you link your **arms**
With a priest or rabbi or Dr. Spock—
That's what we call the Civil Rights Rock!
   They dance a half-chorus.

BOY:

Put your little foot down in Alabam',

GIRL:

Support your local p'lice dog in Birmingham,

BOY:

Raise your banners high like at Valley Forge,

GIRL:

Then you strike a pose
And thumb your nose
At Lurlene and George!

BOY:

Wiggle when the billy clubs hit your legs,

GIRL:

Jump around the street dodgin' rotten eggs

ALL:

Come from Harvard or Yale or Antioch,
Come on, do the Civil Rights Rock—
I said Rock!

SQUARE:

Hey, gang, have you heard? Professor Higgins just flunked Gabrilowitz, our star quarterback, the big game is only an hour away, and the alumni are demanding a victory. What are we gonna do?

BOY:

We're all gonna get together and give a big cheer.

SQUARE:

For Gabrilowitz?

ALL:

NO!

SQUARE:

For good old Busby College?

ALL:

NO!

SQUARE:

What else is there to cheer for?

GIRL:

For our Cause.

SQUARE

What cause?

ALL:

Any cause!

Roar, students, roar

Until you shake 'em up in Orange County;

Make love instead of making war,

Give a cheer, oh,

You can be a hero if you

Burn your draft card,

Burn your draft card,

Tell them you won't go—

Yell loud and clear like Mario

Sa-vi-

Oh come to college,

Live with a dame;

Papa will hate it,

Ain't that a shame!

GIRLS:

Hail to the dirty-shirt set,

BOYS:

Hail to the mini-skirt set,

GIRLS:

Wave pom-poms to Wayne Morse

BOYS:

And foot-*balls* to L.B.J.!

ALL: (*Add vocal group*)

Buckle down,

Make Berkeley buckle down;

We can win in Berkeley,

Make 'em buckle down,

We will shock those birds

With some dirty words,

Scare the pants off ev'ry Cap and Gown!

Ev'ry day in Berkeley it's a gas;

Though we go to Berkeley,

We don't go to class!

If we make our point

We will own this joint,

We can win in Berkeley,

We can make 'em buckle down!

Berkeley

Buckle
Down!
Yo!

(*BLACKOUT*)

(*from* WGAw NEWS, 1967)

HOLLYWOOD GOES TO WAR

"In case of an air raid, go directly to RKO—they haven't had a hit in years."
ANONYMOUS WIT, 1942

"My draft status is 8-T—that means I go when the Japs are in the lobby."
GEORGE JESSEL, 1943

OPEN ALL NITE—SPECIAL SWING SHIFT SHOW
THEATRE MARQUEE, 1943

AFTER the third preview of *All Quiet on the Western Front,* the studio heads were still nervous. "There's no relief," one executive complained. "Isn't there some way you can manage to give it a happier ending?"

"Well," smiled director Lewis Milestone, "we could have the Germans win the war."

(*from* THIS WAS HOLLYWOOD, *by Beth Day, Doubleday, 1960*)

LELAND HAYWARD

Long before Pearl Harbor a bunch of us in Hollywood who were nuts about flying decided we ought to do something to help, so we organized a flying school down in Arizona, in Phoenix. It was called Thunderbird Field, and we got a batch of contracts to train young British kids how to fly for the R.A.F. It was a Lend-Lease deal.

We were always in debt down there—my partners were Bert Allenberg, Bill Goetz, Brian Aherne, Jimmy Stewart and Phil Berg— and we grew so damned fast and expanded the facilities even faster. Nobody made a dime. We did the whole thing as our contribution to the Allied side. Finally we got lucky. Somebody down in Washington got us a loan from the R.F.C.—Reconstruction Finance Corporation —which bailed all us guys out, and then we were okay.

One day we got word from Darryl Zanuck that he wanted to make a picture with Tyrone Power called *A Yank in the R.A.F.* and he wanted to use Thunderbird Field as a background for the picture. We figured that was a great idea and we told Darryl sure, we'd co-operate. Obviously, we couldn't charge Fox any fee, so Darryl asked us what we needed, and we told him those British kids needed recreation facilities. Arizona gets damned hot, and how about some swimming pools?

That was okay with Darryl. By the time the Fox people got through, we had ourselves four swimming pools—two at Thunderbird I, another at Thunderbird II and a great big one, eighty-five feet long, at Falcon Field. That's how big we were by then.

Came the end of the war, and all of us owners sold out Thunder-

259

bird, and in return for their loan the R.F.C. guys took possession of the physical facilities.

I was sitting in my office in Beverly Hills one day when a guy came in from the R.F.C. He was very upset. In the original specifications on the deal we'd made with R.F.C., there was no mention of swimming pools. Now he'd been down there and found four pools. I said, "Take 'em, you're welcome to 'em." Oh, no. The government doesn't operate that way. The property had to revert to the R.F.C. in exactly the same state it had been in when we'd made the contracts four years before.

When I explained the four pools were a gift from Fox, that didn't cut any ice at all. This guy was adamant. "Those four pools must be removed," he told me. I was pretty damn busy trying to run my agency, and I got bored with this. I told him, "If you want the pools out, take 'em out. You're the boss now."

One evening about a month later, just as it was getting dark, a bunch of huge trucks came rolling up Coldwater Canyon and they stopped in front of my house. A truck driver got out and rang my doorbell.

"You Leland Hayward?" he asked.

"Sure, why?" I said.

"We've got some equipment here belongs to you," he said. And I'm standing there on my lawn while these guys start unloading six trucks' worth of filtration equipment, diving boards, steps, ladders and pipes and Christ knows what else you need for four swimming pools, all over my place! The pools had been filled in, and that damn R.F.C. guy was really finishing up his contract to the letter!

During the war years, most of the leading men were drafted or enlisted, and producers were hard put to come up with male actors who could carry films. Middle-aged character men, 4-F's and even slightly effeminate types found studio doors wide open and desperate producers beckoning them in.

Henry Blanke, one of Warner Brothers' most capable producers, was filming *Old Acquaintance*, which went on to win all sorts of awards. He was stopped on the studio street by an Eastern executive, who raved over the progress of the picture. "I saw some rushes yesterday, and Bette Davis was absolutely marvelous," he said. "Bette is great!" said Blanke. "And I thought Miriam Hopkins was fine, too," said the exec. "Miriam is giving the performance of her life!" said

Blanke. "And then there's your leading man, John Loder," said the exec.

Blanke shrugged. "Victory casting," he said, and walked away.

One of the legends most fondly recalled by those film technicians who served during World War II with the Signal Corps, first at its base at Fort Monmouth, New Jersey, and later at the Signal Corps Photographic Center in the old Paramount studios in Astoria, Long Island, concerns Private Carl Laemmle, Jr.

"Junior" Laemmle was drafted many months before Pearl Harbor. When his California board tapped him for service, he was nearly past draft age. But he was a bachelor, and he accepted his country's call to arms without complaint.

Despite the fact that he'd had many years experience as production head of Universal, where he had been associated with the making of such films as *Frankenstein* and *All Quiet on the Western Front*, the Army, with its peculiar logic, did not put Junior into any position of importance; it kept him a simple GI.

On the day that he arrived at Astoria from Monmouth, so goes the legend, Junior presented himself and his orders in the office of the Astoria commanding officer, at that time Lieutenant Colonel Paul Sloane. Sloane had been for many years a producer in Hollywood, and had, in fact, been one of Laemmle's staff at Universal.

Junior, delighted to see his former employee, greeted him cheerfully with an outstretched hand. "Paul! How the hell are you?" he inquired.

"Junior," said Sloane, a bit embarrassed, "I'm a lieutenant *colonel*."

"That's great!" said Junior. "How've things been going with you?"

"Junior," said Sloane in an undertone, "you're supposed to *salute* me."

"I am?" asked Junior. "Okay, why not?" And he saluted Sloane. "Now what are you up to around here, Paul?"

"Junior," whispered Sloane, "I am your commanding officer. I am in command of this post."

"You are?" asked Junior. "Gee, that's great, Paul." He leaned over, impressed, and said, also in an undertone: "You've really got a good thing going here, Paul—don't fuck it up!"

The Signal Corps had operated a motion-picture section since the days of the First World War, when it was known as the Fort Monmouth Photographic Unit. Early in 1942 General H. H. Arnold decided to establish a motion-picture unit that would serve the Air Force. Jack L. Warner was commissioned a lieutenant colonel, and he set about recruiting directors, producers, actors and all sorts of technicians to serve as GI's and to staff the First Motion Picture Unit. The Air Force took over the old Hal Roach studios on Washington Boulevard in Culver City and turned it into a thriving military post.

There is in the Air Force archives at Maxwell Field, Alabama, a completely documented official history of the F.M.P.U. at "Fort Roach," as it was fondly named. ("GHQ of the CBI theatre," said one wit, "Culver City, Burbank and Inglewood." Others referred to the unit as "The Flying Typers.") And there still exists the unit's massive film output, which will stand as a record of its accomplishment. F.M.P.U. personnel staffed combat camera units that went out to every war theatre and sent back a vivid record of air war. Hollywood technicians in khaki turned out such brilliant documentaries as Colonel William Wyler's B-17 film, *The Memphis Belle,* and Captain Norman Krasna's *Wings Up.* Literally hundreds of reels of valuable training films were made in Culver City, brilliant trail-blazing techniques in animation were devised, vitally needed recruiting and propaganda films were turned out—and the Air Force was well served by F.M.P.U.

On a less documentary level, however, some of the daily incidents at Fort Roach seem, in retrospect, to resemble certain scenes from Joseph Heller's *Catch-22.* The case of the missing Messerschmitt is one of them, recalled by Edward Anhalt, who is today a successful screenwriter, but then a lieutenant at Fort Roach serving as an unwilling supply officer.

"I did sign for a lot of equipment," he remembers. "Blackmailed into it by senior officers who threatened to ship me to Alaska if I didn't. I managed to account for most of the stuff by keeping my ears open for air crashes. When a B-17 would go down off Catalina, it always unaccountably had two movieolas on it. One of the items I signed for was a German Messerschmitt, flown into Scotland under the radar by two defecting Luftwaffe men.

"The end of the war came, and finally I went back to civilian life. I completely forgot about the Messerschmitt. Along about 1955 I was living at the Chateau Marmont Apartments on Sunset Boulevard when a Colonel Grauman called me.

" 'Of the feet-in-the-concrete Graumans?' I asked.

" 'No,' he responded. 'Of the military-intelligence Graumans.'

"It seemed I owed them $175,000.

"Eventually I appealed to a brigand of my acquaintance, who finally located the Messerschmitt. It was on the back lot of MGM, where it was serving as a mock-up."

Over the years the legend of Anhalt's missing Messerschmitt was passed from person to person and was actually used as the basis of a film comedy (switched, in typical Hollywood story tradition, to the story of a missing Navy destroyer).

Nunnally Johnson recalls that after a tour of Texas army bases with Groucho Marx during World War II, Harry Ruby said, "God is going to have to answer to His maker for this part of the country."

"We were going back East during the war," said Gene Thompson. "I was working on Groucho's radio show, and it was going to be broadcast from New York. The train we were on was loaded with various movie people, who were making whistle-stop appearances on behalf of Roosevelt's campaign for re-election—it was 1944.

"Claudette Colbert was on the train, and Joel Pressman got on. He was a commander in the Navy, and her husband, and they hadn't seen each other for a long time—he'd been overseas.

"Well, there was a lot of socializing, but not by Commander and Mrs. Pressman. They stayed locked in their compartment for the three days it took to travel East. It was Groucho who hung on the compartment door a little sign which read: ISN'T THIS CARRYING NAVAL RELIEF A LITTLE TOO FAR?

At a war-bond art auction held in Beverly Hills, Eddie Cantor and Georgie Jessel were two of numerous "guest" auctioneers.

Jessel stood up and indicated a picture he was to sell, one with a patriotic motif. Before the bidders were allowed to offer their prices, Jessel made a short speech in which he related the time, during the depths of the Depression, when he was playing Washington, D.C., and was invited to the White House to meet the President. "When I left the White House," Jessel said, "I went to the nearest telephone, and I called my mother, and I said, 'Hello, Momma, this is Georgie.'" At this point Jessel took out a handkerchief and wiped his eyes. "I said, 'Momma, you don't have to be ashamed of your son Georgie— the President himself said I was good!'" Jessel blew his nose, wiped his eyes, and said, "Now, what am I bid?"

When he had finished his stint, Jessel sat down, and Eddie Cantor rose. "Ladies and gentlemen," he said, "I am going to try and sell you a painting. I'll be very straight about it—I'm not an emotional type of person like my friend George Jessel. As a matter of fact, Jessel is so emotional, he cries at card tricks."

The unquestioned high point of Irving Berlin's *This Is the Army,* the World War II GI musical show, always came in the second act.

Berlin himself, in a World War I uniform, would re-create a scene from his earlier soldier show *Yip, Yip, Yaphank!* and then, with a group of veterans from that show, he would sing two choruses of his famous song hit "Oh, How I Hate to Get Up in the Morning."

Came the afternoon when Mr. Berlin was due to record this moment on film for color cameras at Warner Brothers. Everything was in readiness. The cameras began to turn, Curtiz called, "Action," and the diminutive Berlin stepped out and began to mouth the lyrics of his song. Synchronizing the movement of his lips to a studio playback record of his song, Berlin pantomimed while the music and the sound of his high, quavering voice echoed through the sound stage.

Two studio stagehands were standing by. One of them shook his head sadly. "You know something?" he said to his friend. "If the guy who wrote that song ever heard *this* guy sing it, he'd turn over in his grave!"

The filming of *This Is the Army,* with a cast of 300 GI's, took place at Warner Brothers Burbank studio. The film was directed by Mike Curtiz, and while the studio assigned its own dance director, LeRoy Prinz, to work on the film, most of the actual choreography was done by the then Master Sergeant Bob Sidney, an outspoken and talented dancer.

One hot afternoon a second assistant director appeared on Stage 12, where Sergeant Sidney was rehearsing a corps of GI dancers in an intricate dance number. "Sergeant," he told Sidney, "LeRoy Prinz says to bring your men right over to Stage 2 and run through the number so he can see what it looks like." Sidney waved the studio minion away and continued with his drilling.

Ten minutes later the assistant was back. "Sergeant," he insisted, "Mr. Prinz says that Mr. Curtiz *himself* will be there in ten minutes—

you've got to get these guys over right away—"

"Look, buddy," said Sidney, mopping his forehead, "we're not ready. Tell them we'll do it some other time."

"But Mr. Curtiz is the director," said the assistant. "Nobody keeps *him* waiting—"

"I do," said Sergeant Sidney. "Beat it, I'm busy."

A few moments later the assistant, now near hysteria, was back. "Listen, Sergeant," he gasped. "Mr. Prinz says to tell you that not only Mike Curtiz but Mr. Jack L. Warner *himself* is going to be on Stage 2 in exactly five minutes, and you'd better be over there to run this dance number for them—*or else!*"

"Listen, you," said Sergeant Sidney with drama. "You can go tell Miss Prinz and Miss Curtiz—you can even tell Miss Warner herself—they can go fuck themselves. *I'm working for Aunt Sam!*"

Jack Rose, who served in the Armed Forces Radio Service, is fond of recalling a program which was prepared for late-night listening all over the world. It was called "Words and Music," and on it the works of great poets were read by such people as Ronald Colman and Dame May Whitty, to the accompaniment of soft symphonic strings.

One evening the credits at the end of the show were intoned by the GI announcer. "Lyrics heard on this show," he said, "were by Percy Bysshe Shelley, Alfred, Lord Tennyson, Robert Browning—and Sammy Cahn."

Actors Victor Mature and Jim Backus were playing in a costume epic of Biblical times, *Demetrius and the Gladiators.* Came lunch break, and Mature urged Backus to join him on a trip downtown to his bank to perform an errand, in a studio car with a driver. Still attired in their Roman centurion costumes, the two actors went to the bank, and their driver fulfilled the errand. Thirst overtook them, however, and they left the parked car and proceeded across the street to a small bar. The barkeep was reading a newspaper as the two actors in Roman Army costume entered and ordered two scotch highballs. Without looking up, he filled their glasses, then turned and, at the sight of two Roman soldiers in a downtown Hollywood bar, he froze. "What's the matter?" queried Backus. "Don't you serve servicemen?"

* * *

The Wit and Wisdom of Hollywood

ART BUCHWALD

The other evening we saw an American film, *The Enemy Below*. It was about a naval engagement in World War II between an American destroyer escort and a German submarine. Robert Mitchum played the captain of the destroyer escort, and Curt Jurgens played the commander of the submarine.

What interested us was that there were no bad guys in the film. Mitchum, of course, was a good guy and so was Jurgens. At the end of the picture, after a duel between the escort and the sub, Mr. Jurgens surfaces and salutes Mr. Mitchum and Mr. Mitchum salutes back and even saves the lives of Jurgens and his executive officer.

It's sad, but there seems to be a trend in Hollywood, now that Germany and Japan are such lucrative markets for films, for the history of World War II to be slowly rewritten, and it's hard to find a bad guy in a war picture any more. (In *The Bridge on the River Kwai* the Japanese commander of the prisoners also turned out to be a pretty good guy at the end.)

If movie business continues on the downgrade in the United States and on the upgrade in Germany and Japan, it may not be long before the Americans become the bad guys and the Germans and Japs the good guys.

We can just imagine a story conference in Hollywood these days.

The Producer: Let's make a war picture.

Assistant Producer: Gee, boss, what an original idea.

The Producer: Nobody's done Pearl Harbor yet.

Assistant Producer: You're the only one with the guts to do it.

Vice-President in Charge of Sales: Let's be careful, though. There could be ramifications.

The Producer: We'll show the Japs planning the operation for months.

Senior Writer: The dirty-dealing double-crossers.

VPICS: Now wait a minute. There can be two sides to the story. A few Japanese can be for the bombing of Pearl Harbor, but let's insert a scene showing the majority are against the whole idea.

Senior Writer: That's going to be a hard scene to write.

VIPCS: You just have to write it. I have to sell it.

The Producer: We'll need a love story.

Senior Writer: A Naval officer is in love with an American girl and they're going to get married on December 7.

VIPCS: Why can't the Naval officer be in love with a Japanese girl? She doesn't like war any more than he does.

Assistant Producer: What's she doing at Pearl Harbor?

Senior Writer: She's sending radio reports back to Japan on the fleet.

VIPCS: No, no, no. Her father is a professor lecturing at the University of Hawaii. She loves her father.

The Producer: Okay, she loves her father, she loves the Naval officer and she loves her country.

Senior Writer: On December 6 we'll show the peacetime Navy having a good time while the Jap planes take off for Pearl Harbor.

VIPCS: We can't show the Navy having a good time or they'll never loan us the ships.

Senior Writer: Okay, the whole Navy is on the alert, all leaves have been canceled and every man is at his gun.

Assistant Producer: We could show maybe two or three enlisted men in a bar, just so we get over the idea that everyone isn't at his station.

The Producer: So the planes approach Pearl Harbor.

Senior Writer: People are going to church.

VIPCS: We could insert a scene showing the Japanese admiral against the raid. He tries to call it off, but it's too late.

Assistant Producer: Because of radio silence.

Senior Writer: We see Pearl Harbor from the air. The battleships and cruisers are all anchored around Ford Island.

The Producer: The Naval officer and the Japanese girl are just about to get married when they look up and see the planes.

Senior Writer: The planes peel off and start their bombing runs, plastering hell out of the ships.

VIPCS: We've got to make sure the audience knows they're only after military targets. No strafing of civilians or any of that stuff.

Senior Writer: The ships start burning in the harbor.

Assistant Producer: The Naval officer has to get back to the ship, but the Japanese girl pleads for him not to go. She says it isn't his business, but he insists it is. He picks up a .30-caliber machine-gun lying in the street and fires at a plane.

Senior Writer: The plane starts strafing the ground and hits both of them. They fall down into each other's arms, but the plane is hit.

VIPCS: The Jap pilot parachutes to the ground next to them, and when he sees what he has done, he asks their forgiveness. The Naval officer salutes him and the Japanese pilot salutes back. At the end of the picture we could show Pearl Harbor as it is today to prove the Japanese didn't do any permanent damage.

Senior Writer: And we could show the graves of the Naval officer and Japanese pilot right next to each other.

VIPCS: It sounds pretty good. I think I can sell it.

The Producer: Now let's discuss a picture about the Bulge.

(from the NEW YORK HERALD TRIBUNE*)*

"After the war," Billy Wilder said, "some Germans wanted to put on a Passion Play. It was while I was in Occupied Germany with the Psychological Warfare Division of the U.S. Army. A carpenter wrote me asking permission to play Jesus. After we screened them, we found out that six of the Apostles were Gestapo men and the carpenter was a stormtrooper. I said, 'Yes—as long as the nails are real.' "

Jack Rose and his partner, Mel Shavelson, were producing a film in Italy, starring Clark Gable and Sophia Loren.

On the first day of shooting, they were making a scene in a tiny eating-place in Capri. The schedule had been planned carefully to begin in October so that the usual crowds would be gone.

The scene involved Gable entering the restaurant, and the filmmakers carefully explained to the patrons that they would have to finish and leave so that the actors could take over. All were agreeable, save for one party of German tourists, who refused to go. No amount of persuasion would get them out.

Finally, in desperation, Rose decided to shoot the scene and include the Germans. The cameras rolled, Gable made his entrance—and, of course, the Germans looked up in awe at Gable and ruined the shot.

Rose came over to the Germans. "You know, you sons of bitches would have won the war if you'd fought it off season," he said.

The biography of Wernher von Braun, the eminent rocket technician, was filmed by an enterprising producer named Charles Schneer and shipped out to the theatres bearing the title *I Aim at the Stars*.

The picture was somewhat less than successful. "It needed a subtitle," cracked one unsympathetic Hollywood wit: *"I Aim at the Stars—But Sometimes I Hit London."*

PRESTON STURGES

One of the most charming characteristics of Homo Sapiens—the wise guy on your left—is the consistency with which he has stoned,

268

crucified, burned at the stake and otherwise rid himself of those who consecrated their lives to his further comfort and well-being so that all his strength and cunning might be preserved for the creation of ever larger monuments, memorial shafts, triumphal arches, pyramids, and obelisks to the eternal glory of generals on horseback, tyrants, usurpers, dictators, politicians, and other heroes who led him, usually from the rear, to dismemberment and death.

(from the prologue to THE GREAT MOMENT, *a Paramount film)*

MR. NUNNALLY JOHNSON OF COLUMBUS, GEORGIA

NUNNALLY JOHNSON of Colum-

bus, Georgia, was a successful newspaperman and short-
story writer in New York before he decided to try his hand
at motion-picture scripting in 1932.

"I had written for The New Yorker," says Johnson.
"Funny thing about that magazine. Over the years it maintained a very strict anti-movie attitude. We had a saying
around town that The New Yorker's critic was only allowed
to like one movie a year—which was in direct contrast to
editor Harold Ross's own tastes. He enjoyed the movies. But
when I suggested to Ross that I was interested in the job
of doing a weekly movie-review column, Ross wouldn't
hear of it. 'Reviewing movies is for women and fairies!'
he insisted."

Ross's loss was Hollywood's gain. A few years later
Johnson had piled up an impressive record of hit movies.
According to Pete Martin, a Johnson fan from way back, by
1948 the sum of the grosses of Nunnally's pictures was already in excess of $100,000,000. And Abel Green, the
knowledgeable editor of Variety, remarked, "The answer to
every producer's prayer is Nunnally Johnson."

Nunnally's latest film, The Dirty Dozen, was a huge financial success. But, as Martin reported, "Nunnally can do
any kind of story you want. There is no one else in the
business who can do so many different kinds of pictures
so well."

He is certainly not to be type-cast, and his list of credits
is awesome. He did such memorable dramas as The House
of Rothschild, Jesse James, The Keys of the Kingdom, The
Desert Fox, the classic film adaptation of John Steinbeck's
The Grapes of Wrath, Tobacco Road, The Mudlark, the
brilliant Three Faces of Eve, and the thriller The Woman
in the Window, to mention a small sampling.

In the difficult métier of comedy and farce, Johnson
was responsible for Holy Matrimony, Mr. Peabody and the
Mermaid, How to Marry a Millionaire, Roxie Hart, Along

273

Came Jones and, more recently, The World of Henry Orient.

Financial gains came swiftly to Nunnally. Joseph M. Schenck, the chairman of the board of Twentieth Century-Fox, who was intimately aware of the large weekly paycheck his firm made out each Friday to Nunnally, remarked, "Johnson is like a child with money. All he knows is that he wants more of it." But David Hempstead, who understood his friend a bit better, said, "Nunnally's shrewdness in business affairs is such that he can walk up to any soda fountain and get a fifteen-cent drink for as little as thirty cents."

Hempstead's analysis is borne out by an incident reported by Pete Martin, who says that at one time Nunnally was involved in a corporate set-up which was amassing large sums for films that he was making.

"You'll be better off," said his agent, the late Johnny Hyde, "as soon as you get out from under that interest."

"What interest?" Johnson inquired.

"On that two million you owe," Hyde replied.

"You'll have to go a long way," Johnson marveled to Martin, "before you find another country where a man can borrow two million dollars without even knowing it."

Over the past four decades Nunnally has delivered himself of many notable comments, some dealing with his own status, others directed at the state of the film industry. To cheer themselves up when *The Grapes of Wrath* lost out on the Academy Awards, Pete Martin reported that Johnson and David Hempstead, his associate, designed and had cast for themselves their own Oscar, identical with the more legitimate trophy, except that their skimpily dressed little fellow wore a derby hat. Not caring, however, to be too specific as to their qualifications for this consolation prize, they contented themselves with the simple claim, engraved on the base: *For being twenty-two years and six months ahead of their time.*

When a crisis meeting was held at Universal-International, and the late Nate Blumberg, who was then head of the company, delivered a speech in which he bemoaned the fact that cash customers were not attending movie theatres in sufficient numbers, it was Nunnally who suggested, "Let's show the movies in the street—and drive the people back into the theatres."

One of Nunnally's most quoted lines had to do with *Tobacco Road,* which he had been assigned to adapt into a film. The play by

Jack Kirkland dealt with very low-class Southern folk of the very best Erskine Caldwell vintage. One evening, at a party at E. E. Paramore's house, an indignant Southern lady confronted Johnson and said to him, "Is that the kind of people *you* come from?"

"Ma'am," said Nunnally, "wheah ah come from, we call that crowd the country-club set."

Erskine Caldwell later complained to Nunnally about the endless reprinting of that line. "I subscribe to a clipping service," he said, "and, you know, I'm paying more for that clipping of your crack than I am for anything about me."

During the years when he operated his own production unit, Nunnally devised his own slogan, which was stamped by postage machine on all mail leaving the office, and which proclaimed: *"Leave the Dishes in the Sink, Ma—There's a Nunnally Johnson Picture in Town!"*

One of Nunnally's close friends from New York newspaper days, Mark Hellinger, arrived in Hollywood to become a writer-producer, and received the following letter:

> Dear Mark:
>
> I meant to stop and welcome you to Hollywood at Chasen's the other night, but I became a little confused as to whether this was the thing to do or not.
>
> It suddenly occurred to me that this would be useless, because I know in my heart that you will not be able to get anywhere out here. You are too tall. With writers, the specifications in Hollywood are not stringent. They may be fat or thin, tall or short, or even medicine-dropper size. But with producers and other executives the rules are strict and inflexible. Unless you can stroll back and forth comfortably under a bridge table, you are doomed from the start. The reason for this is fairly clear. As Alva Johnston pointed out, the title "little Napoleon" in Hollywood is equivalent to the title "Mister" in any other community. Obviously no studio is going to groom a man for high position whom it has to refer to as a "veritable middle-sized Napoleon." This is the only place I ever heard of where the citizens practice stabbing themselves in the back in their spare time just by way of gymnasium work-outs. I could go on like this at some length, but I am called to a story conference with some friends and I just have time to put on my groin-cup.
>
> I hope for the best for you.
>
> Nunnally

The Wit and Wisdom of Hollywood

During the late Thirties there was a gathering of Hollywood wits at the Garden of Allah apartments. Among those of Johnson's acquaintance who were in attendance were Charlie Butterworth, Robert Benchley and Julius Epstein, all of whom, as the evening rolled on, engaged in humorous infighting.

One young lady, the date of one of the males present, found herself completely ignored. In an effort to make herself and her presence felt, she picked a book off a shelf, ostentatiously sat down in the middle of the living-room floor, and proceeded to read. For a few moments her performance went disregarded by the assembled humorists, but finally Nunnally rose and crossed over to the lady.

"I don't blame you a bit," he remarked sympathetically. "It's such a boring evening, isn't it?"

It was at about this time that Johnson compiled and had posted on his office wall the following professional scale of fees:

For reading a story, with one word comment	*$5 a page*
For same, without comment	*$10 a page*
For listening to a story while dozing *	*$500*
For listening to a story jovially described as "just a springboard"	*$10,000*
For listening to a story while wide awake	*$1,000*
For reading stories, plays or scripts written by actors or actresses to star themselves	*$25,000*
For attending amateur performances in a converted shoe store on Highland Avenue to "catch" promising new material	*$10,000 (and transportation)*
For looking at talented children	*$500*
For talking to same or their mothers	*$50,000*
For meeting "new faces" (Male)	*$100*
For same (Female)	*$1*
For same (Female), door closed	*No charge*

---

* *In cases of close friends or warm acquaintances acquired in saloons late the night before, charges are doubled.*

Groucho Marx and Nunnally are very close friends. They enjoy each other's humor and each other's company. Over the years the two men have developed certain signals to communicate their feelings during dinner parties. On one occasion Groucho was amazed to see Johnson get up and leave without even signaling an SOS. He caught up to his friend later and asked him the reason for the sudden retreat.

"Because of what the hostess said to me," said Nunnally.

"What did she say?" demanded Groucho.

"She pointed to Sid Luft and said, 'That's the most interesting man in Hollywood.'"

"All you could do is leave," Groucho agreed.

On another occasion Nunnally remarked, "Movie actors wear dark glasses to funerals to conceal the fact that their eyes are not red from weeping."

One of Johnson's most famous contretemps was *l'affaire Louella Parsons.*

The Saturday Evening Post, to which Nunnally had contributed many short stories prior to his journey Westward, had commissioned an article on the famous gossip columnist, to be written by Thomas Wood. When the Wood manuscript came into the *Post* office, however, the editors judged it to be a bit rough.

"Louella's husband, for instance," recalls Nunnally, "the famous Dockie—Dr. Martin—who was a proctologist, was revealed to be so popular that his nickname was 'Old Velvet Finger.' And in fact the suggestion was that the piece be called 'Velvet Finger's Wife.'"

The *Post* editors asked Nunnally to help them out with a certain amount of diplomatic rewriting, and he obliged, on an anonymous basis. When the article finally appeared, it was bylined Thomas Wood, but Hollywood is a very small town. Everyone in range of a studio commissary knew that Nunnally had worked on the article. "It was the worst-kept secret in town," Nunnally admits.

"The day it hit the stands, Louella appeared in Darryl Zanuck's office, weeping and furious. 'I expect you to fire him!' she told Zanuck, who was my boss.

" 'I can't do that, he has a contract,' said Darryl.

" 'If he worked for *me,* I'd fire him!' cried Louella. And she stamped out in a rage.

"Zanuck sent for me. He was very ambivalent about the situation. 'Why did you get me mixed up in this?' he asked. 'Louella has a lot of power.'

" 'What power?' I asked him. 'She hates me more than anyone in town—and she can't get me fired, can she?'

"Harry Brand, who was the head of 20th's publicity department,

277

was in on the meeting. 'But, Nunnally,' he said, 'after all Louella's *done* for you—'

" 'What has she done for me?' I demanded.

" 'Well,' said Brand, 'when you were picked up for drunken driving, she didn't print the item in her column, did she?'

" 'She didn't have to,' I told him, 'seeing as how her city editor had put it in headlines all over the front page!'

"It was a few days later that Louella counterpunched," says Johnson. "I had just married Dorris Bowden, and one day we picked up the paper and Louella had written, 'I saw Dorris Johnson the other day. Poor Dorris. Before her marriage, she looked so lovely . . .'

"That," Nunnally says with admiration, "was *really* shooting around a corner!"

"I remember when John Ford came to make his first picture at Fox," says Johnson. "Up to then Ford had been at RKO, where he had everybody so frightened of him that the executives used to flip coins to see who would have to sit in the projection room and listen to Ford's blasts about the daily rushes."

Ford began shooting one of Nunnally's screenplays, *The Prisoner of Shark Island*, which was the true story of Dr. Samuel Mudd, the physician who set the leg of John Wilkes Booth after the assassination of President Lincoln. The title role was played by the late Warner Baxter.

"We went to the projection room to watch the rushes, and Zanuck asked me about Warner Baxter's accent—it was some sort of phony Southern drawl that was all wrong, and I told him it was lousy.

" 'Tell Ford to stop Baxter from using it, then,' ordered Zanuck. I sent word on down to Ford to this effect, but when we went to see the next day's rushes, there it was again, that same lousy accent. Baxter was evidently enjoying it.

"Zanuck was now getting angry. He asked me if I'd told Ford, and I said I had, and Darryl said, 'Okay, we'll go down and find out what's going on.'

"We came down to Ford's set. Zanuck walked right over to Ford and demanded to know why Ford hadn't obeyed his orders about curbing that lousy accent.

"Ford turned around and glared at Zanuck. 'Now look,' he said, 'if you don't like the way I'm doing this show, I'll quit.'

" 'Are you *threatening me?*' yelled Zanuck. 'Don't you threaten to quit! *I* throw people off sets! *Nobody threatens me,* do you understand?'

"Ford shut up, and went over to talk to Baxter.

"I remember, a few days later, I was out cruising on somebody's boat," adds Johnson. "There was a whole batch of us aboard, including Ford, who hadn't yet seen me. Somebody asked John how he and Zanuck were getting along.

" 'Oh,' said Ford, very casually, 'Darryl and I had a little talk, and after that there was no more trouble.'

"A couple of seconds later Ford turned around and he noticed me sitting there, for the first time. 'That's right, isn't it, Nunnally?' he asked, finally.

"I just nodded."

Another one of Johnson's close friends is the song-writer Harry Ruby.* Nunnally is fond of quoting Ruby's letter of a few years back.

". . . for a long time," wrote Ruby, "I've been worried about the problem of growing old and not having enough money for my old age. So about two years ago, I found a way to provide for my golden years, and I must say, it's given me a lot of satisfaction. I got myself a piggy bank, and every morning I slip a $100 bill into it. I never miss doing this each day. It's so easy—everyone should do it. Now I find I have $76,800. And I could kick myself for not having started it earlier."

"And then," says Nunnally, "Harry got very sick and went to the hospital. He wrote me the following:

"I don't know whether or not you knew it, but I was very ill last summer. For a while, I thought I was a goner. I woke up one night in my hospital bed, and I saw, standing there, a tall man, wearing a white robe, with a long white beard.

I said, "Who are you?"

He said, "I am the Holy Ghost."

I said, "Where are the Father and the Son?"

He said, "They're out of town."

I'm not a religious man, but it's things like this that make you stop and think. Love Harry.

When Johnson finally took the plunge and became a director of his own film scripts, he encountered Henry Hathaway, a veteran at directing whose latest film is *True Grit*.

* Letter from Harry Ruby to the author: "Quite a few years back, while dining at my table, the one and only Alexander Woollcott kept staring at me across the table. I finally said, 'Aleck, why do you keep looking at me like that?' He said, 'I can't help it. I keep looking at you because you look like a dishonest Abe Lincoln.' "

"I hear you're going to direct," said Hathaway.

"Well, I'm going to take a crack at it," said Nunnally.

"You'll be no good," said Hathaway. "You're not a bastard. To be a good director, you've got to be a bastard. I'm one, and I know it. Look at John Ford, or George Stevens, or Willie Wyler—all bastards! But I know you, Nunnally—you won't ever fight. Something comes up, you'll compromise."

"Well," said Nunnally, "maybe I'll have to give in on a little thing every once in a while—"

"You compromise once a day," warned Hathaway, "and it's thirty-six times in one picture!"

"Later on," says Johnson, "I went to London to film *The Mudlark*, and I ran into a British film crew which had just finished doing a picture with Hathaway. Henry had left behind him a trail of hate. At the end of the picture he called his English crew together and made a little speech. He said, 'We've been together forty days, and we've had our rows. We've had our fights. We've worked together. There have been differences, but I'd like to say this. I want you to know— you are the lousiest crew I've ever had in my whole life!'

"That night the producer said, 'We've got to do some retakes, Henry.'

"I thought, 'Oh, my God—poor Henry. They'll drop something on him sure as hell.' And it would have served him right."

"Then," says Nunnally, "there came a time when I decided to give up directing, and I remember that moment. I was directing a picture on location in Sicily. It was about two o'clock in the morning. My God, it was cold. There was only one actor, Joe Cotten. We were out in an open field and there was an enormous rock there. And he, Joe, was supposed to be a radio reporter creeping across the field, getting near a battle, to get the sound of battle. After he'd gone through it, I was shaking with cold, and it was slippery, and I said, 'All right, let's put the camera here.'

"And just then I said to myself, 'What the hell am I doing here? Two o'clock in the morning. In Sicily. At the age of sixty. On a slippery rock. On a cold night. Saying, "Put the camera here!" Oh, no. This is the end of it. From now on, let somebody else say, "Put the camera here." I'm going to be home in bed!'

"And so, at the end of that picture, I said, 'That's all for directing. I will resume my role as a writer.'

"I was telling this to Groucho Marx one night," he continues. "Groucho said, 'It happened to me. We were making a picture called

A Night in Casablanca. This was the final day of shooting. We were on a very short budget. We had to finish up that night. It was about midnight. And here I was, hanging by my knees, upside down. I said exactly the same thing: "What the hell. I'm sixty-two years old. I've got enough money. What the hell am I doing, hanging by my legs at two o'clock in the morning," or one, or twelve o'clock— whatever the hell it was. That's all. That's all, brother. From now on, the rest of you Marx boys can go on, but include me out. I mean, I'm through with that kind of stuff.' "

In 1968 Nunnally returned to Hollywood. In a letter to his good friend Bob Goldstein, he reported on various goings-on in the film capital: "I went to the dinner for Jack Warner, a real smasher [Warner's seventy-fifth birthday]. Sinatra was the M.C., and they'd have been better off with the gateman. Very breezy, very inside, and very lousy, with even more no-laugh jokes than Jack. This chap Ashley [the new production head of the Warner–Seven Arts company, Ted Ashley] really has guts. After a showing of clips from all the big Warner Brothers pictures from Rin-Tin-Tin to *Camelot* he announced proudly that the New Regime had already finished two cheap pictures, one under budget. That's getting out of the starting gate like greased lightning! . . . Eight or nine hundred guests, with good food by Chasen, and all the old-timers ever heard of—Henry Hathaway, George Stevens, Norman Taurog, Harry Brand and Sybil, and I suspected that the whole thing was a trap and that when we senior citizens started out of the building we would be mowed down by machine guns manned by bearded boys. . . ."

In another letter Nunnally jovially replied to a recollection of how he had loathed the title song in *Born Free*, at the preview of that picture: "I'd forgotten about the *Born Free* song, but it is right in line with my usual perceptiveness. Long ago at 20th-Fox, I was reading one of the innumerable synopses that were distributed each week and I paused when I came to the name of the hero: Rhett Butler. Undiscouraged, I pressed on. But when I came to the name of the heroine, Scarlett O'Hara, I dropped the whole matter. I had no intention of getting mixed up in another version of Terry and the Pirates and the Dragon Lady and Lace. What fools they were to think they could hoodwink me with rot like that!"

In a conversation with the compiler of this book, in the winter of 1970, Nunnally remarked, "You know, nobody ever wrote about Hollywood with any seriousness until Scott Fitzgerald did *The Last Tycoon.* Up till then, the level of Hollywood satire was all of the

Kaufman-Hart school—you know, the *Once in a Lifetime* comedy. They all had the same characters—the drunk writers, the stupid producers, the arrogant directors . . ." Nunnally paused, and then added, "who are all still here, too!"

In the winter of 1970 he also announced his formal retirement from the motion-picture business. Helen Hayes, an old friend, wrote from New York: "I'm puzzled by your announcement. How does one formally retire?" "Very easily," said Nunnally, in reply. "I simply put on my white tie and tails—and I retired."

SAM GOLDWYN
PROUDLY
PRESENTS

BACK *in 1937, Alva Johnston wrote a brief biography of Goldwyn for the* Saturday Evening Post. *It was later published in book form by Random House, and in it Johnston wrote:*

"The election of Woodrow Wilson changed Samuel Goldwyn from a glove salesman to a movie magnate. The Wilson Administration lowered the tariff on skins. Sam thought that would take the profit out of gloves. He looked around for some other line and picked the movies. That was in 1913. . . .

"Sam has had more fights than any other man in Hollywood. Because he is a rebel and a trailblazer in the use of the English language, he is the central figure of a great comic legend. . . .

"But most of those who hate him or laugh at him will say, 'I admire Sam.' The routine is to ridicule Goldwyn for a while and to denounce him for a while, and then to credit him with 'an instinctive love of beauty,' and 'complete' or 'almost complete artistic integrity.' The ablest people in Hollywood, generally speaking, admire Goldwyn the most. . . . It is almost a fad in Hollywood today to rave about Goldwyn's taste. He commands respect because of a seeming contempt for money when he is in a mood to lavish it in the pursuit of what he regards as perfection. He suffers and agonizes to get 'the Goldwyn touch': those who work for him suffer and agonize with him. . . ."

Mr. Johnston wrote this about Goldwyn thirty-three years ago, when the motion-picture business and Hollywood were a thriving center of commerce. Since then, most of the king-size power brokers who ran the game, made the rules and had a tight lock on the operation have folded up and moved on. But the longer one wanders through the elephants' graveyard that is Hollywood, to examine its artifacts and to listen to the vivid recollections of Hollywood survivors who staffed the once-thriving jute mills and salt mines, the more it becomes obvious that of all the now-legendary big bosses—Mayer, Warner, Laemmle, Zanuck, Thalberg, et al—none will leave behind a more vivid and lasting set of heiroglyphics for future audiences than the one man who remained for half a century fiercely independent and his own man—Sam Goldwyn.

"Over the years," said Arthur L. Mayer in Merely Colossal, one of the few books ever written on the movie business that is not only authentic but witty, "Goldwyn has had the highest batting average of any producer. He has been responsible for occasional potboilers, but he has to his credit such memorable films as Dodsworth, Wuthering Heights, Stella Dallas, The Little Foxes, Dead End . . . and The Best Years of Our Lives. . . . He was, moreover (and still is), one of the few picture producers who was an expert not only in making pictures but in distribution, publicity and sale to the public. In this, like the description of Alexander Woollcott, Goldwyn was 'a sensitive, creative artist with a fine sense of double-entry bookkeeping.'"

Certainly, in all those years no other Hollywood personality has ever been as footnoted, annotated, quoted (and misquoted) as Sam Goldwyn. For openers, there are all those legendary malapropisms. ("I can answer you in two words. Im Possible!" "A verbal contract isn't worth the paper it's written on." "Let's bring it up to date with some snappy nineteenth-century dialogue." And the most famous of all: "Gentlemen—include me out!") Whether he actually said them or not, to deny their authenticity is now useless. They're Goldwyn's, and they'll always be Goldwyn's.

"One of my few claims to distinction within the industry," wrote Mayer, whose career began with Goldwyn fifty years ago in New York, "is that I am apparently the only person in it who, man or boy, never heard Sam utter a Goldwynism. I was, however, on the ground floor of one. He advised me once, 'First you have a good story, then a a good treatment, and next a first-rate director. After that, you hire a competent cast and even then you have only the nucleus of a good picture.' Since then I have seen this story so often in print rewritten by press agents to 'only the mucus of a good picture,' that I now tell it that way myself.

"That a first-rate publicity representative can often improve on the original product, however, cannot be denied, and there is no higher example than the curtain *line of the celebrated meeting between Goldwyn and George Bernard Shaw, during which Sam tried to sell Shaw on the idea of coming to Hollywood. 'The trouble, Mr. Goldwyn, is that you are only interested in art,' Shaw is supposed to have said, 'and I am only interested in money.' As an ardent admirer of the great vegetarian, I am, nevertheless, pleased to report that the real author of that neat and excellent line was the rare-steak eater, publicist and lyricist Howard Dietz, who was at that time working for Goldwyn.*

"There is a story—quite untrue, like most Goldwyn fables, but not entirely untypical of the great man—that one of his henchmen once wrote an ad for a forthcoming picture which read simply: 'The directorial skill of Mamoulian, the radiance of Anna Sten and the genius of Goldwyn have united to make the world's greatest entertainment.'

" 'That,' Sam is supposed to have said, 'is the kind of ad I like. Facts. No exaggeration.' "

From here on, then: Mr. Goldwyn. With no exaggerations—they're not needed—merely facts.

Back in 1919 Goldwyn produced films starring Will Rogers, his favorite being *Jubilo*, based on a Ben Ames Williams story about a lovable tramp. Rogers was appearing in New York when he received word from Goldwyn's office that Sam had decided to change the title of the picture. He sat down and composed the following telegram to Sam:

THOUGHT I WAS SUPPOSED TO BE A COMEDIAN BUT WHEN YOU SUGGEST CHANGING THE TITLE OF JUBILO YOU ARE FUNNIER THAN I EVER WAS. I DON'T SEE HOW LORIMER OF THE POST EVER LET IT BE PUBLISHED UNDER THAT TITLE. THAT SONG IS BETTER KNOWN THROUGH THE SOUTH BY OLDER PEOPLE THAN GERALDINE FARRAR'S HUSBAND. WE HAVE USED IT ALL THROUGH BUSINESS IN THE PICTURE BUT OF COURSE WE CAN CHANGE THAT TO "EVERYBODY SHIMMY NOW." SUPPOSE IF YOU HAD PRODUCED "THE MIRACLE MAN" YOU WOULD HAVE CALLED IT "A QUEER OLD GUY." BUT IF YOU REALLY WANT A TITLE FOR THIS SECOND PICTURE I WOULD SUGGEST "JUBILO." ALSO THE FOLLOWING:

A POOR BUT HONEST TRAMP
HE LIES BUT HE DON'T MEAN IT

The Wit and Wisdom of Hollywood

A FARMER'S VIRTUOUS DAUGHTER

THE GREAT TRAIN ROBBERY MYSTERY

A SPOTTED HORSE BUT HE IS ONLY PAINTED

A HUNGRY TRAMP'S REVENGE

THE VAGABOND WITH A HEART AS BIG AS HIS APPETITE

HE LOSES IN THE FIRST REEL BUT WINS IN THE LAST

THE OLD MAN LEFT BUT THE TRAMP PROTECTED HER

WHAT WOULD YOU HAVE CALLED "THE BIRTH OF A NATION?"

WILL ROGERS.

Goldwyn kept the original title.

(*from* THE AUTOBIOGRAPHY OF WILL ROGERS, *Houghton Mifflin,*
1949)

It was in his early years as a film-maker that Goldwyn became convinced that to make top-drawer pictures, one must go to the source, the author. He signed up a group of contemporary writers, including such respected ones as Rex Beach, Rupert Hughes, Gertrude Atherton, Robert W. Chambers, and even imported from Belgium the great Maurice Maeterlinck, who had written *The Life of the Bee* and *The Blue Bird,* among other highly esteemed works.

Goldwyn's idea was less successful in execution than it was in concept. His eminent authors were paid extremely well, but their work was generally unusable. When Maeterlinck sent Goldwyn a thirty-page synopsis of an idea for a film, Goldwyn read it and reeled. "My God!" he is supposed to have said. "The hero is a *bee!*"

"When the distinguished Belgian author left his office after his unsuccessful fling at the movies," reports Arthur Mayer, "Goldwyn put his arm around his shoulder. 'Don't worry, Maurice,' he said. 'I'm sure you'll make good yet.'"

But throughout his producing career Goldwyn continued to employ the services of the very best. Famous writers who wrote for him included Robert E. Sherwood, Lillian Hellman, Sidney Howard and even Thornton Wilder, who labored on a Goldwyn screenplay during the Thirties.

King Vidor, the director, in his book *A Tree Is a Tree,* reports on a conversation between Goldwyn and Wilder over an adaptation Wilder had done:

Mr. Wilder: I presume you have read my little effort.
Mr. Goldwyn: Yes, yes—Mr. Wilder—your little, er, yes, I have, sir.

288

Mr. W: And what do you think of it, sir?

Mr. G: Well now—the character of Sir Malcolm—

Mr. W: Precisely. I am afraid I didn't do so well by Sir Malcolm.

Mr. G: Not so well—Mr. Wilder.

Mr. W: I'm afraid he turned out psychologically immature. Philosophically, a bit of a—

Mr. G: (Smiling pleasantly and trying his best to be polite) Yes, psychologically, he made me feel—

Mr. W: (Interrupting) I think I know exactly what you mean—

Mr. G: And philosoph—well, frankly, Mr. Wilder, *Sir Malcolm is a horse's ass!*

Goldwyn struggled violently and heroically to make Anna Sten, a European import, into a female box-office star. Whether it was her lack of talent or her inability to be understood by American audiences due to her thick accent, Miss Sten never made it.

It was during the shooting of the third Sten film, *Wedding Night,* which co-starred Gary Cooper and was directed by Vidor, that Leonard Praskins, a Hollywood wit, referred to the picture as "Goldwyn's Last Sten."

Vidor continues: "Gary Cooper and Anna Sten were putting forth a valiant struggle [with dialogue], getting nowhere fast. Goldwyn began to fidget in his chair, and finally, losing his patience, interrupted the rehearsal.

" 'Do you mind if I talk to them?' he asked me. For the moment, he appeared to have taken on the impressiveness of a Knute Rockne.

" 'Go ahead, coach,' I said.

"He made an eloquent plea for effort and co-operation. He told, as is usual at these moments, of the dwindling receipts at the box office. He said his whole career was staked on the success of this picture. Then, reaching his climax, he said, 'And I tell you that if this scene isn't the greatest love scene ever put on film, the whole goddamned picture will go right up out of the sewer!' He turned and strode from the stage as rapidly as he had arrived."

Vidor reports that for years Sam referred to his own picture as *Withering Heights,* and that when Sam handed the director a copy of *The Best Years of Our Lives,* he casually remarked that "this is written in blank werse."

Bob Parrish, the director, relates the story of Goldwyn and Joel McCrea, who for seven years was under contract to Sam and made many successful films for the Goldwyn organization. The contract came to an end, and McCrea decided to free-lance. The parting was an amicable one, and in the best Hollywood tradition Goldwyn gave a farewell luncheon at his studio for McCrea. Many guests were invited.

After luncheon Sam stood up and said, "And now I should like to bid farewell to my good friend Joe McCrail—"

One of Goldwyn's aides leaned over to whisper, "Sam—it's McCrea—"

Goldwyn glared at his aide. "I've been paying him $5,000 a week for seven years and you're trying to tell me his name?"

Once, when Goldwyn was recuperating from a rather severe illness, up at William Randolph Hearst's magnificent ranch at San Simeon, he failed to join Hearst's other guests for several days, preferring to stay in solitude, in a guest house. He was finally coaxed by Marion Davies to mingle with the others at the main establishment.

"I tell you, Marion," Sam sighed, "you just don't realize what life is all about until you have found yourself lying on the brink of a great abscess!"

Abel Green, the editor of *Variety*, is the source of more authentic Goldwynisms. For many years, he reports, Goldwyn was never able to position properly the name of Bosley Crowther, the *New York Times* film critic. Inevitably, he emerged as "Boswell Carruthers."

And when Arthur Hornblow, Jr., the film producer, sired an infant son, Goldwyn called to congratulate Hornblow and to inquire what name the Hornblows intended for the child. Hornblow informed Sam that the son would carry on the family tradition and be called Arthur Hornblow III. "Why Arthur?" inquired Sam. "Every Tom, Dick and Harry is called Arthur!"

And it is also a Hollywood legend that when Goldwyn accepted an Academy Award for his picture *The Best Years of Our Lives*, he made a brief speech in which he referred to his female star "Miss Virginia Mayer" (translation, Mayo) and "that talented fellow Hugo Carmichael" (translation, Hoagy).

Mrs. Ann Frank, the wife of Mel Frank, himself a successful writer-producer, was once employed as a secretary in Goldwyn's office. She was present in Goldwyn's office when Sam called in a male assistant who had been in his employ for many years. "Listen to me," complained Goldwyn, "we've got twenty-five years' worth of files out there, just sitting around. Now what I want you to do is to go out there and throw everything out—but make a copy of everything first!"

There were times when Goldwyn was capable of great wisdom, succinctly put.

Over the years, Goldwyn story conferences were fabled for their rhetoric and noise level. One afternoon Sam was guiding a visitor through the Goldwyn studio, and they passed a row of writers' offices. In one of them two of Sam's current writers were holding a story conference with a director. The conversation was contained and polite, and the sound quite bearable. "Amazing," said Sam's guest. "Here I'd always been told that story conferences were loud and uproarious affairs, but these men are working very quietly." "From quiet conferences come quiet pictures," said Sam.

One evening when David Selznick was an executive producer at MGM, his telephone rang. It was Goldwyn calling. "David," said Sam, "you and I are in terrible trouble!"

"What's the matter, Sam?" asked Selznick anxiously.

"You've got Gable," said Goldwyn, "and I want him."

Goldwyn not only made impressive dramatic films, but over the years he turned out many musical comedies, starting with the great Eddie Cantor, including his opulent *Goldwyn Follies*, and finally starring Danny Kaye in a succession of successful box-office attractions.

Nat Perrin and Arthur Sheekman worked on several of Goldwyn's musicals of the Thirties, including Eddie Cantor's *Kid from Spain* and *Roman Scandals*.

"Goldwyn liked to have his writers involved in all phases of production," Perrin recalls. "Casting, costuming, the works. I remember one day when Sam called us and said he wanted us to come down on the set. His designer was going to present us with his ideas for slave-girl costumes, Roman style.

"The designer wasn't merely going to show Sam a few sketches —he had a sense of showmanship about the whole thing. We went down to the sound stage with Sam, and there was a small platform set up, with curtains, and some chairs. We sat down, and the lights went down, and then from behind the curtains there was the sound of a gong being struck. Music began to play from behind the curtain, and then it parted, and there were soft-colored lights. One by one, the girls came forward very dramatically, each one of them wearing a different slave-girl costume; she'd turn and model, bow, and then disappear, and then another, and another. Finally, the curtains closed, we heard the gong again, and then the lights went on.

"The designer who'd put this whole thing on came out, and he walked over to Sam. 'Well, Mr. Goldwyn?' he beamed.

" 'The show was great,' said Sam, 'but the costumes stink!'

"We shot a long sequence in *Roman Scandals* in which Eddie Cantor, as a slave, was being put up for auction in Rome. In the crowd of potential buyers there was a very ugly woman, and we'd worked out a comedy bit where she fancied Eddie and led the bidding for him. Eventually we did a bit where Eddie, in a desperate attempt to fend her off, used ventriloquism and bid against her, and it was pretty funny,' says Perrin.

"When Sam saw the rushes in the projection room, he didn't think it was right. The visual emphasis was all wrong, he wanted the comedy focused on Eddie, and he sat there and told us that he wanted the whole sequence shot again, which would cost a lot, but that didn't matter. It wasn't right, and Sam couldn't accept mistakes.

"Cantor couldn't understand Sam. He kept arguing that it would be better to take the picture out and show it to a preview audience, and then make retakes, if we had to.

"Sam persisted. He wanted the whole sequence redone. Cantor kept arguing, and finally Sam said, 'Eddie—it's no use! You've got to take the bull by the teeth!'

"We always caused a certain amount of confusion around Goldwyn," Perrin continues. "All the time we worked for Sam, he would refer to us as 'The Boys.' At the same time Sam had another writer there, DuBose Heyward, who wrote *Porgy and Bess*. Sam would ring his secretary and tell her, 'Get me DuBose'—which came out De*Boys*—and she'd ring us up, and we'd come trotting up to his office. In we'd go, and Sam would look up and ask, 'What can I do for you, boys?' and we'd say, 'You sent for us, Sam,' and he'd call in the secretary and say, 'I wanted De*Boys*,' and she'd say, 'That's who I *thought* you said you wanted, Mr. Goldwyn,' and he'd say, 'Not the boys, De*Boys!*'

"He spoke in that high-pitched voice, with just a trace of an accent, and he could never refer to Heyward as anything but De-Boys. As a matter of fact, he once made a promotional trailer for one of his pictures, in which he spoke directly to the movie audience, telling them how proud he was of the picture. We all went down to the projection room to look at it, and when the lights came on, Sam turned to me and he said very seriously, 'Do I talk with an *accent?*' "

Al Newman, the great musical conductor, was once assigned by Goldwyn to write a piece of special music for one of his pictures. When the music was run off for Goldwyn, the sound technicians made a mistake and ran the sound track backward. Goldwyn was immensely impressed by the result and called Newman to congratulate him on the novel and intriguing sounds he had created. Newman could never summon up enough courage to inform Goldwyn of what had happened. The music stayed in the picture—backward.

At a meeting in Goldwyn's office, where his sales manager was present, Sam held forth to his staff on his own credo of production. "I know I can put in cheap pictures," he said, "but I don't want 'em. I want pictures with quality—and *heart!*"

The sales manager nodded affirmatively and added, "Fellows, I've been closer to the pulse of the ticket-buyer than anybody else in this room—or in this industry—and I can tell you, Mr. Goldwyn is absolutely right. You have to appeal to the old ticker!"

"I don't care about tickets!" said Goldwyn. "I want to appeal to the *heart!*"

Seeking to recover the conversational ball, the somewhat embarrassed sales manager then said, "You're absolutely right, Mr. Goldwyn—you have to appeal to the old ticker!"

"George," said Goldwyn impatiently, "you're talking about heart —and I'm talking about box-office!"

Harry Tugend, also a very successful comedy writer-producer, was hired by Goldwyn to do a Danny Kaye picture, the script of which was to be a musical-comedy version of a previous Goldwyn comedy success, *Ball of Fire*. Tugend worked for some time on the script, and then he brought in a first draft.

Goldwyn sent for Tugend, and when Tugend arrived, he indicated the script. "Tugend," he said, "this is lousy!"

"What exactly is wrong with it?" asked Tugend.

"Here I'm paying you big money, and what did you do?" demanded Goldwyn. "All you did was change the words!"

"It was tough writing comedy for Sam," says Tugend. "At any given time he had several scripts in work, and when you discussed yours with him, he would constantly confuse the characters you'd written with characters in the other scripts. Besides, I found out that Sam's grasp of a script wasn't too strong when it was in screenplay form. His real genius came when the film was shot and he could see it in the projection room. There, he had an instinctive feel for what was right and wrong. And the very worst thing you could say to Sam was that something was in bad taste.

"Every day," adds Tugend, "Sam presided over a table in his executive dining room. He was finishing up *Best Years of Our Lives*,

293

and one day he stopped me at lunchtime. 'Listen, Harry, I'm going on Bob Hope's radio show. You're a clever writer—what should I say?' he asked.

"I thought for a minute, and then I suggested the following. 'You have Hope ask, "Well, Mr. Goldwyn, how have things been going since I left your studio?" and then you answer him, "Bob, since you've left, we've had the best years of our lives." That way you'll get in a good plug for the new picture.'

" 'Marvelous!' said Sam. 'Thanks a lot, Harry.'

"I left and went back to my office, and a few minutes later Sam's head of publicity came into the dining room. Goldwyn called him over. 'Listen, Tugend is a clever fellow and he has a great idea for me,' he said. 'I go on Hope's show, and he asks, "Well, Mr. Goldwyn, how've things been going since I left your studio?" and then I say, "Bob, since you left, things are better than ever!" ' "

Goldwyn was enormously fond of the late Ben Hecht and greatly respected that writer's talents and opinion. One evening Hecht was a dinner guest at the home of Irving Brecher, a fellow Hollywood writer. Midway during dinner the doorbell rang, and when Brecher answered it, there stood Sam Goldwyn. Goldwyn had not met the Brechers socially, and he excused himself for intruding, but he knew that Hecht was at the Brecher home and might he please speak for a few moments to Ben—it was most important.

Brecher ushered Goldwyn and Hecht into the living room and closed the door on the two men. For some time they remained inside. Evidently Goldwyn had a script with serious problems, he needed Hecht's advice and counsel, and he sat with Hecht while the writer read Goldwyn's material.

An hour or so later Hecht had come to a decision. He told Sam that the script was unsalvageable and that he could not help him. "That's what I wanted to find out!" said Goldwyn. "Thanks very much for helping me, Ben."

He got up and started for the door. He waved away the Brechers' invitation to stay and have coffee or dessert. "No, thank you," he told them, "I must be going, thanks for everything."

Brecher and Hecht accompanied Goldwyn to the front door. As Goldwyn started out of the house, he turned to Hecht. "Lovely place you've got here, Ben," he said. And then, to Brecher, "Young man, may I give you a lift somewhere?"

The late Don Hartman, another talented writer-producer, was

employed by Goldwyn on a Danny Kaye musical comedy. An argument developed between Hartman and Goldwyn, one which became so serious that both parties called in legal assistance. Litigation loomed on the horizon. The lawyers took over, and Goldwyn persuaded Hartman to continue work. "Let the lawyers settle it," he insisted, and Hartman agreed.

One afternoon Hartman, a brilliant writer but an erratic driver, gave Goldwyn a lift home from the studio. He dropped Sam off in his driveway and then, in turning his car around, he inadvertently backed into Goldwyn, knocking Sam flat on the pavement. Hartman jumped out of his car and helped the somewhat dazed Goldwyn to his feet. Apologizing profusely for his carelessness, he started to help the older man into the house.

"This is absolutely awful!" he cried.

"It's all right," soothed Goldwyn. "I know you didn't do it on purpose, Don!"

"I know," groaned Hartman, "but who's going to believe it?"

One of Goldwyn's elegantly simplistic lines concerned Howard Dietz, who had left him to go to work for MGM. "I ran into Howard Dietz last night," he remarked to a friend. "He was having dinner at my house."

David Miller, the director, and his wife sailed for London on the *Queen Mary*. They discovered Mr. and Mrs. Goldwyn were aboard. That evening the Millers entered the dining saloon and came up to the Goldwyns' table. Goldwyn looked up. "Why, hello there, David," he said. "You going to Europe?"

The stories concerning Goldwyn's passion for perfection are repeated wherever film technicians gather. No one, however, ever defined his attitude better than Sam did himself.

"I went to work for Sam on *The Secret Life of Walter Mitty*," says Ken Englund, "and at the time he was preparing *The Bishop's Wife*. One day we were in a script conference and he interrupted it to go down on the stage to inspect a new set that had just been finished for that picture, so he insisted I come along."

"Sam looked it over and told the art director the set was all wrong—it was the interior of a bishop's house, and it was too flashy. 'Tear it all down and build another one,' he ordered, and no amount of argument could change his mind. He didn't think it was right, and that was that. Wasn't up to the Goldwyn standard.

"What was involved was maybe $100,000 in added production costs, and I was pretty impressed that he could spend so much just like that. I told him so.

"Sam nodded. 'The banks couldn't afford me,' he said. 'That's why I had to be in business for myself.' " (It was several days before the actual filming of *The Bishop's Wife* that Goldwyn received word from his leading lady's agent that she could not make the film. She had, it seemed, just discovered that she was expecting a child. Goldwyn is reported to have called the actress' husband on the phone and said, "You know what you did? You didn't just screw her—you screwed *me!*")

"One day at lunch," continues Englund, "I ran into Sam, and he cheerfully announced, 'Well, I just bought *Billion Dollar Baby* for $100,000. I thought it was worth it!'

"Another time he had teamed me with Everett Freeman on a script. We worked for a few weeks, and the pages we sent up to Sam were very satisfactory—he kept telling us we were doing a fine job and he was very pleased with us.

"One noon we decided to go off the lot for lunch. As we started across the lawn, I heard Sam calling, 'Boys! Boys!'

"We turned around, and there was Sam, showing the studio to a couple of Eastern men in dark suits, obviously bankers. 'I want you to meet these two,' Sam said to the visitors. 'Say hello to my favorite writers, Ken Englander and Everett What's-His-Name.' "

For many years Goldwyn nurtured the idea of making a large-scale outdoor spectacle based on the exploits of the famous 7th Cavalry in the early days of the Western frontier. At one point he sent for Norman Reilly Raine, a writer and long one of *The Saturday Evening Post's* reliables, suggesting that Raine would be uniquely suited to write him a good script.

Raine was interested and intrigued by the notion. Goldwyn thereupon had his story department send up stacks of treatments and screenplays which had already been written by previous scripters at Goldwyn's behest. "I want you to take all these away, go to Palm Springs, read everything, digest it all, at my expense, of course, and then come back here and we'll discuss the project further," said Goldwyn.

Raine agreed and went off with the stack of material. After a week or so he was back in Goldwyn's office. "All right," said Goldwyn. "Tell me what you think of the material."

"I'll be very honest with you, Mr. Goldwyn," said Raine. "I've read everything and I don't know what you need *me* for—there are at least five or six good pictures here in this stuff."

Goldwyn nodded. "That's right," he said. "But all those writers forgot one thing. I hate Indians."

There is also the classic story of author Eddie Chodorov. Goldwyn was engaged in preparing a film about life in Russia, to be called *North Star,* and there was considerable script trouble.

Pat Duggan, then Goldwyn's story editor, suggested Chodorov for a rewrite. Chodorov, who had written the Broadway play *Kind Lady,* as well as many successful films, seemed like a good choice, and Goldwyn instructed Duggan to find him and bring him into the office for a meeting.

Chodorov was located; he was vacationing in Maine. Duggan called him on the phone and persuaded him to come down to Boston, thence to take a train to New York, and finally to travel out to California, at Goldwyn's expense, for conferences.

Upon his arrival at the studio, Chodorov was handed the latest draft of the script, which he read and pondered. When Sam inquired as to his reactions, Chodorov was firm. The script, in his opinion, was unsalvageable. Whereupon, at Goldwyn's expense, he returned to his interrupted vacation in Maine.

Some years later, when another Goldwyn project was in preparation, Goldwyn's story editor, a replacement for Duggan (who had gone on to become a producer at Paramount), suggested that Eddie Chodorov was available to work on it.

"Chodorov?" cried Goldwyn. "Never! He was associated with one of my worst failures!"

On another occasion Sam was recommending his latest film to a friend. "I want you to be sure and see my *Hans Christian Andersen,*" he urged. "It's full of charmth and warmth."

One morning he called Harry Tugend to tell him he had seen a remarkable film the evening before. "You'll love it," he said. "It's called *Black Neurosis.*" (It was, of course, *Black Narcissus.*)

Norman Krasna insists that the story of Goldwyn on the Hillcrest golf course with his friend Harpo Marx is absolutely true.

"One afternoon Sam and Harpo were playing a round," says Krasna. "Goldwyn's caddy carried a bag of clubs with several new putters with which he'd equipped himself. They got to the green, and Sam tried out one of the new putters. He missed his shot and furiously tossed away the putter.

"Harpo picked up the putter and put it quietly into his bag. When they came to the next hole, Harpo took out Goldwyn's putter, used it, and sank his ball.

"Then it got to be like a scene from a picture. Goldwyn was impressed. 'Say, Harpo,' he commented, 'that's a very nice putter you've

The Wit and Wisdom of Hollywood

got there. Mind if I try it?'

" 'Why not?' said Harpo.

"They got to the next green. Goldwyn borrowed the putter, and this time he sank his shot. 'This is a great putter!' he exulted. 'How about selling it to me, Harpo?'

"And with an absolutely straight face, Harpo sold Sam back his own putter."

Not content with gambling huge sums of his own money on whether or not the public would pay to see his films, Sam was exceedingly fond of card games. One evening he was seated in a game with a few film-colony cronies. The subject of legal problems arose— a couple of the players were involved in court actions and were bemoaning the endless complications.

Goldwyn nodded. "Well," he said, somewhat piously, "I'm happy to say that *I*'ve never been involved in a lawsuit."

The other men stared at him. One was Don Hartman. "Sam—how could you say that—after what we went through?" A second player chimed in. "You and I had a lawsuit once—remember?" And a third player reminded Sam that his lawyer had been in touch with Sam's only a week or so before.

Goldwyn nodded and then he shrugged. "Present company excepted," he said.

Unlike so many of his contemporaries, Sam has always been a generous giver. He established scholarships to the U.C.L.A. film school, and worthy charities have always benefited from his open-handedness.

At a fund-raising luncheon Irving Brecher found himself seated next to Mr. and Mrs. Goldwyn. The menu consisted of some sort of the customary hotel-style creamed chicken. Sam got up to make an important phone call, but reminded his wife Frances that he could not eat such a rich dish. Could she possibly arrange for something simpler?

While Sam was out telephoning, the toastmaster began to call for pledges. In the name of Sam and herself, Frances Goldwyn pledged $200,000.

Sam tiptoed back into the dining room and took his seat. A moment or so later the waiter placed a pair of simple broiled lamb chops before him. Goldwyn began to eat.

Brecher couldn't resist making a small joke. He leaned over and said, "Mr. Goldwyn, if I'm not mistaken, those lamb chops just cost you $100,000 apiece."

"Can't help it," said Goldwyn. "Doctor's orders."

298

One of the Goldwynisms that George Axelrod remembers most fondly was Sam's exclamation, "It's spreading like wildflowers!"

"There's a certain poetic justice to it," says George.

When Axelrod established his own production company, he rented office space at the Goldwyn studios. One day he encountered Goldwyn, who remarked in passing, "We ran Blake Edwards' new picture last night."

"*The Party?*" asked Axelrod.

"No, just five people," said Goldwyn.

"He had an enormous capacity for work," says David Golding, who served as Goldwyn's press agent for many years. "Once Sam came to New York and I met him up at his hotel room at nine in the morning. We sat and worked out various ad campaigns, made phone calls, did all sorts of important business, and then, around five in the afternoon, Sam said, 'Goulding'—for all those years I was always Goulding—'I think I'll take a shower.' He went inside, took a shower, came out a couple of minutes later, completely revived, and said, 'Well, what's new?'

"Then there was a period when he was making *Guys and Dolls*," says Golding. "Sam insisted that Frank Loesser, who'd written the Broadway show, be in residence while the picture was being shot. Frank was a definite night-person. He really couldn't adjust to the regular Goldwyn 9:00 A.M.–6:00 P.M. routine. And Sam couldn't understand why if *he* could put in such a day, Loesser could not.

"Anyway, Frank would arrive at the studio sometime around ten, check in, grab the trade papers, and head directly for the Formosa Restaurant, right across the street, and there he would warm himself up with a therapeutic breakfast—a couple of martinis and some ham and eggs. Only then would he be ready to cope with Sam and all of his energy. (Goldwyn was then in his early seventies.)

"Well, one bright morning Frank arrived. He grabbed his trades and ducked out onto the sidewalk, and he ran into me. 'C'mon, quick, let's get over to the Formosa,' he muttered. 'If Sam sees me out here, I'm finished.'

"We started across the street to the Formosa. Sam's office looks out on the street, and then I heard his voice, calling out behind us, 'Frankie! Frankie!'

"'Ignore him,' muttered Loesser, and dragged me toward the restaurant.

"'*Frankie!*' persisted Goldwyn. We'd almost gotten to the Formosa doorway, when Sam changed his tune."

"'Money, *money!*' he called.

"Which broke us both up. 'How can you turn *that* down?' groaned Loesser, and he went back to Sam, who was beaming triumphantly from his office window."

Another one of Goldwyn's passions over the years has been his croquet. There is an apocryphal story of his bringing one of his youthful associates over to the house for a game. In the course of the match the young man trounced Goldwyn badly. "Why aren't you in the office paying attention to your job?" demanded his angry boss.

Iz Diamond, Billy Wilder's longtime partner and collaborator, has another authentic Goldwyn story. "At the time that Charlie Brackett and Billy were working on the screenplay of *Ball of Fire* for Sam," he relates, "Wilder came up with the idea of making the life story of Nijinsky, the famous ballet dancer. (Years ahead of his time. It is currently being prepared by Harry Salzman as a film vehicle for Nureyev.) Billy was very enthusiastic about its potential for the screen, and he went into Sam's office to tell him about it.

"Sam listened intently as Billy told him about Nijinsky—his early ballet triumphs with Diaghilev, and finally he came to the tragic ending, in which the dancer goes mad and ends his days in a Swiss sanitarium, suffering from the delusion that he is a horse.

"Sam, to say the least, was very upset. 'What kind of story is this—the hero *thinks he's a horse?'* He waved Billy out of his office as if Billy were the one who'd gone mad.

"Billy realized it was a lost cause, and started out, but he stopped at the door. 'I didn't tell you the ending, Sam,' he said. 'The guy not only thinks he's a horse—but he also goes on to win the Kentucky Derby!'"

And it was Wilder's earlier partner, Charlie Brackett, who was once involved in a crisis on Sam's croquet court.

According to reliable witnesses, Sam played to win, and in order to win games, which involved side bets, he was not above minor infractions of the rules. Brackett played with Goldwyn for many years, and then one day he lost his temper. "Sam! That's enough!" he is supposed to have cried. "I've been playing with you for years and years, and I've been watching you cheat, but this time you've gone too far! I quit!"

The two men glared at each other, and then Goldwyn said, "As I recall it, Brackett, you were also a big Stevenson man."

Groucho Marx is fond of recalling how each time he encountered Goldwyn over the many years he lived in Hollywood, Sam waved and greeted him by asking, "How's your brother Harpo?"

This ritual went on until finally Groucho met Goldwyn one evening and became tired of the greeting. "Listen, Sam," he snapped,

"I've been meeting you for years, and all you've ever asked me is how is Harpo. When are you going to ask me how *I* am?"

"Oh, sometime I will," smiled Goldwyn. "But in the meantime, how's your brother Harpo?"

Porgy and Bess, the Gershwin-Heyward classic folk opera, became one of Goldwyn's largest-scale film projects. At one point during its preparation for the screen, Goldwyn hired N. Richard Nash, a young playwright with extensive theatrical experience, who preferred to work at his home in the East.

Goldwyn kept in constant touch with Nash by telephone, and one morning at 2:00 A.M. the phone rang beside Nash's bed. It was, as usual, Goldwyn, who wished to discuss some script changes. Nash groaned wearily. "Mr. Goldwyn," he protested, "do you have any idea what time it is?"

"Just a second," said Goldwyn, in California, and then Nash heard him say, "Frances, Mr. Nash wants to know what time it is."

Mr. and Mrs. Goldwyn were invited, a few winters back, to luncheon at the Palm Springs home of Frederick Loewe, the composer. Luncheon was scheduled for twelve noon, and Sam is a punctual man. He is also an early riser, a taker of long walks, and a man who is more than ready to eat lunch at twelve noon.

The Goldwyns arrived at the Loewe house and were ushered into the living room. There ensued conversation. No lunch. As time passed, Sam began to glance at his watch.

There seemed to be a certain amount of trouble in the Loewe kitchen—food was not ready to be served. Anxious to placate his hungry guest, Loewe went to his grand piano, sat down, and began to play a medley of some of his more famous songs, written with Alan Jay Lerner, from *Brigadoon* and *My Fair Lady*.

When he had finished, and luncheon was ready, Goldwyn beamed on Loewe. "You know, Fritz," he said, "you've got five or six possible hits there?"

At a Beverly Hills dinner party, Goldwyn held forth on the subject of filth in current films. "In all my years in this business, I've never seen anything like what they're putting out and trying to sell as entertainment. I ran a picture last night in my own home—disgusting! I wouldn't show it to anybody—I'd be ashamed to!"

Billy Wilder politely inquired the name of the offending film.

"It was *Hello, Dolly!*" said Goldwyn. "An absolutely filthy picture!"

Wilder was puzzled. "I don't see how it could have been *Hello, Dolly*," he remarked.

"I know what I saw!" insisted Sam.

"But, Sam," said Wilder, "you couldn't have seen it. It hasn't been released yet—Zanuck is still cutting it."

"Look, I'm telling you I saw *Hello, Dolly!*" said Sam. "Filthy!"

"Could you give us an idea what the story was about?" asked Wilder.

"Terrible!" said Sam. "All about these young girls in show business—and taking drugs, and having affairs to get ahead—"

"Sam," interrupted Wilder gently, "if I'm not mistaken, I think the picture you're referring to is called *Valley of the Dolls.*"

"Isn't that what I told you?" demanded Goldwyn. "*Valley of the Hello Dollies!*"

If, then, as Alva Johnston's biography states, it was the Woodrow Wilson administration's tariff decision that brought Sam Goldwyn of Gloversville, N.Y., down to New York City and into the movie business, then it certainly follows that American audiences of the past fifty years owe Woodrow Wilson a large debt of thanks. For if Sam had stayed in the glove business, who would have given us *The Squaw Man* and five decades' worth of good films, all of them somehow stamped with that "Goldwyn touch"?

And who would have given us all these great Goldwyn stories? For, as Sam himself might say, "Who would want to laugh at a glove salesman?"

> *Ken Englund's recollection of the collaborative task involving himself, James Thurber and Goldwyn during the preparation of* The Secret Life of Walter Mitty *was written in 1963. It is herewith reprinted for the benefit of future generations of film buffs and Thurber fans. It should also be carefully studied by various film critics and the entire staff of* Cahiers du Cinéma *(somewhat misguided intellectuals who persist in propounding a theory that all good films are made by directors working tout seul, without any assistance from other sources, such as cutters, producers and writers).*

My desk is strewn with rusty paper clips and discarded daydreams because I have just opened—for the first time since 1946—a dusty faded file labeled: THURBER-GOLDWYN-ENGLUND PRODUCTION NOTES AND CORRESPONDENCE, December 1945 to April 1946.

On the top of the pile is a carbon of my memorandum to Mr. Goldwyn dated April 1, 1946.

302

Dear Mr. Goldwyn: Relative to my Phone Conference with James Thurber re: Mitty Final Shooting Script dated March 15th.

Mr. Thurber phoned me last night and we talked for approximately an hour. He is primarily upset over the fact that there are not enough dreams. He feels that's what the picture's about—dreams, and that's what the audience is going to enjoy.

I explained that The Molly Malone Dream had a mood similar to The Spy Dream, so that's why it was felt in certain studio quarters that the latter dream should be eliminated. . . .

Thurber felt, however, that it doesn't matter at all how close or how far apart the dreams were in the picture, and that the factor should not be taken into consideration. A day-dreamer dreams when he gets the chance. . . . He says that the dreams are the best part of the script and feels very strongly that they should not be touched, but also feels very strongly that there should be more of them, that The Third Act particularly needs them. . . .

There were two major schools of thought. The Pro-Thurber Dream Group—Thurber, McLeod, Max Wilkinson, Goldwyn's Story Editor, and myself—stood shoulder to shoulder and agreed with Jim that the dreams were the best part of Mitty. Stoutly and sincerely opposed were the anti-Dream studio-based contingent who felt that the Dreams themselves were "too literary"—"too smart"— "too subtle"—"too *New Yorker!*"

At least a dozen times during those embattled days I had to listen to them quote that master satirist George Kaufman's famous crack, "Satire in the theater is something that closes Saturday night!"

They were all for keeping the Dreams—but at a minimum, and "joking them up," making them a farcical springboard for Danny Kaye's expert antics. Not caring that in the process the legitimate character of Walter Mitty might be turned into an unbelievable meaningless marionette, and the psychological essence and meaning of Mitty would then evaporate into thin studio air.

The anti-Dream division had a forthright answer ready: "The timid inhibited character of Thurber's Walter Mitty is too limiting for the multi-faceted exuberant talents of Danny Kaye. His other musical-comedy films were hits because the slim stories harnessed his talents—they didn't hobble them! All he needs is a picture frame that's fresh and an amusing starting point and he'll take off all by himself like a rocket—and let his own mad quips fall where they may, inside or outside the story. To hell with Mitty's character! It's only a peg to hang a Kaye vehicle on anyway. That's the only reason Goldwyn bought that Thurber piece in the first place!"

But it wasn't! Mr. Goldwyn, the uneasy headmaster presiding over these schools of opposing thought, although trying to compose the creative differences of opinion, began as a strong pro-Dream man.

So did Danny Kaye and his talented lyricist wife, Sylvia Fine.

However, like Mr. Goldwyn, they began to worry when the Calamity Janes and Johns continued to spread the gospel of disaster: "If Danny hews to the story line, the real Kaye will be lost and the picture will be nowhere—except in the red! Who cares about the handful of Thurber devotees?"

During one of our early closed-door preliminary story debates in Mr. Goldwyn's office on this same point, I made my customary pitch for a believable story line to make the Thurber Dreams psychologically valid.

"Ken," sighed the exhausted, exasperated Mr. G., "I can't keep listening to you on this point! Frankly, let me tell you something for your own good as a writer in Hollywood. Outside of a few thousand people in Manhattan, you are the only one in the rest of America that ever reads that *New Yorker* magazine!"

I admitted ruefully that I was a member of the elite, but argued that Thurber's tale was now well known to millions of delighted readers of *Reader's Digest* who had virtually overnight come to treasure the True Mitty. People who had never read or heard of Thurber instantly recognized a secret part of themselves in wistful Walter, the frustrated Everyman who compensated for his prosaic everyday humdrum existence by daydreaming of an adventurous, romantically exciting world where he is always the gallant, brave, victorious Hero. I showed my suspicious producer a copy of a later issue of the *Digest* quoting readers from all walks of life who had written their praises of Mitty. . . .

Mr. Goldwyn was amused and touched, but his rebuttal was valid. To break even on a big A picture in color, he would have to appeal to a greater segment of the American public than even the combined readership of *Reader's Digest* and *The New Yorker*.

I finally got his message. In terms of story content and script, we'd have to play it down the middle. In short: Do our level best to make Walter Mitty come to life, but also do our best to provide a practical platform for the varied talents of Danny Kaye.

Everett Freeman and I labored on a treatment. The slight story as it stood on paper, delightful as it was, was in fact a mere incident, not a story that could provide the plot for an entire two-hour film. It was clear that to solve the problem we would have to invent a plot.

René Clair, who was shooting a picture on the Goldwyn lot at that time, turned out to be a Thurber fan and tried to persuade Mr. Goldwyn to make a more intimate, naturalistic "little" Continental-style comedy, retaining as protagonists the middle-aged henpecked Husband Hero and the dominating relentlessly unromantic Mundane Wife.

Clair, of course, had cinema visions of a warmly mellow middle-aged star like Raimu, or his American equivalent, playing Mitty. But again, to be practical, Raimu was dead and where was his American equivalent? Victor Moore? Charles Butterworth? One was too old and the other was already in Comedians' Heaven. Besides, Mr. Goldwyn had already signed young, equally talented Danny Kaye to play our Mitty, which by *force majeure* changed the hero to a younger, white-collar worm henpecked by a dominant mother.

Goldwyn agreed to this major change, but warned us that if we couldn't get a screen story out of the Thurber property soon, he'd drop the option on it and find another, more suitable, story for Kaye.

We tried to create a believable world for our Hero where he could live a life of quiet desperation—not too easily stifled by a bossy mother and a blustering pompous know-it-all employer, Mr. Pierce, a publisher of lurid pulp magazines, who took all the credit for Walter's good ideas.

We gave Walter a selfish bird-brained fiancée, Gertrude Griswold, with a battering ram of a mother, Irmagard, setting the psychological scene for Walter's dreams, born of frustrations at home and at work.

We still had a long way to go. Mitty, on the surface, was "a passive character." A mouse in life who was a man only in his fantasy world. He was no virile doer; he was primarily a reactor to situations. We all felt a secret terror that, if not handled carefully, Mitty could be dull. And "dull" is an unprofitable word in the picture business.

We had the wrong girl set in our screen story now—Gertrude, the girl Walter is about to marry. Now we had to invent the right one—the type Walter was constantly dreaming about.

We found our heroine—and Walter's—in Jim Thurber's Court-room Dream:

> Pandemonium broke loose in the courtroom. A wom-an's scream rose above the bedlam and suddenly a lovely, dark-haired girl was in Walter Mitty's arms. The District Attorney struck at her savagely. Without rising, Mitty let the man have it on the point of the chin.
>
> "You miserable cur!"

She became Rosalind Van Hoorn, seemingly an accomplice, but actually the pawn, of a desperate band of international criminals led by the diabolically sinister brain of Dr. Hugo Hollingshead.

The melodramatic spine of the screen story was designed to save the hero from a mundane marriage to Gertrude by bringing to life Rosalind, the girl of his dreams, who is surrounded by villains he must vanquish to get to her. This leads to his liberation in the third act, where he puts his new-found strength and courage to the test and tells off all those truly frightening villains in his life: his mother, boss, fiancée Gertrude and Irmagard, his castrating mother-in-law-to-be, along with another of his detractors, Tubby Wadsworth, an arrogantly athletic rival for Gertrude's hand. As Thurber himself later analyzed it: "The crooks were nothing compared to the women he's got to face!"

Our goal, obviously: the Comedy of Catharsis. The mouse be-comes a man. Walter Mitty stops daydreaming and starts doing—making his own dreams come true at the fadeout.

We wrote two rough drafts, and Mr. Goldwyn, accompanied by his charming and enthusiastic wife, Frances, took the second screen-play to New York for James Thurber's perusal and a tea-party script conference in Goldwyn's Waldorf Tower suite—Frances pouring, Thurber's wife, Helen, acting as his "eyes."

Helen read him the draft, and the next day Thurber announced that the script was "too melodramatic". . . .

When Pat Duggan, vice-president of Goldwyn Productions, gave us this far-from-stimulating report, Everett Freeman accepted an assignment at another studio; we went our separate ways.

Some thirteen days later I was called back to work. Mr. Goldwyn wanted to try again, but he did feel the script needed a great deal of work.

I asked him to be more specific.

"I'll be specific!" he thundered. "I hate the last sixty pages!" He handed me my plane ticket to New York.

While I checked to see if it was round trip, he softened, gravely shook my hand, wished me well and assured me that I would be able to handle Thurber "because, Ken, you are charming."

When I reached the door of Apartment 8-D at 410 West 57th Street, New York, the next morning, I wasn't at all sure what my playing attitude should be.

Should I enter all smiles—that he would not be able to see—and shower the great Thurber with compliments about his work, playing the humble and inferior role of the Hollywood hack?

Should I come on strong? A crass West Coast Marco Polo from Rajah Goldwyn who paid damned good money for a mere wisp of a literary property that must by some miraculous process be fashioned into a profitable picture?

I rang the buzzer and decided to play it by ear.

James Thurber opened the door.

I quickly noted that he, too, would play it by ear, for he was almost completely blind.

After meeting his wife, Helen, who affably asked me what I ate for lunch, Mr. Thurber and I sat alone in the living room of his cozy, comfortable apartment, facing each other.

He kept studying me, his wispy mustache twitching occasionally, peering at me through—as he explained it—"a gray mist." I don't know how he managed to discern that I too, had had serious eye trouble in my youth, but he did. He "saw" that my left eye muscle was weak. I admitted that it didn't always focus and function properly, and immediately we began to chatter like two biddies about our special and highly original symptoms. Jim merrily thought that we'd make "a perfect pair of bookends for Mr. Goldwyn's home library!" Naturally we put off talking about the script as long as we could. . . .

When I got back to my hotel I found this telegram:

PLEASE CALL GOLDWYN IMMEDIATELY YOU FINISH WITH THURBER TODAY AT STUDIO OR HOME CRESTVIEW ONE TWO EIGHT THREE SIX REGARDS

PAT DUGGAN

Mr. Goldwyn's voice came at me loud and clear from three thousand miles away.

"Well, Ken, how is it coming?"

This, incidentally, has been the standard greeting to screenwriters throughout the ages, spoken always in a suspicious, accusing tone of voice.

"What?" I floundered. "Oh—we're getting along fine, Mr. Goldwyn—couldn't be better! It's coming—fine!"

Mr. Goldwyn got down to business. Thurber's very able and tough agent, William Herndon, was asking a thousand dollars for every day I would have to spend with his illustrious client.

"Do you think you can finish with Thurber in a week? How far did you get today? What sequence are you on in the script?"

"The script?" I stalled. "Oh . . . well, at the moment I'm just getting his general ideas about the over-all problems. . . ."

"You have ten days at the most! I've set the shooting date for March fifteenth! Goodbye, Ken!"

It was indeed "Goodbye, Ken" if Thurber didn't cooperate in the salvaging of at least some of what was already written, because this was already the fourth of December!

The next day Thurber and I got right to work. And here I think that I can report best by quoting story notes and correspondence, and excerpts from Thurber's own letters. His consideration, tact, diplomacy and gentlemanly regard for the feelings of others are clearly exhibited in his own words.

December 19, 1945

Dear Mr. Goldwyn:

Ken Englund and I completed our work on the WALTER MITTY script late yesterday evening, after devoting long days and going over the story with a microscope and a fine tooth comb from beginning to end.

I believe we have accomplished what you had in mind, which I am confident is also what I myself wanted to achieve. . . . Mr. Englund is taking complete and copious notes to Hollywood which he will present to you for your approval or disapproval. I feel sure that he can explain what we have done to your satisfaction, much better than I could in a letter from so long a distance. It was a pleasure to work with him. . . .

. . . there is nothing that can be done at this late date about the melodrama, as such, except to blend it more realistically and more humorously with the dreams and with Walter's day to day life with his Mother and his Fiancée. The melodrama still remains the spine of our structure, but I feel, and so does Ken Englund, that it no longer sticks out, but that it has been more ingenuously inter-laced with the Dreams and the private life of our Hero.

. . . the changes we have suggested not only enrich the credibility of the story but, I believe, add considerable to its humor and to what you describe as the warm quality of the first sixty pages.

The Mother still remains a tyrant and a domineering woman but audiences everywhere will find her recogniz-able. I think this is also true of Gertrude and of Gertrude's Mother, Irmagard.

We must eliminate what was for me the most unbeliev-able scene in the whole script—the scene with Dr. Hol-lingshead in which Dr. Hollingshead convinces Walter that *he has never seen Rosalind* and has not been involved with any Crooks at all.

To elaborate this point briefly: This scene also struck Elliott Nugent as unbelievable and even dangerous be-cause, as Elliott said, "Now everybody will believe that Walter Mitty is crazy, and all of your values of Walter as a mere daydreamer will be lost as soon as the audience sus-pects that he is in fact insane."

As for the Firing Squad Daydream, I think it's inte-grated in the story now in a perfectly plausible way. . . .

I feel that I have learned a great deal in a short time about some of the problems that face a motion picture pro-ducer and a motion picture writer. Let me thank you again for selecting Ken Englund to work with me on this story, and let me say once more that I am enthusiastic about the picture. . . .

Sincerely yours,
JAMES THURBER

The Firing Squad Dream which Jim refers to here was the poignantly comical last daydream in his original story of "The Secret Life of Walter Mitty." Everett Freeman and I had altered it to fit the screen story and further the plot action psychologically, so that the scene would not only be Thurber fun but have its roots in Walter's inner torment. For his boss was the commander of the firing squad. This was expanded in New York with Thurber's help to include Rosalind, who, as a beautiful Red Cross nurse, ran into the scene at the finish and cradled the hero's head in her soft, warm lap. Mitty, the gallant spy, wearing a contented smile on his face, was now happy and secure even in death.

The Spy Dream, the most admired by all at the beginning, became a studio bone of contention. It was out one moment, in the next.

One of our big problems was one of timing and mechanics. The Dreams couldn't come too close together in a film because they could become repetitious, with diminishing comedy results.

Another problem was that Danny Kaye was enormously effective in his comedy song numbers; we had to remind ourselves from time to time that this, after all, was still a musical comedy.

Prior to my flying trip to see Thurber, Goldwyn asked me to talk with Sylvia Kaye and get her views because it was her job to write Danny Kaye's numbers. Sylvia was completely cooperative. She still had faith in the Thurber Dreams—even if some of the studio group didn't—and we agreed that Danny in a daydream satirizing a French couturier, "Anatole of Paris," could provide the basis for a number that wouldn't destroy the continuity and would also include the beautiful Goldwyn Girls—in a reasonably plausible manner.

I wasn't as eager to integrate a comic German music teacher in Mitty's R.A.F. Desert Ace Reverie, but Sylvia's arguments were valid. The number was one of Danny's strongest. It had been tested on the night-club circuit and was sure-fire. It afforded Danny an excellent tongue-twisting opportunity to imitate all the instruments in an orchestra; if he knew he had this old sturdy standby nailed down for his first song, he would feel secure. So would Mr. Goldwyn, who "loved the number." What's more, this R.A.F. Dream had been under attack as being "dated" and "satire that was familiar and old hat."

I tried a new idea out on Sylvia Fine—an Irish "informer"-style dream that would lyrically move the plot forward psychologically and sentimentally and give Mitty a different style of dream in the third act. I suggested tactfully that Sylvia write a song *like* "Molly Malone."

"Why not use 'Molly Malone'? It will be great for Danny!" reacted Sylvia. And so the problem of the three necessary numbers was solved to Mr. Goldwyn's satisfaction—and Jim Thurber's.

And now to backtrack just a little. When I left New York, reluctantly, after our ten-day think session, I had a briefcase crammed with my handwritten notes, some in Thurber's large scrawl, scribbled on both sides of his favorite unlined yellow paper.

We were in complete agreement on using the following Dreams:

I. THE SEA DAYDREAM
To quote from the Revised Shooting Script of 3/14/46, a NARRATOR'S VOICE is heard over the scene of a storm at sea:

"Somewhere off the South China Coast, in the worst ty-
phoon in forty years, the little schooner India Queen
ploughed through an ocean gone mad. . . . Straining engines went ta-pocketa-pocketa-pocketa, driving the tortured
vessel forward. Up on deck Captain Walter Mitty stood
astride his bridge barking orders. . . ."

2. THE HOSPITAL DAYDREAM

"—and Mitty the surgical genius, entered the breathless
hush of the operating room, the tense silence broken only
by the sound of the huge anesthetizing machine going ta-
pocketa-pocketa-pocketa. There were whispered introduc-
tions. . . ."

DR. BENBOW: Dr. Remington, Dr. Renshaw, and this is Dr.
Pritchard-Mitford of St. John's Hospital, London . . . Dr.
Walter Mitty.

They exchange nods and continue with the operation.

DR. REMINGTON: Read your book on Streptothricosis. A
brilliant performance, sir.

DR. MITTY: Thank you.

DR. PRITCHARD-MITFORD: Didn't know you were in the
States, Mitty. Coals to Newcastle, bringing me up here for
a Tertiary.

And so on—Rosalind making an appearance as the "striking blonde
nurse" who "looks up at Walter through moist sapphire eyes."

BLONDE NURSE: Doctor, do you . . . will he . . . ?

DR. MITTY (nods): Your brother will play the violin again.
I grafted new fingers on him.

In a burst of emotion, she kisses his hand, but Mitty draws
it away and pats her shoulder.

DR. MITTY (gently): There, there, Miss Cartwright. You'll
want some rest now.

BLONDE NURSE (untying his gown): What about you?
You've been on your feet for thirty-six hours.

[And remember this is a good fifteen years before Ben Casey and
Dr. Kildare!]

3. THE R. A. F. DAYDREAM

NARRATOR'S VOICE: The Spitfire dived through the clouds,
its machine guns belching lead. . . . Oblivious of the omi-
nous ta-pocketa-ta-pocketa of his failing engines, Wing
Commander Walter Mitty, the most feared man in the en-

tire R.A.F. Desert Patrol, clung to the tail of the Messerschmitt.

GERMAN ACE (fearfully): Gott in Himmel, it's Walter Mitty
—I'm a lost man!

NARRATOR'S VOICE: Mitty's jaw was a grim, straight line as
he gave the Jerry three more lethal bursts and watched him
go down in flames!

When Wing Commander Mitty enters the French-Arab café
in Abd-el-Fez, his uniform is rumpled and torn, a white silk
muffler knotted carelessly at his throat. As he crosses toward the bar, the young officers greet him boisterously and
his Colonel breathes a visible sigh of relief to see that the
best man in his squadron is still miraculously alive.

YOUNG BRITISH PILOTS (ad lib): There's Commander Mitty,
fellows! He made it! . . . Good old Mitty! . . . How
many this time, old chap?

Mitty casually, modestly, holds up five fingers. The pilots
cheer and Mitty joins his Colonel.

COLONEL: Good show.

MITTY: Thank you, sir.

COLONEL: That makes seventy-three, doesn't it?

MITTY: Seventy-one, sir. Two were only probables.

COLONEL (anxiously): I say, old man, you're wounded.

MITTY (pouring a brandy): Just a scratch, sir. I set the
bone myself. . . .

4. THE MISSISSIPPI RIVERBOAT DAYDREAM

NARRATOR'S VOICE: The paddlewheels make a pocketa-
pocketa sound in the water as the boat churns along the
moonlit river. . . .

While Gaylord Mitty, the Gentleman Gambler, cool and im-
placable, wins all from a decadent Southern dandy of the
Old Civil War South (who looks like his hated rival, Tubby
Wadsworth) at a game of cards in the riverboat's salon.

TUBBY (desperately): One more hand, Mitty!

MITTY (coolly fingering his chips): With what, Colonel?
Ginger snaps? (He starts to rise.)

TUBBY: Wait—I know you're in love with my fiancée. I'll
play you one hand for her!

MITTY (scornfully): You'd pluck a star from the heavens
and fling it on the soiled cloth of a gaming table?

TUBBY: If I lose, I'll go North. Is it a wager?

It is, and Gaylord Mitty wins the lovely Southern belle who stands, two large magnolias in her hair, on the stern deck.
NARRATOR'S VOICE: The scent of honeysuckle was strong in the air; the plink of banjos could be heard over the gentle lapping of the paddlewheels as they went pocketa-pocketa-pocketa in the moonlit waters. Gaylord Mitty squared his enormous shoulders, and called her name softly.
MITTY: Miss Gertrude . . .
The belle turns and we see it is not Walter's fiancée, Gertrude! It is his Dream girl, Rosalind!

5. THE FIRING SQUAD DAYDREAM
Walter Mitty lights a cigarette as he comes out of the Chinese restaurant with his party: Mother, fiancée, mother-in-law-to-be and his boss, Mr. Pierce. It begins to rain. Walter stands up against the wall, smoking. He puts his shoulders back and his heels together. . . .
WALTER (scornfully): To hell with the handkerchief!
He takes one last drag on his cigarette and snaps it away. . . .

6. THE FAMOUS DRESSMAKER DAYDREAM
NARRATOR'S VOICE: Completing last-minute preparations for the greatest show of his dazzling career, Anatole Mitty, known wherever hats are worn as "Anatole of Paree," flitted about his world-famous salon in the Rue de la Blanc Mange! Today he would unveil his newest creations, and so excited was he that his little heart was beating pocketa-pocketa-pocketa under his hand-embroidered vest. . . .

7. THE IRISH DAYDREAM
Leaning against a lamppost in the murky, drizzly Dublin night is Walter O'Mitty, wearing a cap pulled down over one eye, a turtleneck sweater, a cigarette dangling from his desperate lips. He slinks along the foggy streets.
NARRATOR'S VOICE: . . . and even while the sirens were still screaming at Bleakmore Prison, Walter O'Mitty, the hunted, had eluded the entire Dublin Police Force in a final mad desire to reach the side of his beloved Molly. . . .
Reaching a tiny house in the slums, O'Mitty recoils in a black Irish anguish at sight of a mourning wreath that hangs from the door-knocker. The door opens and an old

313

silver-haired Irish lady stands there wiping away tears with her apron.

OLD IRISH LADY (staring in fright): Walter O'Mitty! They're lookin' for you!

WALTER (thick Irish brogue): Mother Macree—she isn't—they didn't—Molly isn't—?

Old Irish lady buries her face in her apron.

WALTER: Oh, the black dogs!

Hounded by the police, and with the cries of passing hucksters coming over the scene as they hawk their wares—"Cockles!" "I've got fresh mussels here! Alive, alive, oh!"—Walter O'Mitty pours out his sad, broken Irish heart in "Molly Malone."

8. THE WESTERN DREAM

In which Walter "Slim" Mitty, the clean-cut cowboy in the white hat, rescues the beautiful blonde cowgirl Rosalind from a fate worse than death at the hands of a bad hombre in a black hat, Toledo Tubby (who bears a close physical resemblance to Tubby Wadsworth).

NARRATOR'S VOICE: And Slim Mitty, the Perth Amboy Kid, strode grimly towards his sworn enemy, Toledo Tubby, the lowest varmint west of the Pecos. . . .

So far so good in terms of Thurber approval of Walter's Dreamland, but when I set foot again on California soil I found that Mr. Goldwyn and the Kayes had asked Phil Rapp to drop work on another film he was preparing for Mr. Goldwyn and help me "funny up the Dreams" so that we would be sure to get laughs.

This secretly dismayed Thurber. His sensitive ears pricked up like one of his own cartoon hound dogs when he learned of this fresh development. He immediately phoned me at home to find out if everything was under control. I assured him it was. Phil Rapp and I had been old collaborators way back in the Golden Age of radio when we wrote the Victor Moore-Helen Broderick-Mary Martin show together in Los Angeles.

The world of comedy writers is indeed a small one. Phil Rapp, Everett Freeman and I had all worked for one of the great pioneers of radio writing, David Freedman, who had also helped in the development of other young writers like Arnold Auerbach and the now successful Herman Wouk.

Convinced that the Rapp-Englund coalition might eliminate some

Dreams and give Walter Mitty baggy pants and a red nose that would light up, Jim developed a set of East Coast super-anxieties. He sent up the following distress signals, addressing a firm memo to Goldwyn's vice-president, Pat Duggan:

> . . . the last fifty pages should not skimp the dream element. To say that dreams slow up the story is to say the locomotive slows up the cow. The dreams are the best Kaye and the best audience appeal. They are new, unique and universal.
>
> The other elements in the picture cannot touch *The 39 Steps* or *The Awful Truth*. Any cutting should come in them.
>
> I will personally undertake to thrash anyone who mangles the dreams. They are wonderful. . . .
>
> Yours,
Jim Thurber

He liked the new Molly Malone Dream in particular, and when I told him on the phone that Phil Rapp had helped me, Jim was reassured. About Phil, that is, but he was still worried that Goldwyn *et al.* would lay heavy hands on the Dreams and add too much obvious corny comedy to the melodramatic sequences.

Some of the Dreams started going out as shooting, under Norman McLeod's direction got under way.

The Firing Squad Dream, everybody's favorite, was shot—but left on the cutting-room floor because it didn't jell on film.

The Molly Malone Dream turned out beautifully, but suddenly a lobby of "outsiders" began joining Goldwyn, McLeod and the Kayes when they viewed the daily rushes at the end of each day. Some were mighty names, like director Howard Hawks, who meant only to be helpful. None of them had anything to do with the making of the film, yet they gave advice as to which Dreams should be retained and which ones "delayed the action."

During this ulcerating period Mr. Goldwyn asked me not to alarm Jim Thurber by reporting that any particular Dream had permanently bit the dust on the cutting-room floor. "Until we've previewed the picture several times with all the dreams in it, we won't decide, I assure you, Ken, what the final version will look like until a week before we open at the Astor. Let me tell you something for your own good, Ken—you worry too much!"

Jim bombarded me with notes and suggestions of new Dreams

I might have ready to replace those that fell by the wayside. He begged me to "ward off the corny contingent."

> What we get too far away from is Walter, the ingratiating little guy to whom nothing ever happens except the humdrum—except in his dream. These romantic, heroic dreams are funny, and touching, because they happen to a man who, in reality, is in an office or tending a furnace or playing bridge badly, like Any Man.
>
> . . . the Anatole Dream loses this quality, because our man at the time of this dream *is* Anatole, in effect. He is the tiger-tamer dreaming of being a lion-tamer. Our Walter's natural dream here would be to imagine himself as Robinson Crusoe, a hermit in a cave, or last man in the world. . . .

Learning from his Hollywood grapevine that the Firing Squad Dream had misfired when it was filmed, Jim fired off a note to me urging that I urge Mr. G. to let us take another shot at it, integrating and retaking the Dream in a new way: and he invented a new Dream.

At this point, some of us at the studio were uncertain about everything. Thurber, reading our wishy-washy minds from three thousand miles away, now began lobbying by mail for a Courtroom Dream that had never been scheduled.

> The value of going into a brief Courtroom Dream in the Doctor's office, while Dr. Bellman, the good psychiatrist, is listening to a summary of Walter's case from Mrs. Mitty, is not only the humor I see in this familiar place of daydreams—*all of us imagine ourselves on trial*—but is the chance to add to Walter's growing concern for himself, and to the Doctor's and the Others' conviction that he is a nut. . . .

By this time there was a good chance that the picture, if all this rough material were polished and shot, might run longer than *Cleopatra.*

Nevertheless, Jim felt it was wise to have daydreams in reserve, waiting in the wings, ready to be shot at a moment's notice, and on March 31, 1946, he revealed his anxiety about the Western Dream. So he rushed me a scrawled outline of a new version. At the same time expressing other misgivings:

Dear Ken:

> I hope to God you can sell them the idea of separating the two climaxes, keeping the major one last—the ironing

out of the love and family problem. We had this identical set-up in *The Male Animal*, and I pleaded for what I plead for in Mitty. In *The Male Animal* we originally settled the hash of the bad trustee and that of the football player in the same scene. Using my idea, we got rid of the trustee first and then settled the triangle, and it made the third act. . . .

In his next directive, Jim reminded me of a Dutch Dream we ad-libbed together in New York that could be inserted in the story in the last reel—as Walter is about to marry the wrong girl, his fiancée, Gertrude. He would dream of himself as Walter Van Mitty saving Holland with his finger in the leaking dyke.

> ROSALINDA: Oh, Walter! Run! Run for your life! It is hope-less, don't you see, my love?
> WALTER: I ask only that you remember me always and leave me something to wear next to my heart!
> The water is rising with perilous rapidity. Rosalinda has nothing but her wooden shoes to give him as a farewell love token, along with a big tearful farewell kiss.
> ROSALINDA: My hero!
> The Dream is terminated abruptly by the impatient Min-ister's words:
> MINISTER: . . . do you, Walter Mitty, take this woman, Gertrude Griswald, as your lawful wedded wife. . .
> And panicky, trapped Walter is back once more in the Perth Amboy world of harsh reality.

About this time during the shooting, Mr. Goldwyn began mailing Thurber the final script pages re-mimeographed daily to include all changes large or minuscule.

To Helen Thurber the morning mail must have resembled a rainbow, because each changed page was run off in different color. However, she would dutifully read each change to her husband, inspiring new valuable contributions to story construction and, more important, ammunition for the beleaguered pro-Dream forces, including those among us who still wanted to avoid comedy that was too low.

On the other hand, contradicting himself, Thurber rushed some lower jokes to Pat Duggan for the scene between Walter and the Psychiatrist—worried himself that maybe some of the scenes were too sophisticated and too light in comedic value.

Even at the midway point in the shooting when half the picture was in the can, Jim continued to sprinkle parsley on the roast. He sent me this telegram from Hot Springs, Va.:

> MAILED AIR MAIL SPECIAL DELIVERY YESTERDAY OUTLIN-
> ING WHAT WE DISCUSSED AND INDICATING SOME DIALOGUE
> ROUGHLY. PLEASE HAVE TWO COPIES OF MY LETTER MADE
> AND SEND ONE TO BILL HERNDON AND THE OTHER TO ME
> IN NEW YORK LOVE
>
> JIM THURBER

As we all know, Jim had learned his trade as an editor of *The New Yorker*. He never stopped trying to improve and rewrite. And he always wanted to give an employer his money's worth. In a letter for Pat Duggan, Goldwyn's story editor, he said:

> Largely due to the well-known Thurber system of handling any matter, I had Herndon on the spot for a time, but the financial arrangement has been worked out to my satisfaction and to his, and I hope to yours.
> "During the days in Virginia when I was making the changes I sent you, I also wrote on yellow paper one or two other brief ideas. Since these were done at the same time in which I wrote the others, it seems only fair to me to con- sider that the $1500 you have agreed to pay for what I sent should also include these two minor items. I simply did not have the time to get them properly arranged but I offer them to you now as an integral part of the work I was do- ing. I do not need to tell you that my interest in the movie is intense and that I still keep thinking about it all the time."

(*Author's Comment:* Thurber had come a long way since our first brain-storming session. At that time I had pointed out that Goldwyn had to reach a mass audience of millions in order to show a profit on the picture. Unimpressed, he had riposted: "All I care about reaching is my twenty thousand readers!")

Another suggestion:

> Walter's scene on page 20 with the enormous bottle of cologne could be made funnier, and a real-life scene which happens to every man who uses a safety razor but which, so far as I know, has not been presented in a movie. I find, on talking to my men friends, that they have all become

318

enormously and comically involved by the following shaving sequence:

A man gets his face all lathered up and his hands all covered with the lather, and then finds he has forgotten to put a blade in the razor. No man, certainly not Walter Mitty, would think of wiping off his face and hands and beginning again. He tries to get the blade in the razor, succeeds only in getting it wet and soapy, and letting it fall into the washbowl. If you have ever tried to get a wet razor blade out of a wash bowl with soapy fingers, you know what I mean. Finally, what you do is snap the razor blade out of the bowl and it falls on the tile floor. A wet razor blade sticks to a tile floor like a leech. Using the nail of the index finger to lift up one end, you put your shoe against the other and in the hope that the razor blade will stand up and you can grab it between your fingers. What happens is that the razor now gets stuck to the sole of your left shoe.

I kept one crisis from Thurber: the title crisis. The New York sales organization of Goldwyn Productions decided that we must create a new title for the picture. *The Secret Life of Walter Mitty* simply was not a film title. "Too long, too literary and not commercial!" So everyone connected with Mitty in Hollywood was memoed by Goldwyn's publicity chief, Bill Hebert, asking us to submit a list of new titles.

For a short and depressing time the working title was "I Wake Up Dreaming." I sabotaged this by depressing Goldwyn with the fact that Fox had recently released a Laird Cregar thriller, *I Wake Up Screaming*. He retaliated by demanding that I "cooperate" and submit a list of new titles I liked.

I submitted: *The Secret Life of Walter Mitty*. And I had my secretary type it twenty-five times. Goldwyn then engaged a company of statistical "experts" who for a huge fee were going to make a man-in-the-street survey, testing titles for the picture in various American cities. Norman McLeod, a strong pro-Thurber man, and I unwittingly torpedoed this new scientific approach to the title problem by shooting off our mouths to the *New York Times* Drama Editor when he called us to get our views.

Norman suggested that the man in the street could hardly give a sensible reaction to a title for a picture he had not as yet seen, and that the people making the film were the only ones qualified to give it a name.

I made the point that if you came up to a strange man in the street and asked him what he thought of *Wuthering Heights*, he might scratch his head and reply that it sounded like a pretty classy subdivision but he wasn't sure he'd want to live there.

We rattled off the titles of other great Goldwyn pictures which didn't mean anything until the pictures themselves gave them meaning: *Dead End,* etc., etc.

Early Monday morning Bill Hebert had Norman and myself on the phone, plaintively asking, "Please, you guys, no more interviews till we get this title thing settled, huh?"

It was settled when Mr. Goldwyn quickly tired of the statistical charts in his office. *Mitty* became the working title, and the final one.

When the picture was cut and sneak-previewed on the Coast, I tried to spare Thurber from learning about some of the unkindest cuts of all. For instance, the pro-Dream faction fought right up to the wire to save the Molly Malone Dream, which bit the dust of Pasadena after our last preview.

Forty-eight hours before the opening day of *Mitty* at the Astor Theatre in New York, I had breakfast with John Fulton, the brilliant Academy Award-winning creator of the special effects of the Dream sequences. He too mourned the loss of the Irish Dream and suggested I dispatch an eloquent wire to Mr. Goldwyn urging him to air-express to us the Molly Malone Dream. There was still time to splice it back in before the opening. In short, let the New York film critics decide whether or not the extra three-minute Dream was one too many.

Suddenly I was the Mouse that became a Man. No longer on the payroll, I was as fearless as Mitty in the last reel. The desk clerk at the hotel was bug-eyed and terribly impressed by my Hollywood derring-do when I handed him one of the most eloquent wires ever written, listing all the reasons why we should retain "Molly Malone" for at least the first day of the premiere. The straight telegram cost me forty-one dollars and some cents.

Talk about Dreams! The film never arrived. But the morning of opening day I received an airmail reply from Mr. Goldwyn:

Dear Ken:
Everyone agrees with me that the Molly Malone Dream holds up the entertainment. The picture plays much better without it. You worry too much.

Very best regards to you, always,
Sam

Jim and I corresponded from time to time and he once suggested I do a Broadway musical dramatization of *Mitty,* but we never saw each other again. That's fate and show biz. Ships and writers that pass in the night. And all too quickly.

I prize a letter he sent me the day after I returned to the Coast. I've framed it. I'm proud of it—to hell with modesty!

Dear Ken:

I have just signed my letter to Sam Goldwyn, a copy of which I am enclosing for your secret and confidential information and guidance.

I hope it does not confuse or conflict with anything you are going to say or may have said to him. I tried to make it a clear statement of our major changes in the script.

I said in my letter to the boss a few little things about you which I hope will not embarrass you. Helen and I both missed you when a day rolled around and you were not here to kick Walter around for another six hours. I realize that it was a great deal of fun to make our changes in Walter's life and destiny, and that a great deal of this fun was in knowing you and working with you. As soon as I find the proper drawing I will send it to you, and if it doesn't arrive until after the holidays, it will still carry my best wishes for a Merry Christmas, a Happy New Year and a good life generally.

I trust that you will finally be able to finish this Mitty script and be allowed to get around to something of your own once more.

> Cordially yours,
> s/Jim
> James Thurber

(*from* THE SECRET LIFE OF JAMES THURBER, *by Ken Englund,*
in POINT OF VIEW)

It is alleged that James Thurber later communicated with Goldwyn to the effect that he felt the picture contained far too much violence and gore. Goldwyn immediately wrote Thurber, "I am sorry that you felt it was too blood and thirsty." Whereupon Thurber replied, "Not only did I think so, but I was horror and struck."

George Axelrod, the playwright and screenwriter, had a series of dealings with Goldwyn some years later regarding the elaboration of some of the Thurber dream sequences which had been left out of the Kaye picture, and which Goldwyn felt might be used for another film.

"It was after a couple of our conferences that I found out that Sam had never read Thurber's original short story," says Axelrod. "He originally bought it from a synopsis.

"There's an apocryphal Thurber story which deals with the time somebody got Thurber to go see a psychiatrist, a member of a profession he particularly loathed," adds Axelrod. "After some consultation on his personal habits, the psychiatrist is supposed to have told Thurber, who had been doodling on a pad, 'Mr. Thurber, I think we can lick this whole drawing thing in about six weeks.' "

TWILIGHT
OF THE GODS

"Tell me, how did you love the picture?"
ATTRIBUTED TO SAM GOLDWYN

"A rock's a rock, a tree is a tree, shoot it in bed."
SAYING, CIRCA 1968

"Boy lays girl, boy meets girl, boy gets boy."
FORMULA, CIRCA 1970

recent years, the role of the director has become so important in the making of films that financial backing is no longer based on the status of a potential star, but on which director will be in charge. "I used to be prejudiced against directors," said the late Isobel Lennart, a prominent screenwriter, "but now I'm bigoted against them."

HOLLYWOOD GOSSIP IN THE SEVENTIES

by Hal Kanter

SHOW BIZ BUZZ: Bob Wise plans prepping another film bio for Julie Andrews, titled *Scar!* This time Julie plays Al Capone. . . . From Rome, new twosome spotted on the Via Veneto: Julie Newmar. . . . Here at home, Raymond Massey donned his old shawl and stovepipe, invaded Stage 20 at Fox to free the cast of *Julia*. . . . Director Dick Fleischer's nephew will read from *Tora! Tora! Tora!* next Saturday at his Bar Mitzvah, Mitzvah, Mitzvah. . . . HAPPY BIRTHDAY to the Grand Canyon, sixteen million years young tomorrow. Warren Beatty will fly a group of his closest girls up to help celebrate. . . . Designer Travilla paged to Monaco by the Rainiers. Grace commissioned him to create new cords for her Princess phones. Travilla sails Tuesday; he does not fly. . . . Warner Bros. leading man Ronnie Reagan, moonlighting as Governor of California, being eyed for similar duties by Arizona, Vermont and Romania. . . . San Diego Poultry Breeders Ass'n commissioned actor-writer Douglas Dick to film an in-depth study of the migratory habits of mallards. John Wayne saw a rough cut and was so impressed, Duke's dickering Diego for Doug Dick's duck doc. . . . Was that Omar Sharif riding the camel down Ventura last night? It was the one with the bumper sticker that says "Golda Meir is a Shiksa.". . . Look for Irving Wallace's new novel—he lost it somewhere between Sunset and Pico. . . . It was Will Shakespeare's 405th birthday last month, and because his *Romeo and J* is still drawing such long lines at the b.o., Joe Levine wants Shakey to pen a sequel, even at his age. . . . Writer-producer Ernie Lehman now claims to have his screen approach to *Portnoy's Complaint* firmly in hand. . . . That's it for today. Tomorrow, too.

(from THE HOLLYWOOD REPORTER, *June 1970)*

The motion picture business has never done anything by halves. Just as money was flung about with wild abandon throughout the lush boom years, so in the austere Seventies has cost-consciousness moved into Hollywood with a vengeance. For years, only "quickie" producers pinched pennies. Today the whole town has become Poverty Row.

In the fall of 1970, Clint Eastwood, a popular star of action films, was engaged in making a new picture for Universal International. Universal provided the finances; Eastwood not only starred in the film, but also produced it.

Eastwood and his production crew were on location in Arizona when there arose an unforeseen production problem, one which involved a question of extra charges to the budget. Said monies could not be spent until they were authorized by Eastwood's partner in the venture, Universal.

Eastwood climbed into a studio car and drove to the nearest telephone, a pay booth in a dusty gas station five miles from his location. Sans silver, he borrowed a dime from the station's owner and made a reversed-charges call to Universal studio. The studio switchboard operator refused to accept the charges.

"Lady," protested Eastwood, "this is Clint Eastwood—and I'm *working* for you people—"

"Sorree, sir," said the Universal operator. "I have to obey the company policy."

"But I can't go ahead with my next sequence unless somebody there authorizes it!" Eastwood cried. "Will you put the production office on?"

"Sorree, sir," said the operator. "Not until *you* pay for the call."

Further production of Eastwood's picture was held up a bit longer while the producer-actor drove back to the location site and borrowed sufficient change from his crew to put through the call.

Paul Mazurski and Larry Tucker are of the new breed of Hollywood writer-director-producers, with *I Love You, Alice B. Toklas* and *Bob & Carol & Ted & Alice* to their credit. One morning Mazurski

326

arrived on a studio sound stage for a rehearsal, obviously in a bad humor.

"You look depressed, Paul," remarked his partner. "What's bothering you?"

"Richard Nixon is my President," sighed Mazurski, "Ronald Reagan is my Governor, George Murphy is my Senator, Sam Yorty is my Mayor, and the William Morris office is my agent—and you want to know why I'm depressed?"

JOSEPH L. MANKIEWICZ

The end of Hollywood was always predictable. There were always financial crises. Someone would come out from the East and announce that the business was in deep trouble, and, literally, what would happen was that they'd reduce the number of matzo balls in Louie Mayer's chicken soup at the commissary from three to two in each portion. Then they'd fire a couple of secretaries and feel virtuous. But the Overhead Club—that was the name I had for those executives who drew down huge salaries and expense accounts all year long and did little to justify their existence—always went right on. Eventually that whole structure of people had to topple.

I remember once, when I was at Fox, writing and directing and producing two pictures a year—which is a lot of work—Spyros Skouras came out. He told me Fox was in deep trouble and everyone would have to take a pay cut—it was a crisis.

Well, I'd been through that before, at Paramount, and at Metro, and I wasn't buying it. I said, "Spyros, I'll tell you when it will be a crisis. It's when some guy in a white shirt with a button-down collar and Brooks Brothers suit comes out here and starts interviewing one of the studio executives, and he says, 'Mr. X, tell me what you do here.' And X says, 'Well, I'm in charge of talent, and I operate the studio stock company.' 'I see,' says the Eastern guy. 'Do you hire and fire these performers?' 'Oh, no,' says X, 'that's Mr. Zanuck's decision. I merely advise him. I let him know when contracts are expiring. I see the actors' agents and work out whatever deals are offered.' 'I see,' says the Eastern guy. 'And do you accept or reject those deals?' 'Oh, no,' says X. 'I leave all that to Mr. Zanuck.' 'And how much do you get a week?' asks the Eastern guy. 'I get $3,000 a week,' says X. 'Well, Mr. X,' says the Eastern guy, 'we have a Harvard Business School graduate who can do all that, and he gets $175 a week.'

"When he says *that*, Spyros," I said, "you'll know it's a *real* crisis."

Mankiewicz made a film at Warner-Seven Arts during the fall of 1969. "It was very strange," he remarks. "All those empty sound stages, and the wind whistling down the studio street. I couldn't get rid of the feeling that any minute I'd look out and see tumbleweeds come rolling past."

CHARLES G. BLUHDORN

As an American I want to see American pictures succeed, and I believe very strongly in the future of the motion picture. As board chairman of Gulf & Western, I oversee all our divisions. One of them is called Leisure Time, and Paramount is just a part of it. We also operate cable TV companies, music companies, recording companies —in Canada the largest theater chain in North America. Movies in cassettes for home viewing will open an enormous market. Satellites someday will relay first-run movies into millions of homes. It's a great challenge. There is a tremendous future in the leisure field. The revolution in the industry is creating unparalleled opportunities for those who want to learn the lessons of the past. From this shake-out in Hollywood will come something sound and firm.

(from LIFE, *February 27, 1970)*

"It's easy enough to make fun of a film distributor today," remarked Arthur Mayer, "but how can you help but feel sorry for the poor bastard? He's faced with the daily decision whether or not to commit large sums of capital to producers who want to make pictures for release a year from now. Now we all realize that exhibitors don't have a clue about what the kids want to see today. How can anyone possibly know what kids will want to see *a year from now?*"

CULVER CITY, Calif., May 3—A mantel clock used as a prop in the Greta Garbo movie *Ninotchka* was the star in the first hour of bidding at the auction today of Metro-Goldwyn-Mayer. It went for $3,750 to a collector who refused to identify himself.

About 3,000 people had filed onto Stage 27 of the studio's sprawling lot here, as David Weisz, the auctioneer, opened the first of 18 bidding days on hundreds of thousands of set decorations, costumes, antiques, pieces of furniture and other props of MGM.

. . . Miss Debbie Reynolds, who starred in 30 MGM films, starting in 1949, said she was bidding to acquire items for a motion picture hall of fame. The actress said she was spending her own money to acquire the first items for the exhibition, but that she hoped other Hollywood people would eventually join her, and that other studios would donate items.

Miss Reynolds said she had borrowed "a great deal of money" from her bank and "I'll spend it." In early bidding, she spent $1,450 for an armchair and a four-piece salon set used in *Marie Antoinette*, a nineteen-thirties film starring Norma Shearer. . . .

The Weisz company paid an estimated total of $1.5-million for the MGM property in January. The studio had decided to sell off its back lots to make better use of its assets. Fifty-one lots in the first hour of bidding went for $5,500 altogether.

(*from* THE NEW YORK TIMES, *1970*)

For many years Al Lewis and Max Gordon were partners. First they produced vaudeville, and later expanded to do Broadway plays. It was customary for Lewis & Gordon to try out their shows during the summertime, in Atlantic City, or Asbury Park, and while Lewis worked with the actors and the author, his wife and family would stay at a local boardwalk hotel and enjoy the beach, the ocean and the pleasant surroundings. With the advent of talking pictures Lewis was lured to California to produce films for Winfield Sheehan, then the production head of Fox Films.

One sunny California weekend Lewis and his wife and their very young daughter, Eleanor, accompanied by their good friend Arthur Caesar, the writer, also a transplanted New Yorker, went for a drive down to the Pacific. As they started back through the placid Santa Monica hills, headed home to the film capital, Caesar turned to young Eleanor. Referring to her new surroundings in Southern California, he joshingly asked the girl, "And when are you going home, my dear?" Eleanor Lewis, a veteran of many summer tryouts, quickly replied, "Oh—when it closes."

That was forty-odd years ago.

Forty-odd years since a little girl in the back seat of an open touring car on Sunset Boulevard inadvertently pronounced Hollywood's epitaph. It took that long for Eleanor Lewis's remark to become truth.

It *has* closed.

The Wit and Wisdom of Hollywood

H. L. MENCKEN (1927)

The bookkeeper of an opera house, alas, is seldom competent to select its repertory or to rehearse its caterwaulers. The movies, today, suffer from that profound and inconvenient fact. The men who organized them as an industry now attempt to operate them as an art—and the result is exactly the same as that which follows when a rich hog fattener, having decided to retire to the country seat, designs his own house, including the wall paper and the steeple, and loads a fowling piece to make sure that the workmen carry out his plans.

In other words, the movies languish as a fine art because the men who determine what is to get into them haven't the slightest visible notion that such a thing as a fine art exists.

. . . But . . . sooner or later, the authors, scenario writers, directors, and actors—that is, those among them who have any intelligence, which is not many—will have to revolt against this bondage. Soon or late the movie as an art will have to emancipate itself from the movie as a vast, machine-like, unimaginative, imbecile industry. . . . The theatre, once beset by the same folly, has been liberated by the so-called Little Theater—that is, by the amateur. The movie, I suspect, will be liberated in much the same way. Some day some one with an authentic movie mind will make a cheap and simple picture that will arrest the notice of the civilized minority. . . . When that day comes, the movies will split into two halves, just as the theater has split. There will be huge, banal, maudlin, idiotic movies for the mob, and no doubt the present movie magnates will continue to produce them. And there will be movies made by artists, and for people who can read and write.

(*from* THE BATHTUB HQAX, *by H. L. Mencken, Knopf,* 1952)

As William Ludwig, for many years a staunch MGMan, remarked to Arnold Auerbach, "They should have kept the props and auctioned off the producers."

MAX WILK

Max Wilk was born in New York City in 1920, the son of Jacob Wilk, who was for forty years a prominent motion-picture executive. After graduating from Yale University, Max Wilk entered the field of film and theater publicity. He has written extensively for films and television, and his accolades include a Peabody Award, an Emmy Award and a Writers Guild Award for his television musical revue, *The Fabulous Fifties*. The most recent of his eight novels are *A Dirty Mind Never Sleeps* (1969) and *My Masterpiece* (1970), and his articles have appeared in such magazines as *McCall's* and *Field and Stream*. He lives in Westport, Connecticut, with his wife and three children.

ONCE, IN YEARS PAST,

there was a thriving factory town called Hollywood. In it were nine or ten large establishments known as studios. In these studios, which were operated by somewhat noisy and aggressive men (and their relatives) who were called producers, was created an interesting form of native handicraft called motion pictures.

This so-called business flourished for half a century in Hollywood and then, without warning, it ended. In recent years, scholars have been attempting to collect relics, artifacts and information about Hollywood and the curious people who labored there.

Max Wilk, prowling through the ruins with a tape recorder, has, fortunately, been unable to gather much practical information about the movie business. Instead, listening to Nunnally Johnson, Joe Mankiewicz, Jack Benny, George Burns, Donald Ogden Stewart, Sam Goldwyn, Groucho Marx, Goodman Ace, the late and fabled Harry Kurnitz and many others, he has unearthed countless examples of what were called, in the old days, belly laughs. Movie fans will find this book hysterical. Serious students, critics, Film Society faithful and the *Cahiers du Cinéma* crowd will find it historical.

Here, for the first time in one place, is a treasury of wit and anecdote from the place where they flourished.